DISLOYAL
OPPOSITION

DISLOYAL
OPPOSITION

HOW THE #NEVERTRUMP RIGHT

TRIED — AND FAILED —

TO TAKE DOWN THE PRESIDENT

★ ★ JULIE KELLY ★ ★

Encounter BOOKS

New York • London

First American edition published in 2020 by Encounter Books, an activity of Encounter for Culture and Education, Inc., a nonprofit, tax exempt corporation. Encounter Books website address: www.encounterbooks.com

Manufactured in the United States and printed on acid-free paper. The paper used in this publication meets the minimum requirements of ANSI/NISO Z39.48-1992 (R 1997) (*Permanence of Paper*).

FIRST AMERICAN EDITION

LIBRARY OF CONGRESS CATALOGING-IN-PUBLICATION DATA

Names: Kelly, Julie, 1968– author.
Title: Disloyal opposition : how the NeverTrump Right tried—and failed—to take down the president / Julie Kelly.
Other titles: How the NeverTrump Right tried—and failed—to take down the president
Description: First American edition. | New York : Encounter Books, 2020. | Includes bibliographical references and index.
Identifiers: LCCN 2020000596 (print) | LCCN 2020000597 (ebook)
ISBN 9781641771146 (hardback) | ISBN 9781641771153 (ebook)
Subjects: LCSH: Trump, Donald, 1946– | Republican Party (U.S. : 1854–) Intra-party disagreements (Political parties)—United States. Conservatism—United States. | United States—Politics and government—2017– | Presidents—United States—Election—2016.
Classification: LCC E912 (print) | LCC E912 (ebook)
DDC 973.933092—dc23
LC record available at https://lccn.loc.gov/2020000596
LC ebook record available at https://lccn.loc.gov/2020000597

Interior illustrations by Elliott Banfield

DEDICATION

To John, Victoria, and Josie

To the late Alice "Kitty" Kelly (May 15, 1947–June 15, 2019),
my mother-in-law and dear friend of 25 years whom I miss every day.

No one is more excited about this book than she would have been.

CONTENTS

Preface / ix

Introduction / 1

1. The Birth of NeverTrump / 7

NeverTrump Hall of Lame / 25

2. Trump Wins, NeverTrump Regroups / 33

3. Useful Idiots for the Left / 47

4. But Gorsuch! / 65

5. Weapons of Mass Collusion / 85

6. NeverTrump's Enemies List / 103

7. NeverTrump Splits Up / 125

8. The Death of the *Weekly Standard* / 139

9. Trump 2020 / 155

Epilogue / 163

Acknowledgments / 169

Notes / 171

Index / 217

PREFACE

As this book went to print in spring 2020, the country was in chaos due to the threat of coronavirus, or, as President Trump called it, the "Chinese flu." After deadly outbreaks consumed parts of China and Italy, US government leaders started to enact harsh measures to combat the virus's spread here. Schools were closed; college campuses cleared out for the semester; public places shuttered; restaurants, bars, shopping malls, and public beaches closed during the height of spring break. The stock market started to crash, erasing all the gains under the Trump era. People were panicked about not just contracting the disease but the short-term and long-term ramifications of locking down the country during an economic boom.

Forecasts for economic growth in the second quarter were unfathomable: Some experts predicted double-digit drops in gross domestic product for the second and third quarters of 2020, just in time for the November presidential election. This, of course, titillated NeverTrump. As I detail in this book, Trump's foes on the putative Right seized on every crisis, every rumor, every scandal, to warn that the end days for Donald Trump finally were upon us. "The Trump presidency is over," declared one NeverTrump writer in the *Atlantic* on March 13, 2020. "It has taken a good deal longer than it should have, but Americans have now seen the con man behind the curtain."[1]

The nonprofit run by Bill Kristol, NeverTrump's leader from the start, grotesquely exploited the crisis in television ads that mocked the president's words as coronavirus cases began to rise.[2] (The group, as I detail in chapter 8, is largely funded by a left-wing billionaire and sworn enemy of Donald Trump.)

The Bulwark, the refuge of former *Weekly Standard* editors and contributors after the publication shut down in December 2018, was flooded with columns that accused Trump of lying about the disease and ignoring its early stages (he didn't). "The country deserves competent and responsible leadership and so, for the country's sake, Trump should lose in November," Kristol wrote in the Bulwark on March 19, 2020. "He probably will lose. But this is by no means inevitable. So we can't be complacent."[3]

The media were apoplectic over Trump's insistence on calling COVID-19 the "Chinese flu." NeverTrump, per usual, played along. "It's vitally important to push back against Chinese propaganda regarding the virus. That can be done directly, by refuting Chinese lies. Dunking on each other, by contrast, seems like a frivolous sideshow," tweeted David French on March 20.[4] NeverTrumpers who had spent nearly four years dunking on Trump, his administration, Republican lawmakers, and Trump supporters suddenly were very worried about hurting the feelings of communist China. David Frum, a senior editor at the Atlantic, instead suggested calling the disease the "Trump plague."

Jennifer Rubin, a *Washington Post* columnist and MSNBC contributor, fantasized that the disease would kill more Republicans than Democrats. Fox News, she falsely claimed, had downplayed the crisis. "There is a particular cruelty/irony that it is their core viewers, the Republican older viewers, who are the most at risk," she said on MSNBC on March 15.[5] She also commended Democrats for canceling campaign events before Trump did. "So, I hate to put it this way, but there will be less Democrat deaths because there will be less mass gatherings. There will be less opportunities for people to congregate and share this horrible disease." Eager to blame any fatalities on Trump, Rick Wilson, a self-proclaimed Republican strategist, started referring to the president as "President Kevorkian."[6]

As of this writing, it's hard to know how the economic and political fallout of the coronavirus crisis will affect Trump's reelection chances. (After instituting a 15-day social distancing policy to try to stem a rise in confirmed cases, President Trump on March 29 announced an extension of that policy until April 30, 2020.) But one thing is certain: NeverTrump will weaponize every aspect of the chaos, including the number of dead, against Trump. Of all the low points of NeverTrump's crusade against the president, it will be the lowest.

INTRODUCTION

Like many of today's writers on the Right, I grew up in a *National Review* household.

My dad was a longtime subscriber and a big fan of William F. Buckley Jr. Raised during the Reagan era, I would occasionally read the magazine, too. It helped shape many of my early political views.

When *National Review* online posted my first article in 2015, it was a huge thrill. Each time my work was published on NRO—and once in the magazine—I thought about my dad, who passed away in 2012, and how proud he would have been. (He also would have been a MAGA man.)

While my dad was more of a typical 1980s country club Republican, I cut my political teeth in the 1990s during the reign of the so-called neoconservatives. A recent college graduate and political junkie, I signed up to volunteer for the 1992 Bush/Quayle reelection campaign. It was basic grunt work: working phone banks, registering voters, delivering yard signs. Even though it was clear President Bush would lose to Bill Clinton on November 3, 1992, it still was a shock. My first political defeat!

One figure emerged from the GOP's political wreckage after Bush's loss: Bill Kristol, who had served as Vice President Dan Quayle's chief of staff. He helped the party regain its footing after Clinton took the White House; Democrats, at the same time, controlled Congress and all the experts were once again predicting the demise of the Grand Old Party.

But Kristol devised a plan to fight First Lady Hillary Clinton's health care plan in 1993. I was working for a newly elected Republican Illinois state senator at the time and became a Bill Kristol fan. When he launched the *Weekly Standard* in 1995, I wouldn't be surprised if I was one of the magazine's first subscribers.

As I continued working in Republican politics in the western suburbs of Chicago, once a Republican stronghold that has skewed blue over the past decade, I continued to follow Kristol and his fellow neoconservatives.

But after Donald Trump declared his candidacy and steadily rose in the polls throughout late 2015 and early 2016, the maestros of what some call Conservative, Inc.—the aristocracy that houses right-leaning think tanks, media organizations, major donors, and former officials of the Reagan and Bush administrations—decided Donald Trump could not be elected. Their opposition to Trump was voiced often in the pages of *National Review* and the *Weekly Standard*, as well as other less-popular publications throughout 2016.

Trump, as we know, shocked the world and won. Plenty of us had our reservations about Donald Trump when we voted for him in November 2016. Many Republican voters, myself included, had supported someone else in the primary. But when he won, barely defeating a treacherous, vindictive candidate who would have spent the ensuing four years seeking revenge against anyone who had ever wronged her, including everyone associated with the conservative movement, it was time to rally behind the president.

But Kristol and his Trump-opposing pals refused to get on board. They couldn't get past their own bruised egos and personal agendas to stand with the president.

They have proudly displayed their defiance under one banner: Never-Trump.

Never has a president been subjected to the vicious, divisive, and self-indulgent intra-party resistance orchestrated by Donald Trump's "conservative" foes. And his detractors aren't only random bloggers and disgruntled party officials and wanna-be contenders: The list of agitators includes two former Republican presidential candidates, esteemed conservative opinion/news outlets, and influential thought leaders. (A detailed list is published in chapter 2.)

From the time Trump announced his candidacy in the summer of 2015 to the point you are reading this right now, NeverTrump has plotted his demise.

———————

And, since the summer of 2015 to the point you are reading this right now, NeverTrump has been wrong about everything: Wrong that Trump wouldn't win the primary. Wrong that Trump wouldn't win the election.

Wrong that Trump wouldn't survive his first year in office. Wrong that Trump wouldn't survive his first term.

They have been wrong that Trump would cause a stock market crash, a recession, and widespread economic misery. They have been wrong that our allies would abandon us. They have been wrong that his hardline tariff policies would launch a trade war, a war that the United States would lose. They were wrong that his saber-rattling in North Korea and Iran would prompt World War III.

NeverTrump, as I explain in chapter 5, planted the very first seeds of the Russian collusion hoax. For three years, and even *after* Special Counsel Robert Mueller found no evidence of collusion between the Trump campaign and the Kremlin, NeverTrump bolstered the destructive scheme. NeverTrump opinion outlets published collusion propaganda as early as March 2016; in the interim—before Mueller issued his report confessing that his team of partisan prosecutors, despite unlimited resources, could not find evidence of a criminal conspiracy—NeverTrump hyped every collusion tidbit and "bombshell" as fact.

NeverTrump offered aid and comfort to the enemy Left during two of the most despicable events in modern political history: the character assassination of Supreme Court nominee Brett Kavanaugh and the media mob against Covington Catholic High School students. As the Left continues to show their true colors—no tactic, no allegation, no child is out of bounds in their unholy crusade against Donald Trump—NeverTrump unflinchingly and willingly plays along.

Despite public claims by some that they have left the Republican Party and despite their collective pivot on nearly every previously held "conservative" belief, NeverTrump, disguised as legitimate voices on the Right, overpopulates left-wing cable news channels, political websites, and publications. NeverTrump's gig as reliable mouthpieces to spew Trump hate from the right flank of #TheResistance has turned unknowns into social media celebrities, revived fledgling careers, earned nonstop hits on CNN and featured columns in the *Washington Post*, and resulted in long-awaited forgiveness for its members' role in perpetuating the Iraq War.

Neoconservatives once tarred as "war criminals" by the Left now routinely link arms with their former antiwar tormentors. It is an insidious kumbaya with one shared purpose: Destroy the Bad Orange Man and everyone around him.

While they claim to be serious people with a strict adherence to "conservative" orthodoxy, in reality they have burned whatever reputations they have left. As I detail in chapter 8, many accept funding from a progressive billionaire who has worked against every policy and principle they've supported for three decades. The flagship of the once-powerful neoconservative movement, the *Weekly Standard,* was shut down under humiliating circumstances. NeverTrump campaigned for Democrats in the 2018 midterm election, which elevated lunatics such as Rep. Rashida Tlaib and Rep. Ilhan Omar to power. Some NeverTrumpers have turned on evangelical Christians in a manner that can only be described as a form of religious bigotry.

Ironically, as NeverTrump claims to represent a swath of Trump-hating Republicans, support for the president among the GOP's rank-and-file has increased since Election Day. NeverTrump members represent no one but themselves while acting as useful idiots for the Left in their selfish crusade against Donald Trump. They have betrayed the party that once provided the platform for their professional success; mocked us as rubes, racists, and cultists; and tormented Republican lawmakers who dare to support the president over NeverTrump's objections.

They are worse than the Left because at least one knows what to expect from the Left. NeverTrump are the most dishonest political swindlers, pretending to be "conservatives" while promoting nonconservative ideology and employing the cruelest tactics of the Left.

———

In February 2017, I wrote a tongue-in-cheek column entitled, "Why I've Decided to Break-Up with Bill Kristol."[1] The piece, published in the *Federalist,* was part parody, part plea. I described my longtime affinity for the former editor-in-chief of the *Weekly Standard,* who had completely gone off the rails since Trump's presidency. (I hadn't really followed his anti-Trump antics before Election Day.)

I complimented my one-time political hero: "I hold out hope that this very smart man will be mugged by reality (as his father famously said), emerge from his Trumpian-Nixonian dystopia, and once again play a valuable role as a thought leader instead of a sore loser still trying to prove he was right," I wrote.

How naive. Little did I know how unhinged Kristol would become. Looking back, his remarks in early 2017 make him look tame compared to the crazed hater he is today.

Others noticed NeverTrump's folly. My friend Kurt Schlichter mocks them as the "Ahoy" crew—named for their yearly cruises that charged patrons a fortune to listen to the dull musings of Conservative, Inc.'s marquee names. These folks were famous mostly for pushing "a bunch of utopian ideas generated by a bunch of people who had done nothing in their life except go to college and write unread position papers while completing a fellowship at the Liberty Forum Coalition for Freedom," Schlichter wrote in his 2018 book, *Militant Normals*.[2] (Schlichter often trolls NeverTrump on Twitter with cruise ship emoji.)

The party's base and its newfound support of working-class voters revolted against Conservative, Inc. "Their real wages were stagnant at best, and the conservatives they had sent to Washington did not seem to care," Schlichter wrote. "Their culture and religion were under attack. Their kids were getting killed in wars no one seemed interested in winning. The people they had sent to Washington did not seem to care about anything important to [normal people]."[3] But NeverTrump, many of whom manipulated the inner workings of Conservative, Inc. for decades, couldn't deal with the fact that they created the void filled by Donald Trump.

———————

Since writing my faux break-up letter to Kristol, I have covered Never-Trump extensively. There are plenty of lesser-known NeverTrump proxies preening on social media and Right-leaning websites, but the leaders include the following: Bill Kristol, Jennifer Rubin, Tom Nichols, David French, Jonah Goldberg, Max Boot, Bret Stephens, Mona Charen, Evan McMullin, Charles Sykes, Rick Wilson, David Frum, the late Sen. John McCain, and Sen. Mitt Romney. (A brief description of each appears in chapter 2.) Romney would become the first US senator to vote to convict a president of his own political party when he voted in February 2020 to convict Trump of the Democrats' abuse of power charge against him.

People would sometimes suggest that those of us covering Never-Trump should ignore them; they don't represent the Republican Party, they don't speak for Republican voters, and they have nothing useful to offer, some on our side would argue. Further, some of NeverTrump's more tepid voices insist their criticism is duty-bound—just calling balls and strikes, people who hadn't found the strike zone in two decades would claim—and part of their professional responsibility. All presidents, after all, deserve scrutiny from their party's stalwarts. Trump is no exception.

All that is true. But, in my opinion, we need to make sure these backstabbers are on record for what they've done, and that is my purpose in writing this book. They not only intend to damage Trump presidency's but seek to divide the country during one of its most unstable periods in history. Instead of serving as honest brokers between a subset of conservatives uneasy about Trump's past or his conduct or his plans to govern, NeverTrump doused unneeded fuel on the raging political fire.

They have not just rooted for Trump's failure; by default, they have rooted for the country to fail.

This book isn't just an account of how badly Donald Trump's foes have behaved since he announced his candidacy. It isn't about score-settling or pointing out all the ways the NeverTrump crowd has been wrong over the past five years. It's a story about disloyalty—how people like me, millions of Republicans across the country, have been betrayed by the influencers we trusted and supported for decades.

For that, they should never have a place in the Republican Party again. This book is a Do Not Resuscitate order for any candidate, office holder, or serious publication that might consider reviving NeverTrump after their usefulness to the Left ends along with Trump's presidency, either later this year or in 2024.

The future will remember NeverTrump as a cautionary tale: the disloyal opposition who tried—and failed—to take down Donald Trump.

CHAPTER 1

THE BIRTH OF NEVERTRUMP

*Donald Trump is a menace to American conservatism
who would take the work of generations and trample it
underfoot in behalf of a populism as heedless and crude
as the Donald himself.*

    —The editors, *National Review*, January 22, 2016

Two weeks before the 2016 presidential election, Bill Kristol had a meltdown on MSNBC.

The *Weekly Standard* editor-in-chief was "practically crying," host Joe Scarborough observed, at the idea that Donald Trump might shock the world and eke out a victory on Election Day. Kristol, raising his voice and with tears in his eyes, nearly leaping out of his chair, accused Scarborough of helping to elevate the candidacy of the Manhattan tycoon. "This show was very tough on Trump in late 2015, early 2016, are you going to pretend that?" Kristol sneered at Scarborough, a former Republican congressman, on October 20, 2016. "If that's your way of rewriting history, that's fine with you guys."[1]

It was an odd display: the former chief of staff to Vice President Dan Quayle, a man who had been a fixture in Republican Party politics for nearly three decades, stifling sobs at the thought that Donald Trump, a Republican, would win the White House. Perhaps the fatigue of sitting on too many think tank panels and writing too many opinion columns and headlining too many cruise ship fundraisers finally caught up with the aging political hand.

After all, Kristol should have been elated. Trump was poised to beat Hillary Clinton, the woman whose health care plan Kristol helped kill in the 1990s.

7

But Kristol's tantrum revealed his frustration that his yearlong, very public effort to sink Donald Trump's candidacy would, like so many of his past political calculations, end in failure. Beltway creatures—the only people who really matter to Bill Kristol—already were mocking his almost unmatched political losing streak; Trump's victory would be Kristol's biggest humiliation of all time.

His tears were for himself, not for the Republican Party and certainly not for the country.

While Kristol would be a new name to many on the Left during the Trump era, he already is well known on the Right. A conservative thought leader and quarterback for the Iraq War, Kristol long had occupied a premium spot in the Republican Party's hierarchy. After Bill Clinton beat his boss in 1992, Kristol helped lead the Republican Party out of the political wilderness at a time when many predicted the GOP was finished.

A series of memos, authored by Kristol, detailed a strategy to defeat Hillary Clinton's universal health care legislation.[2] Clinton's plan went down in flames in late 1993 before a bill even made it to the floor of the Democratically controlled US Senate. The following year, in large part due to the demise of the Clinton health care proposal and fear it could be resurrected, fired-up Republican voters elected a Republican-majority House of Representatives for the first time in 50 years.

Kristol's memos morphed into the *Weekly Standard*, a thin but influential magazine that debuted in 1995. It featured several top-notch conservative writers; the publication was a must-read in the Bush White House and served as a crucial organ of pro–Iraq War propaganda before, during, and after the deadly conflict. The animating ideas of neoconservatism, a political philosophy conceived by Kristol's father, Irving, played out in the pages of the *Standard*.

Kristol was a regular on Sunday news shows and even earned a spot in the *New York Times* editorial pages. He was a Beltway-accepted promoter of conservative thought and Republican Party politics.

But when Trump won the Republican nomination for president against his wishes, Kristol turned on the insubordinate party that had powered his gravy train for decades. He became the self-appointed leader of what evolved into "NeverTrump," a small assortment of embittered, parochial "conservatives" enraged over Trump's candidacy. Consumed with their self-importance and alarmed at their potential demotion within the GOP, they pledged to crush the brash interloper who had never edited a very important magazine or toiled at a very important conservative foundation.

Acting as a political Praetorian Guard of sorts, this group behaved as though they, not elected officials or—ew, gross—Republican voters, called the shots. NeverTrump leveraged their long-cultivated Rolodex of powerful press contacts to hit cable news shows and Twitter to express their displeasure about Trump's candidacy.

Interestingly, the early battle between Team Trump and Team Kristol would be a proxy between the old guard and a national GOP agitated at its gutless party leadership; party faithful saw little daylight between Beltway Republicans and Democrats. A Queens-born international businessman who in no small measure owes his success to his father versus a Manhattan-born political guru who in no small measure also owes his success to his father—not exactly the head-to-head challenge that loyal Republicans asked for in 2016. But there we were.

"To Trump, Kristol is the rigged system he's fighting against, the personification of an elite establishment overdue for a rude awakening," noted Michael Crowley in a July 2016 profile on Kristol. "And, of course, Trump's not entirely wrong about that."[3]

Kristol started trolling Trump shortly after he launched his campaign from the luxury hotel in New York City that bears his name. Throughout the last half of 2015, Kristol predicted Trump's campaign would end before the ball dropped in Times Square; he even started a Twitter hashtag—#PeakTrump—to assure his followers that The Donald's days were numbered.[4] (It was a warning he would give repeatedly throughout the Republican primaries, general election, and Trump's first term as president.) "From the beginning of the billionaire's campaign, there has been no better contra-indicator of whether a given controversy would affect Trump than Bill Kristol's Twitter feed," one writer for *New York* magazine presciently noted in January 2016.[5]

That same month, Kristol joined like-minded conservatives in what will forever be considered the establishment's declaration of war against Donald Trump and his supporters.

BUCKLEY'S BRETHREN TAKE AIM AT TRUMP

On the eve of the 2016 Republican primary season, nearly two dozen conservative influencers took to the pages of *National Review*, the conservative movement's most esteemed magazine, to contribute to the publication's infamous "Against Trump" issue.[6] Every page was devoted to discrediting the rogue candidate at the time leading an impressive field of Republican governors, senators, and business executives.

Known for its mantra, "standing athwart history, yelling Stop," the publication founded by William F. Buckley Jr. in the 1950s attempted to stand athwart the accelerating freight train of Donald Trump's presidential candidacy and yell to his supporters, "'Don't you dare."

Contributors included Kristol, broadcaster Glenn Beck, columnist Cal Thomas, scholar Thomas Sowell, and a handful of George W. Bush administration officials. It was a collection of some of the most powerful and revered names in the conservative movement at the time.

"Donald Trump is a menace to American conservatism who would take the work of generations and trample it underfoot in behalf of a populism as heedless and crude as the Donald himself," wrote editor-in-chief Rich Lowry and his colleagues. And that was kind compared to the other rants featured in the issue.

In fairness, *National Review* editors and contributors had reason to suspect Donald Trump was not one of "them." A brash billionaire with political pals on both sides of the aisle and no record of fealty to conservative principles—"gaping holes" in his record, the *NR* editors truthfully surmised—Trump deserved legitimate scrutiny by Republican Party stalwarts. Bill and Hillary Clinton, after all, had attended Trump's wedding to Melania.

Trump's views on foreign affairs and social policies important to conservatives over time were erratic if not alarming. Pro-life conservatives were justifiably concerned after he suggested in 2015 that it was "possible" he once donated to Planned Parenthood.[7] Further, his stance on gun control was unclear, as he once called out NRA-funded Republicans and boosted a ban on so-called "assault rifles."[8]

But the "Against Trump" issue came across as a vanity project that smacked of both desperation and arrogance. Commentary veered from sober analysis to self-serving moralizing. Some contributors regurgitated the Democrats' most inflammatory charges against Trump, including accusations he was a racist, a sexist, and an Islamophobe—pure irony from thought leaders of a political party accused of the same wickedness by the Left for decades.

"Trump has made a career out of egotism, while conservatism implies a certain modesty about government. The two cannot mix," warned longtime conservative commentator Mona Charen, unwittingly making the pro-Trump case for conservatives who think the two are not only compatible but essential.

"Should his election results match his polls, he would be, unquestionably, the worst thing to happen to the American common culture in my lifetime," complained John Podhoretz, editor of *Commentary* magazine, the publication run for more than 30 years by his father Norman Podhoretz, the distinguished (and pro-Trump) public intellectual.

They—accurately—interpreted Trump's support as a bootheel kick to the collective groin of the weak, eager-to-please, and largely incompetent conservative ruling class. "If Trump were to become the president, the Republican nominee, or even a failed candidate with strong conservative support, what would that say about conservatives?" asked *National Review* editor Rich Lowry and his colleagues.[9]

In the succeeding 10 months, Lowry would get his answer. And it would require not more condemnation of Trump and his conservative backers but a long look in the mirror.

Concern over Trump's shaky conservative street cred wasn't their only beef: Trump's demeanor, mannerisms, and thrice-married status offended the Brahmin sensibilities of the *National Review* class. "Can conservatives really believe that, if elected, Trump would care about protecting the family's place in society when his own life is—unapologetically—what conservatives used to recognize as decadent?" asked Russell Moore. "It is not just that he has abandoned one wife after another for a younger woman, or that he has boasted about having sex with some of the 'top women of the world.' It's that he says, after all that, that he has no need to seek forgiveness."[10] (There is no record of similar concerns about John McCain's admitted infidelity or extramarital affair with and subsequent marriage to a much younger woman. In a 2008 interview with CNN's John King about McCain's history of cheating on his first wife, who had been badly injured in a car accident while he was in captivity in Vietnam, McCain told King that "the responsibility is mine" as to why the marriage failed.)[11]

But the magazine's gambit didn't work; in fact, it backfired in a spectacular way, unleashing a tide of pent-up resentment between rank-and-file Republicans and party masters. Frustrated by the GOP's failure to derail the far-left agenda of President Barack Obama despite winning control of the House of Representatives in 2010 and the Senate in 2014, Republican voters were out of patience and in no mood to take marching orders from conservative commanders who lacked a plan to defeat Hillary Clinton in November 2016.

National Review's plea not only fell on deaf ears, it likely contributed to Trump's ascendancy. "Many now believe the reason Trump won both the primary and national election is precisely because publications like *National Review* and the *Weekly Standard* coddled and encouraged a Republican Party that not only betrayed conservatism but turned on what was once its own base by becoming the party of Washington insiders courting favorable press from pundits," Breitbart News noted after the election.[12]

Mark Steyn, a onetime contributor to *NR*, mocked the publication for its outdated fealty to the Morning-in-America era and droning wistfully about how the Gipper would not approve of The Donald. But Ronald Reagan, Steyn noted, could never be elected governor of California today. "The past is another country, and the Chamber of Commerce Republicans gave it away," Steyn wrote. "Reagan's California no longer exists."[13]

After the release of "Against Trump," the leading GOP contender wasted no time trolling *National Review*. "The late, great, William F. Buckley would be ashamed of what had happened to his prize, the dying National Review!" Trump tweeted on January 21, 2016.[14] The battle lines had been drawn between the Republican elite and the GOP's most flamboyant party crasher. And the rank-and-file's rebuke against the former would be swift.

One week after the release of the "Against Trump" issue, the tycoon barely lost the Iowa caucus to Texas senator Ted Cruz. (Trump would go on to win nearly every other contest.) The Republican National Committee rescinded an invitation for *National Review* to help moderate one of the debates.[15] The "Against Trump" issue, rather than scare off Republicans from voting for Trump, had the opposite effect.

(A few years after his publication, Lowry and others expressed regret about the issue as it spurred what would become known as the Never-Trump movement. "I wish they'd never come up with that phrase," Lowry told the *New York Times* in October 2019, referring to NeverTrump.[16] Brent Bozell III, a contributor to the "Against Trump" missive who later became a Trump ally, told the *Times*, "Had I known this was going to be perceived as the bible of the anti-Trump movement, I never would have written it."[17])

Trump was unfazed by *National Review*'s condemnation. If anything, the thrashing by buttoned-up, tight-assed, tone-deaf "conservative" scolds motivated Trump to push back even harder. And he went right for the jugular, saying the quiet parts out loud, as they say, related to the Republican Party's biggest failures in a generation.

THE RECKONING OF THE IRAQ WAR

On a debate stage in February 2016, Trump spoke what was—up until that point—considered blasphemy in the Republican Party. Standing just feet away from former Florida governor Jeb Bush, Trump declared that the Iraq War had been a mistake and that America's 13-year-long military involvement had destabilized, not liberated, the Middle East. Then, in typical Trump style, he went a step further. "They lied," he roared from Peace Center in Greenville, South Carolina. "They said there were weapons of mass destruction, there were none and they knew there were none. There were no weapons of mass destruction."[18] The crowd mostly booed.

The next morning on Fox News, Trump continued his tirade. "The Iraq War was a disaster," he told the morning news hosts, including Tucker Carlson, who had opposed the war. "We spent two trillion dollars, thousands of lives, wounded warriors who we love... what do we have, nothing? We have absolutely nothing."[19]

Trump's roast of the Iraq War would be the most significant challenge to conservative orthodoxy in years; it resulted in a group therapy session for large chunks of the Republican Party who would reassess their attachment to widely accepted slogans that had, by and large, been empty vessels for failed policies. According to polling in 2015, most Republicans still believed the Iraq War was the right thing to do.[20] By 2018, less than half of Republicans believed the US succeeded in achieving its goals in Iraq.[21] (More recriminations about the war would continue into Trump's first term.)

Trump's tongue-lashing for the perpetrators of the Iraq War would be a harbinger of things to come from his candidacy and presidency. No issue was off-limits, no accepted truth too sacred to challenge. It is an approach that to this day appeals to rank-and-file Republicans and some

Democrats while rankling urbane, effete backers of the Democratic Party and NeverTrump fussbudgets.

THE PARTY'S OVER

By May 2016, Trump locked up the nomination, to much widespread pearl-clutching by the party's top tier. Trump crushed his opponents, winning a record number of Republican votes while besting the previous record held by George W. Bush in 2000, in another ironic slap at the Bush dynasty.

The Republican establishment was rocked to its neoconservative core.

But it was the post-primary conduct of NeverTrump that deepened the fault lines between the conservative establishment opposed to Trump and conservative voters who overwhelmingly supported him. Trump gave voice to long-simmering anger about Republicans' complicity in unfettered illegal immigration, unfair trade agreements, and endless foreign war, matters that had been ignored by Washington's political class for more than a decade. Conservatives were especially alarmed at the Left's takeover of academia, the news media, Hollywood, and the corporate world while conservatives were unable to halt the incursion.

The once-patriotic heartbeat of the Republican Party had been put on a bypass machine by party leaders, who seemed more concerned about the plight of illegal immigrants than of American citizens who had been gradually displaced—occupationally, culturally, academically, and socially—in their own homeland.

Trump, with his gaudy but genuine slogan to "Make America Great Again," made an unapologetic commitment to put America's interests first. It was a scolding as much as a promise. To the neoconservatives who ruled the Republican Party, Trump's MAGA mantra disemboweled the internationalist Bush Doctrine, a post-9/11 foreign policy approach that had resulted in protracted war in several countries, with dubious, deadly outcomes.[22] To Democrats, MAGA posed a direct hit to the undercurrent of anti-Americanism that had animated the party for years.

Trump openly antagonized the power base of both political parties— that, of course, was the real threat to establishment conservatives.

So, rather than coalesce around the Republican nominee in preparation for a brutal general election against a well-funded Democrat hostile to conservative views and values, GOP stalwarts fortified their ranks in a

galling rebuke of party acolytes. The very same people who had long prof-
ited from their affiliation with Republicans—who sold them books and
headlined fancy fundraisers and consulted on campaigns and led them
into treacherous wars—turned on their patrons in an ugly way.

"Make sure he loses," bow-tied George Will advised beleaguered conservative voters in a June 2016 interview. "Grit [your] teeth for four years
and win the White House."[23]

Will, channeling Reagan in another slap at Republican voters, changed
his voter registration from Republican to unaffiliated because, as he told
Fox News's Chris Wallace, "the party left me."[24] He later would join other
alleged "conservatives" who either endorsed Hillary Clinton or rooted for
Trump's defeat.

Kristol's desperation to thwart Trump prompted him to make the first
in a series of embarrassing moves: Around Memorial Day, he hinted that
he had an independent candidate who would pose a serious challenge to
Trump in the general election. Speculation swirled. Trump responded
on Twitter, calling Kristol a "dummy" and warned that conservatives
could "say good bye to the Supreme Court" if a conservative independent
jumped in the race to take votes away from the Republican nominee.[25]

But Kristol's secret candidate turned out to be David French, an unknown writer at *National Review*. (French later would emerge as a leading figure in the NeverTrump movement.) The political commentariat
on both sides mocked Kristol's attempted subversion. Vox referred to
French as a "random dude off the street"[26] and *GQ* called French a "random blogger" who had refused to allow his wife to drink, use Facebook,
or have phone conversations with men during his one-year deployment
as a military lawyer to Iraq.[27]

But Kristol's tease would be short-lived and crash in a mortifying
fashion. French, in his hallmark self-aggrandizing style camouflaged with
a veneer of nonexistent humility, declined to run. "I'm grateful for the
opportunity to serve my country, and I thank God for the successes I've
had as a lawyer and a writer, but it is plain to me that I'm not the right
person for this effort," he wrote.[28] French's refusal to run wouldn't be the
last humiliation that Kristol would suffer before Election Day.

With time and options running out, NeverTrump plotted how to overthrow the Republican presidential candidate during the Republican National Convention. Delegates planning to attend the party's convention in

Cleveland were urged to abandon Trump. One group, Delegates Unbound, produced a 30-second television commercial featuring a split screen with competing video clips of Trump and Ronald Reagan. The ad urged convention delegates to "choose your values, follow your conscience."[29]

National Review helped make the case that defections were allowed—there was some legal haggling about whether party rules permitted delegates elected to represent a specific candidate to switch. The drastic measure, one *National Review* contributor insisted, would be necessary in order to salvage the party's chances in November. "Discontent with Trump remains high," wrote John Fund on July 10, 2016. "He languishes in the polls behind a weak Hillary Clinton, his fundraising numbers are anemic, his campaign shambolic. Despite previously promising to do so, he has refused to release his tax returns...Many delegates believe damaging material from his tax returns will leak out of the federal government in October."[30]

Kristol, as would be his habit for the entirety of Trump's first term, imagined a farfetched scenario where Trump would go down in flames. He suggested that delegates should support either two-time loser Mitt Romney or Ohio governor John Kasich, who suspended his 2016 presidential campaign in May after only winning his home state. "They need to have a conversation very soon and agree that one of them will announce this week that he is willing to compete for the nomination after the convention has disposed of Donald Trump," Kristol daydreamed in the pages of his magazine a week before the convention. "It's even conceivable both could announce their willingness to serve, and that they intend to let the delegates choose between them and anyone else who chooses to compete."[31]

Of course, that didn't happen. The effort to oust Trump caused only a minor fracas on the convention floor a few days before Trump's acceptance speech.[32] He won the needed number of votes with little resistance.

But the number of establishment Republican and conservative defectors continued to mount. Sen. Susan Collins, a Republican from Maine, wrote an op-ed for the *Washington Post* in August 2016 to explain why she would not vote for Donald Trump.[33] Former Minnesota congressman Vin Weber wondered aloud whether Trump was a "sociopath" in an interview outlining his various reasons for opposing Trump's candidacy.[34] (Weber later would be caught up in Special Counsel Robert Mueller's investigation into Trump-Russia election collusion as prosecutors scrutinized his lobbying work on behalf of Ukrainian interests.)[35]

A long list of former national security experts who once served Republican presidents, including former CIA director Michael Hayden and former Homeland Security secretary Tom Ridge, signed on to a letter pledging not to vote for Trump. "From a foreign policy perspective, Donald Trump is not qualified to be President and Commander-in-Chief," concluded the architects of the lengthy wars and foreign conflicts that had disillusioned so many rank-and-file Republicans and that Trump promised to end. "Indeed, we are convinced that he would be a dangerous President and would put at risk our country's national security and well-being."[36]

Trump's erratic campaign helped reinforce the narrative that he was unprepared to lead the country and would be a reckless commander in chief. By late August, Trump had named his third campaign manager, longtime Republican strategist Kellyanne Conway.[37] Hillary Clinton's fundraising machine was reaping daily windfalls. Prospects for a win in November looked grim; NeverTrump was already looking forward to a Trump-free future.

With summer winding down, Trump as the official Republican presidential candidate, and high-profile Republicans refusing to launch a last-ditch bid, NeverTrump scraped up someone even lesser known than David French to oppose Trump in the general election: Evan McMullin. The former CIA undercover agent and congressional staffer succumbed to recruitment efforts by Kristol and Rick Wilson, a self-proclaimed Republican campaign strategist, to take on Trump as an independent. The single, childless Mormon with a laughably thin political resume would act as the moral foil to Trump, they predicted. Conservatives would have no justification for choosing an amoral business mogul from New York City over a goody-goody from Utah.

Even the *Washington Post* touted McMullin's clean-as-a-whistle image, offering glowing admiration for his courage to take on the evil magnate: "To understand that optimism, you have to understand Evan McMullin," cooed Josh Rogin in September 2016. "Unlike his backers, he's not trying to save the Republican Party or the conservative movement. He's doing what he has always done, volunteering for service to play whatever role he can to fight what he views as a threat to America. In this case, that threat is Trump."[38]

McMullin's candidacy started to pick up some endorsements from anti-Trump conservatives, but his long-shot effort appeared to be in vain. That is, until NeverTrump received a gift that even Bill Kristol couldn't screw up: the infamous *Access Hollywood* tape.

THE OCTOBER SURPRISE

On October 7, 2016, the *Washington Post* posted a recording of a private conversation from 2005 between Trump and *Access Hollywood* host Billy Bush.[39] The exchange included lewd comments about women; Trump bragged that, because of his fame and wealth, women "let you do" anything, such as "grab them by the pussy." (The tape, perhaps not coincidentally, dropped shortly before WikiLeaks released hacked emails of Clinton campaign manager John Podesta.)

Trump apologized for the language he had used, but the damage to his campaign appeared to be fatal. House Speaker Paul Ryan, who had been hostile to Trump's candidacy from the start, disinvited the candidate to an event and said he would no longer campaign for Trump. The move reignited the feud between the two: Responding on Twitter, Trump advised Ryan to "spend more time on balancing the budget, jobs and illegal immigration and not waste his time on fighting Republican nominee."[40]

Republicans who had endorsed Trump started to demand that Trump abandon his candidacy and defer to Mike Pence, the Indiana governor and Trump's ticket mate. "It would be wise for him to step aside and allow Mike Pence to serve as our party's nominee," Sen. Deb Fischer (R-NE), a Trump supporter, tweeted the day after the tape went public.[41] Other high-profile Republican women, including Hewlett-Packard CEO Carly Fiorina (who exited the 2016 Republican primary early) and Rep. Barbara Comstock (R-VA), joined Fischer's plea.[42]

Gov. John Kasich (R-OH) bragged that he was right all along about Trump's temperament and character—Kasich is on his second marriage to a younger woman and has a reputation as a hothead[43]—and promised to help rebuild the Republican Party after Trump lost.[44] David French, the self-appointed religious scold of NeverTrump, blasted Trump voters on *National Review*'s website for blaming the media's last-minute hit job: "If you're a Trump fan, this one's on you. Your eyes were open: You were warned, and you took the plunge anyway. You should be furious at two people today: Donald Trump and yourself. It's time for some soul-searching," he preached.[45]

Hundreds of Republican candidates and lawmakers withdrew their endorsements. A stable of *National Review* writers, including Jonah Goldberg and Dan McLaughlin, committed to McMullin.[46] Others promised to write in a candidate or vote for Hillary Clinton.

But the tide of outrage from the Republican establishment played right into Trump's hands: Just as with the "Against Trump" missive, voters viewed the rebuke as another way for party elders to thwart their choice. It would not stand.

In fact, some Republicans were forced to promptly reverse themselves after facing backlash from their constituents for abandoning Trump. Less than three days after tweeting her demand that Trump exit the race, Fischer backtracked and restated her support for the Republican ticket.[47] "The quick reversals back to Mr. Trump's camp vividly illustrated Republicans' predicament as they grapple with a nominee whom some of their core supporters adore, a Democratic candidate their base loathes—and a host of voters who believe that Mr. Trump is self-evidently unsuited for high office," wrote Jonathan Martin in the *New York Times* on October 11, 2016.[48]

It would be a harbinger of which side Republican voters would take when faced with a choice between Trump and old-line party leadership. The *Access Hollywood* matter also served up another opportunity for Trump to remind Americans, especially younger voters, exactly who the Clintons were.

In a gutsy piece of stagecraft, Trump hosted a pre-debate press conference on October 10 with four women, including Paula Jones and Juanita Broaddrick, who had accused Bill Clinton of sexual assault and rape. (Broaddrick also claimed that Hillary Clinton had threatened her.) The stunt was a display of Hillary Clinton's immense political baggage and her own husband's predatory sexual behavior; it also served as a stark visual that, had Trump been running against anyone besides Hillary Clinton, his prospects might not have been so bright.

To twist the optics knife even deeper, Trump attempted to seat the victims in his box for the debate, which would have placed the women near the former president; the debate commission prevented the move.[49]

And it was during that debate in St. Louis that Trump, unbowed by the scandal besieging his campaign, murmured his most memorable comment of the general election. When Clinton remarked that she was relieved Trump was "not in charge of the law in our country," Trump, not missing a beat, responded, "because you'd be in jail."[50]

That moment stood in sharp contrast to the debate between Mitt Romney and Barack Obama four years earlier when Romney fumbled his face-to-face encounter with Obama over the president's lies about the Benghazi terror attacks. Confronted by debate moderator Candy Crowley, who sided with Obama's misleading version of events by insisting he *did* call the deadly assault an act of terror (he had not), Romney stammered to condemn the Obama administration for its egregious excuse that a YouTube video sparked the spontaneous attack.[51] Romney's stumble on the debate stage a month before Election Day deflated Republican voters and contributed to his losing a very winnable race in 2012.

Trump, on the other hand, managed to survive a blow that would have tanked the campaign of any other candidate—a feat not unnoticed by Republican voters weary of Romney-esqe timidity. By the beginning of November, Trump had as much support among likely Republican voters as Clinton had among Democrats.[52] Further, according to an ABC News/ *Washington Post* poll taken just days before Election Day, 97 percent of Trump voters had an unfavorable view of Clinton, the exact percentage of Clinton voters who felt the same about Trump. "This depth of animosity is unprecedented in available data from previous elections," the pollsters observed.[53]

No kidding.

But hundreds of Republican and conservative leaders remained opposed to Trump.[54] Sen. Lindsey Graham (R-SC) announced he would vote for McMullin, an act of pure silliness. French threatened to shame believers to do the same. "I'll be calling on Christians to support a candidate who possesses real integrity," French said of McMullin.[55]

Dozens of one-time party heroes, including former secretary of state Colin Powell and former national security advisor Brent Scowcroft, pledged to vote for Clinton. Some news outlets reported that former president George H.W. Bush and his wife also would pull the lever for Hillary Clinton.[56] (The Bushes and Clintons had developed a chummy relationship, something that Republicans, especially conservatives, viewed as a betrayal.)

ELECTION DAY: STORM THE COCKPIT OR DIE

Meanwhile, conservatives were reconciling their personal aversion to Trump's style with their genuine fears about the consequences of a Clinton presidency. An anonymous essay published in September 2016 described, using a stark analogy, the choice before conservatives on Election Day. "The Flight 93 Election," referring to the doomed airliner that crashed in a Pennsylvania field on September 11, 2001, after passengers wrested control of the jet from Islamic terrorists, made the conservative case for Donald Trump. [57]

The 4,300-word piece detailed the multiple failures of the conservative hierarchy; the "whole enterprise of Conservatism, Inc. reeks of failure," the unnamed author wrote. "Its sole recent and ongoing success is its own self-preservation." The essay described the prospective doom posed by a Hillary Clinton presidency and the reasons why conservatives would be justified in voting for a presidential candidate, who, by nearly every measure, contradicted the airbrushed avatar of a true conservative leader.

Writing as Publius Decius Mus in the *Claremont Review of Books*—it initially was published at the *Journal for American Greatness* website, now *American Greatness*, for which I write—the author directly challenged arguments made by marquee conservative influencers against the election of Donald Trump while advocating a vote for Clinton or a third-party candidate:

"Let's be very blunt here: if you genuinely think things can go on with no fundamental change needed, then you have implicitly admitted that conservatism is wrong. Wrong philosophically, wrong on human nature, wrong on the nature of politics, and wrong in its policy prescriptions. The alleged buffoon is thus more prudent—more practically wise—than all of our wise-and-good who so bitterly oppose him. This should embarrass them. That their failures instead embolden them is only further proof of their foolishness and hubris."

The writer presciently warned that the Clinton machine would "be coupled with a level of vindictive persecution against resistance and dissent hitherto seen in the supposedly liberal West only in the most 'advanced' Scandinavian countries and the most leftist corners of Germany and England." Little did he, or anyone outside of the Obama White House or Clinton team, know that a Stasi-like cabal of political operatives were already using powerful government tools to sabotage Trump's presidential campaign, a scheme that would escalate after he won.

Then this parting shot: "Trump, alone among candidates for high office in this or in the last seven (at least) cycles, has stood up to say: I want to live. I want my party to live. I want my country to live. I want my people to live. I want to end the insanity."

The essay outraged the conservative intelligentsia, mostly because it was clear the writer was of their ilk. Kristol outed the identity of the writer—Michael Anton, a former Bush speechwriter—and NeverTrumpers subsequently piled on. (More on this in chapter 6.) In his criticism of the piece, Jonah Goldberg, unwittingly making Anton's point, admitted, "I am the first to concede that if Hillary Clinton wins it will likely be terrible for the country," but the Republic will not in fact literally die like the passengers on Flight 93.[58]

Point missed.

So while pragmatic conservative thinkers like Anton recognized the cataclysmic future under the reign of Hillary, NeverTrump, shamefully, continued their opposition to the Republican nominee while bracing for another Clinton presidency.

A few days before the election, Kristol predicted that Clinton would win by a larger margin that Obama had won by in 2012. "I think there's probably a little more hidden Hillary Clinton vote than hidden Donald Trump vote," Kristol said in an interview on MSNBC on November 4.[59] In another one of his Trump-related delusions in the same interview, Kristol claimed that "many working class white women"—it's unlikely Kristol knows any—"whose husbands are enthusiastic for Trump but don't want to pick a fight at home who might go into the ballot booth and vote for Hillary Clinton."

And as the polls were about to close on Election Day, Kristol again predicted the outcome would be like 2012.[60]

THE NOVEMBER SURPRISE

Hours later, Kristol would join a dozen other commentators on the sprawling set of ABC News as the vote totals gradually indicated Donald Trump would be the next president of the United States.

Realizing that another political prediction would crash and burn, Kristol struggled to explain what was about to happen while proving, once again, he had learned nothing. "He doesn't agree with [Republican House Speaker] Paul Ryan on entitlement reform, the heart of the congressional Republican agenda," Kristol said at around 1:00 A.M. on November 9 as the country awaited the final verdict. "He's got a very different view of immigration, of trade. Is he really going to go ahead with the trade policies he talked about? We're in even more unchartered waters than we really think."[61]

With that final quip, Kristol was uncharacteristically correct.

An hour later, the major network news stations called the race for Donald Trump. The country—and the world—was stunned. The Republican Party would never be the same. And NeverTrump suffered another loss at the hands of Donald Trump.

There would be many more to come.

The
NeverTrump
Hall of Lame

Banfield

The de facto leader of NeverTrump kept his well-documented political losing streak intact during the Trump era. Kristol's predictions about the "end days" for Trump were wrong every single time. A paid propagandist for both the Russian collusion hoax and the impeachment crusade, Kristol also supported Democratic candidates and declared in February 2020, "we are all Democrats now." His contemptuous campaign against Trump and the GOP propelled the demise of the *Weekly Standard*, the magazine he founded in 1995.

The phoniest conservative of all the so-called conservative NeverTrumpers, Rubin, a columnist for the *Washington Post* and an MSNBC contributor, eventually alienated even her onetime allies in NeverTrump. She encouraged violence against Trump associates, peddled phony Russian collusion, and rooted for Democrats to take back Congress in 2018. She reversed herself on every previous opinion including climate change, the Iran nuclear deal, and tax cuts, just to name a few.

The male version of Rubin—he also writes for the *Washington Post* and appears on MSNBC—Boot renounced his past views in a desperate attempt to please his new allies and paymasters on the Left. Trump forced Boot to confront his own "white privilege," Boot revealed. The Russian immigrant claimed that because of Trump, he no longer felt welcome in America. Boot became so unhinged toward the end of Trump's first term that he was calling *National Review* writers white supremacists.

After twice failing to win the White House, Romney settled for the consolation prize of junior senator from Utah. Before taking office in January 2019, Romney authored an editorial in the *Washington Post* pledging to stop the president's worst impulses. He worked to thwart Trump's agenda on every issue from border security to foreign affairs. Romney is the only senator in history to vote to convict a president of his own party. In 2019, reporters uncovered his burner Twitter account: Pierre Delecto.

An unknown until Kristol floated his name as a rival to Trump in 2016, French leveraged his NeverTrump credentials to earn newfound fame. French, a columnist for *National Review*, routinely ridiculed evangelical Christians for backing Trump, insisted the government declare war on white supremacy, and pushed Russian collusion fiction. French supported the Democrats' impeachment effort and commended Sen. Mitt Romney's vote to convict the president. For his insufferable lecturing and proselytizing, French is often referred to as Pastor French. He left *National Review* in 2019 to join the *Dispatch*.

★ ★

Jonah Goldberg

Once a fixture at *National Review*, Goldberg left the publication in 2019 to form his own outlet, the *Dispatch*, with fellow NeverTrumper Stephen Hayes, the former editor of the *Weekly Standard*. His predictions of doom about Trump's presidency never materialized. While helping promote suspicions about Russian collusion, Goldberg insisted that anyone who believed in a "deep state" operation to oust Trump was a promoter of conspiracy theories. Trump brought impeachment upon himself, Goldberg argued, because he's a man of low character who can't act presidential.

CHAPTER 2

TRUMP WINS, NEVERTRUMP REGROUPS

The Never Trumpers rarely self-reflected about why their party had not won the popular vote in five out of the six last elections, or why the last Republican president had left office with near historic unpopularity, doubled the debt during two terms, and passed arguably progressive legislation. Like the Resistance, Never Trumpers failed in all their political aims at removing or delegitimizing Donald Trump.

—Victor Davis Hanson, *The Case for Trump*

In its post-election issue, the *Weekly Standard* published a clear-eyed editorial about Donald Trump's victory.[1] Editor Stephen Hayes acknowledged that after years of threats, voters finally delivered the comeuppance long deserved by the ruling class. Barack Obama failed to make good on nearly all his promises; the Iran deal was a billion-dollar debacle, health care costs were skyrocketing, and the economy remained weak, among other troubles.

Hayes reiterated the *Standard*'s "early and often" opposition to Trump but pledged to play fair moving forward for the good of the country. "Wanting him to succeed, we'll offer him good-faith advice. When he governs as a conservative, we'll support him enthusiastically," Hayes wrote. "If we see the old Trump, we won't stint on criticism; and if he rises to the occasion, as all Americans must hope he will, we won't hold back praise. In short, we were wrong about Trump's electoral prospects, and we hope to be even more mistaken about the kind of president he'll turn out to be."

Other NeverTrumpers appeared to offer sincere promises about how they would cover the Trump presidency. Taking a conciliatory tone in the hours after Trump officially won, *National Review*'s Jonah Goldberg admitted he had been wrong about a Clinton victory and pledged to "do my best to support Trump when I think he's right, and I will continue to criticize him when I think he's not," he wrote on November 9, 2016. "As I've been saying for 18 months—that's my job."[2]

With Trump headed to the White House, it initially looked as though NeverTrump might disband, cut their losses, and swallow a few ounces of their oversized reservoir of pride. It was one thing for NeverTrump to sound magnanimous after the whooping they took from their one-time Republican devotees. It was quite another to accept a drastically reconfigured Republican Party led by Donald Trump.

NeverTrump would have to own up to fomenting the rank-and-file's uprising. Would NeverTrump confront the root causes of Trumpism and their own culpability? Further, would NeverTrump rally the fragmented party and protect the will of the electorate against an enraged Left sworn to go to any extreme to reverse the election results?

It wasn't just that so many NeverTrumpers abandoned the Republican Party's presidential candidate when the party needed them most. Many endorsed a third-party candidate with no shot of winning; some backed Hillary Clinton. They had burned their own reputations in service of frying Donald Trump. Even if they decided to stay in the Trumpified GOP, who wanted them?

The detailed election results were, after all, a harsh repudiation of establishment Republicans and Conservative, Inc. The Donald had achieved what no Republican presidential candidate had achieved since Ronald Reagan in 1984: With the exception of Illinois and a slim loss in Minnesota, Trump swept the Midwest. While the commentariat—and the enraged Clinton campaign—downplayed Trump's margin of victory in Michigan, Wisconsin, and Pennsylvania, the outcome in those three states was stunning.

In 2012, President Obama beat Mitt Romney in Wisconsin by seven percentage points, even though Romney's running mate, Paul Ryan, was a native son. Trump, on the other hand, won the Badger State by nearly one percentage point. The Manhattan mogul won nearly half a million more votes than Romney won in Pennsylvania and Michigan alone.

Trump won Ohio and Iowa, states that Barack Obama won twice, by comfortable margins; he came within striking distance in Minnesota. More than 200 counties, mainly situated in the Midwest and Rust Belt, that twice voted to elect Barack Obama flipped to Trump: These so-called "pivot" counties would represent the new base of the Trumpified Republican Party. (Trump continued to court voters in the region throughout his first term by holding dozens of rallies and stumping for candidates.)

The Democratic Party's fortified Blue Wall crumbled. Despite years of polling and focus groups, consultants' advice, and conservative commentary about how to earn back working-class voters, the Republican Party could not come up with a winning formula.

In 2008, Reihan Salam and Ross Douthat, *Atlantic Monthly* writers at the time, forewarned that the Republican Party's fixation on economic issues and failure to connect with "Sam's Club" voters would keep a Republican out of the White House indefinitely. "Globalization and the rise of knowledge-based economy, growing outsourcing and the demise of lifetime employment, the expansion of credit card debt, the decline of retirement and healthcare security, the pressure from below created by unprecedented illegal immigration—all of these developments of the last three decades have made American workers feel more insecure, even though they're materially better off than ever before," they wrote in their book, *Grand New Party.* "And there's no question that the Republican Party has failed to adequately address these concerns, or that the GOP's emphasis on economic growth over economic security has made working-class life more unstable than it otherwise would have been."[3]

They continued. "Some combination of the populist Left and the neoliberal center is likely to emerge as America's next political majority even so, if the conservative movement can't find innovative ways to address the anxieties of working-class America."[4] (Douthat is a reliable Trump critic from his current perch at the *New York Times.*)

Not only did the conservative movement fail to find policies that would appeal to the so-called "Sam's Club" constituency at a national level, they failed to nominate an attractive salesman. John McCain and Mitt Romney had no natural connection to working-class voters—nor did they try to cultivate one.

So the very same clique of Republicans opposed to Trump's candidacy in 2016 had struggled to make a Republican presidential candidate attractive enough to win blue-collar whites in the Heartland to flip those states from blue to red: Donald Trump figured it out in less than 18 months and basically on his own. In 2012, Barack Obama won 51 percent of non-college graduates; in 2016, that exact same percentage voted for Donald Trump.[5]

"Before Trump, few politicians saw an opening in defending the forgotten working class of the interior, which may have been far larger than believed," wrote Victor Davis Hanson in his 2019 book, *The Case for Trump*. "And predictably, after the 2016 election, head-scratching experts sought to reexamine why their so-called exit polls had missed the impending Trump surge."[6]

There was plenty of head-scratching data for the political class to digest, especially for NeverTrumpers inclined to view Trump's election as an aberration—merely a revolt against the Clinton machine—rather than the relief valve of years of pent-up dissatisfaction with GOP leadership.

According to an exhaustive CNN exit poll with nearly 25,000 respondents, 81 percent of self-identified conservatives voted for Trump; so did 80 percent of devout Christians.[7] (Evangelicals would be repeatedly attacked in a vicious way, particularly by NeverTrumpers such as David French, for supporting Trump. The targeted harassment would not have been tolerated had it been aimed at any other religious group.)

Republicans' rebuke of international trade policies, centerpieces of both Bush administrations, was resounding. Of those who said that international trade takes away US jobs, 64 percent voted for Trump, a consensus that not long ago would have been attributed to Democratic voters, not Republicans.

Trump overwhelmingly was viewed as the candidate of change. Two-thirds of American voters said the country was headed in the wrong direction; 68 percent of that group supported Trump on Election Day. Trump won independents by four points.

In another stunning act of defiance, Trump did not campaign on two policies that had long represented the core of the Republican Party's agenda: entitlement reform and debt reduction. And it was fine with Republican voters. In the end, Trump earned as much support from Republicans as Hillary Clinton had from Democrats.

With the post-election results smacking them right in their smug faces, NeverTrump would be forced to assess the smoldering wreckage of the Republican establishment, debris that had their names and ideas all over it. Canards about the advantages of free trade and illegal immigration were on the top of the trash heap. So too was the unquestioned use of the American military to police unstable nations across the globe in pursuit of vague goals with deadly consequences.

The bill of particulars that Trump supporters handed over to the castrated Republican establishment was long and damning.

"Trump might be vulgar and ignorant, but he wasn't responsible for the many disasters America's leaders created," wrote Tucker Carlson in his 2018 book, *Ship of Fools*. "Trump didn't invade Iraq or bail out Wall Street...Trump's election wasn't about Trump. It was a throbbing middle finger in the face of America's ruling class...Happy countries don't elect Donald Trump president. Desperate ones do."[8] Carlson, a product of the neoconservative political era, emerged as an antidote to the largely neoconservative NeverTrump claque.

ANOTHER KRISTOL COLLAPSE

For Kristol, Trump's victory earned him one more participation trophy in his long Hall of Shame overstocked with political mistakes that has become something of a running joke among the professional commentariat. "The larger question about Kristol is how much it matters that he's been wrong as often as he has been," observed Paul Farhi in the *Washington Post* in February 2016. "Stock-market columnists, weather forecasters and horse-racing touts might never survive so many blown calls. But Kristol hasn't just survived his errant predictions, he's thrived."[9] But here was Kristol, wrong again, and in a spectacular way.

Kristol's poor soothsaying made several year-end lists tallying the worst political predictions, including his claims that Trump would lose the primaries, lose the general election, face a viable third-party candidate, and face an uprising at the Republican National Convention.[10] He was like a forecaddie who could never find the ball in the rough, miscalculated the yardage, misread putts, and never replaced the pin but the country club refused to fire him.

In his pre–Election Day post in the *Weekly Standard*, Kristol sounded ready to redirect his energies if Trump was the victor. "After Election Day we should mostly look forward and not back," he wrote. "There will be too much work to do to spend much time on retrospectives or recriminations. But before we all move on, I do want to reiterate one last time, to allies I've had the privilege of working with and to opponents I've had the pleasure of fighting: #NeverTrump."[11]

After the race was finally called on November 9, 2016, he encouraged his fellow NeverTrumpers to be "magnanimous losers," as if they had an alternative.[12] But that call went unheeded; Kristol's own humility was short-lived. As Trump's transition team prepared to take the reins of government, Kristol organized the remaining NeverTrump holdouts.

Their motivation was obvious from the start: Act as the disloyal opposition to a president of their own (alleged) party while portraying themselves as the moral betters to Trump and his "deplorable" backers. That collective stunt would be a way to resurrect stalled careers and gain long-sought acceptance from the Left. (It would also be a pathway for redemption for the disastrous Iraq War. More on that in chapter 5.)

Groveling to Democrats and their cutouts in the news media—particularly on the pages of the *New York Times* or the sets of CNN and MSNBC—would help these now-inconsequential political players get the attention they no longer deserved.

They would finally get invited to appear on all the cool shows hosted by all the cool people like Bill Maher and Jimmy Kimmel and Stephen Colbert and Whoopi Goldberg.

Their tarnished reputations as warmongers would be buffed to a shiny new patina; even George W. Bush, the most vilified Republican president since Richard Nixon, got a free makeover from most of the Left's media cosmetologists after he bashed Trump and cozied up to the Obamas.

Kristol's NeverTrump roster was filled with failed campaign consultants, B-list "conservative" commentators, fading political columnists, and Bush family loyalists. (Some I had never heard of until they jumped on the NeverTrump bandwagon.) None had ever run for public office before 2016, and their political credentials were as unimpressive as their ability to forecast election results or to win foreign wars.

The short list, with Kristol at the top, includes the following:

DAVID FRENCH

Unknown until Kristol teased his fake presidential candidacy, David French quickly realized that acting as a holier-than-thou "conservative" Trump foe would boost his indistinct punditry career. (He started writing for *National Review* full-time in mid-2015.)[13] According to the memoir he wrote with his wife, the reason French signed up to serve as an army law-yer in Iraq in 2006 was because "I've always thought the theme of my life was that I was a patriot." French views his anti-Trump gig as his patriotic duty while he appears on liberal cable news channels and the pages of liberal rags to satisfy the Left's unquenchable appetite for Trump-loathing sound bites.

A practicing Presbyterian, French frequently scorns evangelicals for electing and continuing to stand by Donald Trump despite numerous scandals, including the Stormy Daniels kerfuffle. French also helped boost the phony Russian collusion storyline while castigating Republicans for exposing the legitimate scandal, the weaponization of President Obama's Justice Department to sabotage Donald Trump.

By the middle of Trump's first term, French was a frequent MSNBC contributor and a columnist for both *Time* and the *Atlantic*. In October 2019, he announced that he would join *National Review*'s Jonah Goldberg and Stephen Hayes, the former editor-in-chief of the now-shuttered *Weekly Standard*, to form the *Dispatch*, an online newsletter.

TOM NICHOLS

The author of *The Death of Expertise* and an academic with no hands-on political experience, Tom Nichols left the Republican Party in 2012 over Newt Gingrich's presidential candidacy. Calling himself a "moderate conservative" (which usually means a pro-growth, pro-war supporter without the pro-life, pro-gun baggage), Nichols "came back [to the Re-publican Party] when the danger of a Trump victory loomed," he wrote in 2018 after he quit the GOP—again.[14] Nichols spent an inordinate amount of time on the Twitter battlefield, cranking out one post after another, usually aimed at Trump and his supporters. He cut ties with the *Federalist* when the online publication became more pro-Trump, but appears regularly in *USA Today*, in the *Atlantic*, and on MSNBC. Nichols voted for Hillary Clinton.[15]

JENNIFER RUBIN

A lawyer with no political background, Jennifer Rubin began writing for conservative publications such as the *Weekly Standard* and *Commentary* in the early 2000s. The *Washington Post* hired her in 2010 to pose as a right-wing "blogger" and act as a foil for the paper's left-wing bias. Shortly after she was hired by the *Post*, the *Columbia Journalism Review* noted that Rubin "characterizes opponents by derision…delegitimizing them rather than engaging them on the substance of their policy preferences."[16] That approach would escalate during the Trump era when, aside from her daily columns at the *Post*, Rubin often appeared on cable news shows to ridicule anyone in Trump's orbit. She openly called for the public harassment of Trump advisors, including press secretary Sarah Sanders, and Trump supporters.[17]

BRET STEPHENS

During his time as a columnist and editorial board member for the *Wall Street Journal*, Bret Stephens was a thoughtful journalist with harsh words for the Obama administration; Trump, as the saying goes, broke him. Like Nichols, Stephens announced his separation from the Republican Party because of Trump's views on immigration, trade, and international policy. He also denounced Republican voters who pointed to Clinton's similar character defects as justification to vote for Trump. "Such deflections are the usual way in which people seek to justify their own side's moral lapses," he wrote in the *Wall Street Journal* in 2016.[18] He prayed Trump would lose so "Republican voters will forever learn their lesson" not to ever again nominate a candidate that Stephens does not approve of.

He left the *Wall Street Journal* in mid-2017 to work for the *New York Times*, a move widely condemned by the *Times'* readership, since Stephens was a so-called "climate denier." In order to please his new leftist masters, Stephens flipped his views on climate, suddenly insisting he believed in anthropogenic global warming; he later would call for the abolition of the Second Amendment.

MONA CHAREN

Mona Charen, the longtime conservative influencer and syndicated columnist, offers her anti-Trump rants in several publications including *National Review*. She is a fellow for the Ethics and Public Policy Center, which houses a number of NeverTrumpers. During an annual gathering of conservatives that had become Trump-friendly territory, Charen blasted the president during a discussion about #MeToo. "I'm disappointed in people on our side for being hypocrites about sexual harassers and abusers of women who are in our party, who are sitting in the White House," she said during a Conservative Political Action Conference (CPAC) panel in Washington, D.C., in February 2018. "And because he happens to have an R after his name, we look the other way."[19] Charen gained instant affection from the Left, later boasting in the *New York Times* about her courage and candor.[20]

EVAN MCMULLIN

One would assume that the candidate who came in fifth place in the 2016 presidential election, only winning an embarrassing 730,000 votes out of the more than 137 million cast, would slink back into anonymity and get a real job. But Evan McMullin and his running mate, Mindy Finn, remained on the national political stage, bolstered by a steady stream of left-wing funding. Frequently overestimating his talent or value, McMullin claimed in 2017 that he had to wear a "light disguise" around the nation's capital and warned that Trump's victory would result in every nightmare scenario from despotism to authoritarianism to a land terrorized by white supremacists.[21]

MAX BOOT

The Russian-born author and historian Max Boot would morph into arguably the most caricatured of the NeverTrumpers, a shameless syco-phant for the Left who used the opinion pages of the *Washington Post* as a confessional to reverse himself on nearly every previously held belief, all in service of blasting Trump and the Republican Party. Boot voted for Clinton; he exited both the Republican Party and the conservative move-ment, although there was scant evidence—aside from his nonstop support for foreign war—that he ever was part of either one.

At the end of Trump's first year, Boot, in perhaps his most cringe-worthy column in a lengthy library of similar screeds, admitted that 2017 was the year he learned about his "white privilege."[22] A few months before Special Counsel Robert Mueller issued his report concluding there was no collusion between the Trump campaign and the Kremlin to influence the 2016 election, Boot listed "18 reasons why Trump could be a Russian asset."[23] In September 2019, he wondered why all of his Trump invective hadn't yet resulted in the president's removal from office. "I am left to ask if all my work has made any difference," he whined.[24]

JONAH GOLDBERG

A longtime *National Review* editor and Fox News contributor, Jonah Goldberg often rejected the formal term "NeverTrump" to describe his political position in the Trump era, but his commentary before and during Trump's first term rightfully earns Goldberg a spot alongside Kristol and company. Goldberg is a fierce critic of the president; when his colleague, Rich Lowry, penned a column rebuking the "delusion" of NeverTrump,[25] Goldberg wrote a harsh response defending "conservative" critics of Trump.[26] Republican voters, Goldberg advised, should consider Trump an "outlier." Nope, not NeverTrump at all.

Goldberg's year-end column in 2018 predicted Trump's presidency will "end poorly" because "character is destiny."[27] He mocked the idea of a "deep state" operation aimed at Donald Trump despite overwhelming evidence:[28] "Trump's coalition is a big tent where people with tinfoil hats get to belly up to the Kool-Aid punch bowl, proudly wearing their QAnon, Pizzagate, anti–Deep State name tags," he sneered in August 2019.[29] Goldberg, however, gave oxygen to one of the biggest conspiracy theories of all time, that the Trump campaign was in cahoots with the Russians to hijack the 2016 presidential election. Even after Special Counsel Robert Mueller admitted there was no collusion between the two interests, Goldberg said in March 2019 that the findings did not "put to rest softer versions of collusion."[30]

CHARLIE SYKES

Before he took on Trump, Charlie Sykes was unknown to Republicans outside of Wisconsin. The "conservative" host of a daily radio program in the Badger State, Sykes interviewed Trump in the spring of 2016 and subsequently declared himself a proud member of NeverTrump.[31] Sykes predicted that Trump would lose his home state in 2016 and take incumbent US senator Ron Johnson down with him. "It's not going to be pretty," Sykes warned in August 2016.[32] (Republican Johnson beat Democrat Russ Feingold by almost four percentage points.) He released a book, *How the Right Lost Its Mind*, in 2017.[33]

Sykes is now the editor of the Bulwark, the *Weekly Standard*'s anti-Trump offspring. Upon the website's launch, Sykes said the reason he is part of the NeverTrump project is because he "is all out of fucks to give."[34]

RICK WILSON

Until Trump's candidacy, Rick Wilson had a thin, unimpressive, and controversial political resume. His most notable accomplishment was producing the infamous ad in 2008 featuring Barack Obama's pastor Jeremiah Wright with clips of Wright bellowing "God damn America" from his pulpit. The McCain campaign distanced itself from the spot: "If you speak against the anointed one [Obama], God will smite you," Wilson explained in October 2008, responding to Obama supporters' criticism of him.[35] Armed with a prodigious dialect of profanity and an eagerness to display his vulgarity on cable news programs at all hours of the day—he called Trump supporters, among other things, "childless single men who masturbate to anime" in 2016—Wilson earned a level of celebrity he never had pre-Trump.[36] (MSNBC had to mute one of his vile tirades during a live interview; this is the same guy who called Trump a "vulgar clown.") Wilson caused an uproar for mocking Trump supporters, referring to them as "Boomer rube[s]" and using a phony Southern accent during a segment on CNN in January 2020. (Host Don Lemon later clarified that he was not laughing at Wilson's ridiculing half the country but at another joke he had made.)

Wilson published his first book, *Everything Trump Touches Dies*, in 2018.

———

In early 2017, several of the aforementioned sworn NeverTrumpers began gathering in Washington on a regular basis to plot their next move to overthrow Donald Trump. Calling their confab the "Meeting of the Concerned," participants also included a few former Republican lawmakers and a handful of DC-based think tank officials. "The Meeting of the Concerned, which has grown all year but consists of just a few dozen people, meets during the work day and does not reveal its member list," *Washington Post* blogger David Weigel reported in November 2017. "Unanimity has been hard to find, even as some members … have become more vocal about the threat posed by the Trump administration."[37] The *Post* later reported that George Conway, husband of Trump advisor Kellyanne Conway, also attended Meeting of the Concerned gatherings.[38]

While Kristol and company represent the starring cast of NeverTrump, a cadre of other Republican lawmakers, conservative influencers, and former bureaucrats plays a supporting role. After he stepped down as editor-in-chief of the *Weekly Standard* in December 2016, Kristol anointed his protégé, Stephen Hayes, as his successor.[39] Hayes, like Kristol, had been wrong about everything in 2016, which in the insulated world of the conservative commentariat entitles you to a promotion. Hayes continued Kristol's anti-Trump legacy at the magazine, eventually turning on Trump-supporting Republicans as well.

Other media figures include Seth Mandel, opinion page editor for the *New York Post* who moved to the *Washington Examiner* magazine in 2018; John Podhoretz, editor of *Commentary*; Ana Navarro, CNN commentator and occasional cohost of *The View*; and David Frum, senior editor of the *Atlantic*. (Frum said in 2018 that "Donald Trump is God's judgment on the United States for not being good enough citizens.")[40]

On Capitol Hill, no Republican lawmaker held more contempt for Donald Trump than the late Sen. John McCain. After Trump derided McCain's captivity during the Vietnam War—"I like people who weren't captured," Trump snarked in 2015[41]—McCain, who failed in 2008 to capture the office Trump now occupies, used his substantial Beltway power and prestige to undermine Trump.

The Arizona Republican bolstered the manufactured Trump-Russia election collusion plotline and represented the decisive vote in the US Senate to block the repeal of Obamacare, even though he campaigned on the issue in 2014. McCain's funeral in September 2018 featured anti-Trump tirades disguised as eulogies. Meghan McCain's emotional speech invoked Trump on several occasions: "The America of John McCain has no need to be made great again because America was always great," she said defiantly, a tantrum met with applause. "We live in an era where we knock down old American heroes for all their imperfections when no leader wants to admit to fault or failure."[42] McCain, as a host of *The View*, routinely criticizes the president.

Senator McCain's close friend, South Carolina senator Lindsey Graham, also thwarted Trump until McCain's death. Jeff Flake, the other Republican senator from Arizona, had to bail on his 2018 reelection bid due to his unpopularity in the state for opposing Trump. Nebraska senator Ben Sasse relished his role as a Trump agitator until his 2020 reelection loomed. Two-time-losing presidential candidate Mitt Romney sought Trump's endorsement in his lay-up Utah Senate race in 2018, then promptly turned on the president when he realized that would be the only way to get attention.

A hodge-podge of House Republicans, Beltway Bushies, and lower-tier writers and editors rounded out NeverTrump as Trump's first year in office began.

At first, they framed their collective mission in patriotic terms. Never-Trump, they explained, would keep an erratic and amoral president in check. Any attempted breach of conservative "principles" would be swiftly condemned on the set of CNN or the opinion pages of the *Washington Post*. Acting as the home stadium referee, NeverTrump vowed to call "balls and strikes" on the Trump administration's at-bats—this from a team of backbenchers who hadn't found the political strikes zone in years.

All in the defense of conservatism, they assured us.

═══════════

But then Kristol tipped his hand. "Obviously strongly prefer normal democratic and constitutional politics. But if it comes to it, prefer the deep state to the Trump state," he tweeted on February 14, 2017.[43] Coincidentally (or not), that was the same day that former national security advisor Mike Flynn resigned amid a deep state–fueled attack based on illegally leaked details of his classified call with the Russian ambassador and an ambush by FBI director James Comey's lackeys.

That tweet made it "Kristol" clear that the animating forces of NeverTrump would not, in fact, promote conservatism—ceding power to nameless, faceless, unelected federal bureaucrats is wholly inimical to the core of conservatism. Empowering government agencies to crush the will of the electorate is what the Left does, not the Right.

Kristol's message would be a harbinger of what to expect from Never-Trump. Rather than fortify a Trumpified Republican Party advancing conservative policies—from federal tax reform to long-promised deregulation to pro-life protections—NeverTrump sided with the Left time and again. Not only would many NeverTrumpers embarrassingly reverse their previously-held views on a number of issues, but they would cozy up to characters far more dubious than Trump, while getting on the dole of leftist funders opposed to every conservative value and policy they had championed for two decades.

CHAPTER 3

USEFUL IDIOTS FOR THE LEFT

Demented and sad, but social.
　　　　　　　　　　　　　—The Breakfast Club (1985)

In 2003, a prominent conservative commentator authored an impressive book that detailed how the Left helped legitimize communism throughout the twentieth century. The writer explained that Democratic lawmakers and presidents, academics, and elite news organizations defended the rise of the Soviet Union as it tightened its iron grip. Their boosterism lasted until beyond the end of the Cold War.[1]

American liberals, the conservative influencer wrote, acted as "useful idiots" for a murderous ideology responsible for the death of tens of millions of people around the world and perpetuated the misery of hundreds of millions more.

The author of the book, entitled *Useful Idiots: How Liberals Got It Wrong in the Cold War and Still Blame America First*, is Mona Charen. Ironically, Charen, as a proud NeverTrumper, would give succor to the Trump-hating Left during his first term in office.

While her coddling of the Left obviously didn't result in the execution and starvation of innocents, Charen and her fellow NeverTrumpers nonetheless reinforced the Left's ranks during one of its most violent periods in modern American history and acted as the Trump era's version of useful idiots for American liberals.

In even more idiotic fashion, NeverTrump did a 180-degree pivot from its very principled conservative perch. This is where NeverTrump's useful idiots fare worse than Stalin's: At least the Soviet Union's American shills didn't pretend to be something they never were.

As it became clear that Donald Trump intended to govern as a conservative, NeverTrump couldn't in good faith, or even bad faith, continue their "principled" conservative crusade against the president. How could they object to tax cuts, deregulation, conservative judicial picks, climate policy rollback, updated trade agreements, and the like from a "conservative" standpoint?

As NeverTrumpers settled into left-wing news and opinion outlets, pleasing their anti-Trump pals at the *Washington Post* and CNN at any cost has been their top priority. This requires a reversal of their previous views on any number of policies and political strategies.

"One of the most amazing outcomes of the Trump administration is the number of neo-conservatives that are now my friends and I am aligned with," confessed MSNBC host Joy Reid in September 2017. "I found myself agreeing on a panel with Bill Kristol. I agree more with Jennifer Rubin, David Frum, and Max Boot than I do with some people on the far left. I am shocked at the way that Donald Trump has brought people together."[2]

Shocked, you say?

In 2007, reporter David Corn, then at the *Nation*, vilified Kristol's espousal of the Iraq War and declared (correctly) that Kristol "ought to have his pundit's license yanked."[3] In 2013, Corn asked why people like Kristol hadn't paid a price for promoting the war under false pretenses.[4]

Just a few years later, united in their common contempt for Donald Trump and everything he represents, Corn and Kristol would share the set as MSNBC pundits. Kristol, the man who excoriated Barack Obama for years, admitted in early 2017 that he would rather endure another four years of President Obama than one term of President Trump.[5]

Trump made strange people into bedfellows.

NeverTrump easily fooled its new followers on the Left to believe that, yes, they represented a large swath of the Republican Party who deep down hated Trump and only voted for him because Clinton was more objectionable. NeverTrumpers assured their distraught soul sisters on the Left that it was only a matter of time before the GOP would see things their way and dump Trump. It was chicken soup for the Trump-loathing soul.

"We have seen a number of people who have been friends and colleagues of ours go pretty strongly in the other direction [away from fundamental conservatism], just embrace big government liberalism because they don't like Trump." That observation, ironically, came from NeverTrumper Stephen Hayes in a podcast interview with Charlie Sykes.[6]

The leftward lurch of NeverTrump happened fast—and nowhere did it happen quicker than on the *Washington Post*'s "Right Turn" blog, occupied by Jennifer Rubin.

RUBIN'S RANTINGS

Her anti-Trump tirades began in 2015.

Disguised as a conservative, Rubin offered Clinton pre-election advice on how to attract Republican voters; that counsel came one year after Rubin listed 20 reasons why Clinton's campaign was on the ropes and possibly doomed to fail.[7]

She fantasized about what would happen to Trump after Clinton defeated him. "That's the best part of this election—it will end and so will Trump's domination of the news," Rubin predicted a few weeks before Election Day.[8] Her post-election ridicule extended to Trump's cabinet picks—she referred to his early nominees as "ignoramuses, billionaires and a few generals"—and his base of support teeming with nativists, white nationalists, and bigots.[9]

One would assume that considering Rubin's support for Hillary Clinton, her contempt for Trump and his conservative backers, *and* her broken political meter in general, the *Post* would have offered that coveted spot to a legitimate conservative, perhaps even a fair-minded columnist without an axe to grind against the Republican president. (Trump tweeted in December 2015 that Rubin was one of the *Post*'s "low IQ people" and "a real dummy.")[10]

And since the *Post* made it clear that it would ratchet up its nonstop negative coverage of Trump during his presidency—the paper introduced its new slogan, "Democracy Dies in Darkness," in February 2017—giving yet another Trump hater prime real estate on the *Post*'s opinion page to rant about everything and everyone related to Trump seemed repetitive.

Except Rubin did not want to jeopardize her sweet spot at the *Post* yet again. In 2013, the paper's former ombudsman advised Jeff Bezos, Amazon's billionaire founder who had purchased the news organization, to fire Rubin. Disclosing that Rubin was the "#1 source of complaint mail" from *Post* readers, Patrick Pexton blasted Rubin's poor writing skills, unoriginal analysis, and overall unprofessionalism. "Her analysis of the conservative movement, which is a worthwhile and important beat that the *Post* should treat more seriously on its national pages, is shallow and predictable,"

Pexton wrote. "Her columns, at best, are political pornography; they get a quick but sure rise out of the right, but you feel bad afterward."[11]

Rubin has employed that same playbook against Trump since late 2015. Stroking Trump foes from the Right would protect her sinecure; she eagerly enlisted in #TheResistance.

Comparing Rubin's views before Trump's election and after his inauguration causes a major case of whiplash. A pitfall of being a political pundit is that there exists an electronic record of your past opinions available for the world to see. As I pointed out in a December 2017 article, Rubin flipped and flopped on a number of issues solely based on their favorability to Trump and his knuckle-dragging base.[12]

An advocate of tax cuts way back in 2013, Rubin criticized Obama's stagnant economy and insisted that the country would "not get robust economic growth and significant job creation with the world's highest corporate tax rate."[13] Four years later, channeling Bernie Sanders rather than Milton Freidman, Rubin called Trump's tax cut proposal a "moral and economic monstrosity" aimed at enriching "the wealthy and big corporations" at the expense of the most vulnerable.[14]

Rubin sympathized with out-of-work coal workers as late as 2014. Correctly concluding that the Democratic Party had been taken hostage by the climate change cabal, Rubin warned that the Obama administration's Clean Power Plan, which sought to significantly reduce carbon emissions, jeopardized the party's Senate majority in that year's election. "Unfortunately for mainstream Democrats, the president and their party are captives to elite, radical environmentalists. It is not only an economic issue, but also reveals the degree to which Democrats are compounding inequality and depressing economic growth."[15]

That compassion disappeared like carbon vapor on November 8, 2016. "While they accuse 'elites' of being out of touch, the GOP climate-change deniers and non-college-educated voters—especially those who reside in poorer, rural and small-town America—are increasingly oblivious to the world outside their ideological bubble," she sneered in June 2017. "Rather than level with voters, their GOP representatives cater to their ignorance and mislead them about the state of science and of our economy."[16]

Her conversion to a disciple of climate science and promoter of the same radical environmental agenda she had slammed a few years earlier was complete with Trump's announcement the US would withdraw from the Paris Climate Accord. Rubin had written several columns condemning Obama's signature international policy agreement; she even accused Obama and Secretary of State John Kerry of using the deal to distract from their failed attempts to defeat ISIS.

But Trump's opposition would be enough to trigger Rubin's epiphany on the issue. "The only difference between then and now is that Trump eventually endorsed Rubin's take in its entirety," Sean Davis wrote for the *Federalist*. "And because Rubin now calibrates her political compass to the opposite of whatever Trump is doing, she feels compelled to vociferously support a vapid agreement she at one time opposed on the merits."[17]

Ditto for the Iran nuclear deal. Before Trump, Obama's Joint Comprehensive Plan of Action (JCPOA) posed a significant threat to national security, according to Rubin, by paving the way for the terrorist-harboring nation to build nuclear weapons in the future.[18] But after Trump announced he would "decertify" the JCPOA, Rubin fretted that the move would agitate the Islamic Republic, not to mention Russia and China.[19] "Putting at risk that deal with really no sort of backup plan, they're just going to kind of bluff their way through and see if the Iranians come back to the table," Rubin commiserated with MSNBC's Lawrence O'Donnell in October 2017. "Our allies are not on board with us, the Russians, the Chinese, so is that another storm that's coming?"[20]

Rubin mocked prayer; urged stricter gun control laws; objected to a repeal of the estate tax; and defended abortion rights. After Rubin's fierce opposition to Brett Kavanaugh's nomination to the Supreme Court, a group of conservative leaders sent a letter to the *Post*'s editorial board, demanding that the paper stop referring to her as a "conservative," while offering to recommend a replacement "who can eloquently and effectively defend the positions held by our President, his party, and the millions of voters who elected him."[21] Rubin dropped the "conservative" descriptor but still occupies the *Post*'s "Right Turn" blog.

NEVERTRUMP FOLLOWS RUBIN TO STAGE LEFT

Bret Stephens has followed a similar route. In early 2017, Bret Stephens jumped ship from the *Wall Street Journal* to the *New York Times*. His hiring sparked outrage among the *Times'* readership; Stephens had been a longtime critic of anthropogenic global warming, now known generally as climate change. That blasphemy, according to the climate cabal, makes one a climate "denier."

"Before he was hired at NYT, Stephens was a source of standard-issue right-wing hackery on climate change," wrote David Roberts at Vox after the *Times* announced Stephens's new gig.[22] Leading climate scientists canceled their *Times* subscriptions.[23] A petition drive to fire Stephens gathered more than 40,000 signatures.[24]

Stephens got the message loud and clear. The same commentator who once compared climate change to religion—"another system of doomsaying prophecy and faith in things unseen," he snickered in 2011—suddenly saw the solar-paneled light.[25] In his debut column for the *Times*, Stephens called the Intergovernmental Panel on Climate Change's claims about the rise in global temperatures "indisputable, as is the human influence on that warming." He tiptoed around much of the fuzziness of climate science but quickly added a pandering disclaimer: "None of this is to deny climate change or the possible severity of its consequences."[26]

When pressed later by fellow *Times* columnist Gail Collins whether he believed global warming is happening and is mostly man-made, Stephens said yes. He hoped that his meetings with climate experts would result in "less ambivalence" on a subject on which he had expressed zero ambivalence for more than a decade.

Unfortunately, Stephens's climate prostrating wouldn't be enough to win converts at the *Times*. He needed something more drastic to preserve his spot there—so he dutifully did what any self-important *New York Times* columnist must do: He called for the repeal of the Second Amendment.

Following the horrific massacre of 58 people in Las Vegas by a mass shooter in June 2017, Stephens admitted that, as a conservative, he never understood the "conservative fetish" for the Second Amendment. Americans don't need all these guns because they kill too many people and, by the way, the government will protect us when needed, he argued. "But [gun ownership] doesn't need a blanket Constitutional protection, either," Stephens opined. "The 46,445 murder victims killed by gunfire in the United States between 2012 and 2016 didn't need to perish so that gun enthusiasts can go on fantasizing that 'Red Dawn' is the fate that soon awaits us."[27]

But one would be hard-pressed to find a more embarrassing Never-

Trump sycophant to the Left than Max Boot. Hardly a day passes that Boot doesn't make a mockery of himself in service of blasting Trump, his family, his supporters, and the Republican Party in general.

Not only has Boot objected to every single "conservative" policy advanced by the president—including the appointment of constitutionalist judges to the federal bench, Trump's exit from the Paris Climate Accord, and overdue immigration reform—he insisted that anyone who backed Trump's conservative agenda "owned" the president's alleged bigotry.[28] "If you want the Trump tax cuts and the judges, you've also signed up for the racism, the misogyny, the amorality, the lawlessness, the deranged tweets, possibly even something close to treason. Trump supporters own it all," he tweeted in December 2017.[29]

Boot, a Russian immigrant who came here as a child, claimed that because of Trump, he felt like he no longer belonged in America.[30] Boot officially quit the Republican Party in 2018—"I don't want to be identified with the party of the child-snatchers," he sneered, referring to Trump's family separation policy—even though there is scant evidence that, aside from his penchant for war, he ever was a Republican.

Once a climate change skeptic, Boot, like nearly every other Never-Trumper, converted to a wild-eyed climate prophet. Conservatives who reject anthropogenic global warming, according to Boot, are willing hostages of the fossil fuel industry. There is little daylight between Boot's delusions of climate doom and those of the most egregious climate propagandists such as Michael Mann or Bernie Sanders. "It is a tragedy for the entire planet that the United States' governing party is impervious to science and reason," Boot lamented.[31]

The Second Amendment, Boot wrote after a tragic massacre at a Florida high school in February 2018, is a "suicide pact" with politicians, Republicans in particular.[32] After Beto O'Rourke suggested an assault rifle buyback program a month before he dropped out of the 2020 Democratic presidential race, Boot thanked O'Rourke for his courage. Comparing "assault rifles" to military artillery, Boot again sneered at "Second Amendment absolutists" who defend the ownership of "weapons of war."[33]

All this, of course, has been rewarded by his new allies on the Left; Boot, like Jennifer Rubin, is a regular columnist for the *Washington Post* and an MSNBC contributor.

NeverTrump expressed little, if any, support for Trump's pro-life advocacy from the Oval Office. In addition to proposing a ban on federal funding for Planned Parenthood, Trump frequently defended the sanctity of life and duty to protect the unborn; he used his international platform to promote anti-abortion policies around the world. "Every child born and unborn is a sacred gift from God," Trump said during his September 2019 address to the United Nations.[34]

Trump's vocal defense of the unborn came at a time when the Democratic Party finally revealed its support for straight-up infanticide. After Virginia state lawmakers considered a bill that would permit the killing of a child even after the mother had given birth, Democratic governor Ralph Northam (supported by many NeverTrumpers over his Republican rival, Ed Gillespie) calmly explained how the "infant would be kept comfortable" as the mother and doctors decided whether or not to murder the baby.[35]

NeverTrumpers, however, waved away the Democrats' slouch toward infanticide. Most were silent about Northam's comments. After Democratic presidential candidate Bernie Sanders seemingly advocated for abortion to halt climate change, Jennifer Rubin warned Sanders that he might want to keep their baby-killing plans quiet. "At a time when progressives have the high ground in abortion politics, citing the cruel and unreasonable abortion bans, Sanders's remark is, to put it lightly, unhelpful," she wrote. "This is similar to how the phony infanticide issue put Democrats on defense...as with Sanders, all the issue did was put the target on Democrats' backs in the battle to determine who gets cast as the most unreasonable side in the abortion fight."[36]

Tom Nichols referred to abortion as a "medical process" and wondered why abortion is such a big deal to conservatives.[37] Even when David French finally gave Trump props for his pro-life advocacy, he added this disclaimer: "I appreciate Trump's pro-life actions, but he can't yet match GWB."[38] When Trump became the first president to speak in person at the March for Life in January 2020, French's blog, the *Dispatch*, gave it a one-sentence mention.

In a nine-tweet thread on the day of the march, French, who jumps on the platform at every opportunity to rant about the president, made no mention of Trump's historic visit to the event.[39]

So, almost en masse, on every issue of importance to devout conservatives, NeverTrump flipped. Rather than defend conservative "principles," as was their alleged raison d'être, NeverTrump converted into propagandists for the pro–climate change, pro–gun control, pro-abortion, anti–tax cut radical Left.

The Trump era ripped the mask off the "conservative" costume donned by so many NeverTrumpers. This tweet by Bill Kristol in November 2017 said it all: "The GOP tax bill's bringing out my inner socialist. The sex scandals are bringing out my inner feminist. Donald Trump and Roy Moore are bringing out my inner liberal. WHAT IS HAPPENING?"[40]

In a lengthy interview with CNBC's John Harwood in 2018, Kristol sounded more like Bernie Sanders than Ronald Reagan.[41] The benefits of Trump's tax cuts, Kristol said, didn't need to be laundered through the corporations that benefited from the rate reduction—the federal government could have handled all of that from Washington! (Many companies announced bonuses for their employees after the cuts went into effect. Horror!)

"Wasn't the whole point of the tax cut to free up money for investment? I mean, the government can just write checks to people. It doesn't have to go through a middleman, you know. Give 'em to everyone, not just the people who work for certain favored companies," said Kristol.

Calling himself a "conservative who's been mugged by Trump" (Kristol's father, a founder of neoconservatism, famously referred to his political transformation as a "liberal who's been mugged by reality"), Kristol then suggested that conservatives' opposition to affirmative action—a defining cog of the movement's platform for more than three decades—was not based on principles of fairness but rather rooted in "bigotry." Ditto for illegal immigration policies.

WHITE GUILT AND RACIAL POLITICS

Borrowing the most mendacious tactics of the Left, NeverTrump readily assigns racist, sexist, anti-Semitic, Islamophobic, and homophobic motives to Trump for any number of policies, comments, and tweets; even events outside of his control, such as the melee in Charlottesville in August 2017, are blamed on Trump for allegedly stoking racial strife.

There is nothing conservative, of course, about evaluating people based on skin color or gender or religion. Further, there is nothing conservative about blaming large groups for the actions of a few. But over and over, NeverTrump aids the Left in painting Trump, his administration, congressional Republicans, and Trump supporters as gay-bashing, Muslim-hating, woman-hating, anti-Semitic white supremacists. Imaginary threats about a surge in white supremacy stoke unnecessary fear in order to gratify their Trump-hating urges.

Specific incidents, while not directly Trump's fault, NeverTrump explains, nevertheless should be pinned on the president because he once made derogatory comments about a Mexican judge and "attacked" a Gold Star Muslim family in 2016. Even Trump's condemnation of kneeling NFL players, a trend started by former quarterback Colin Kaepernick, are racial "dog whistles" to his knuckle-dragging base of white nationalist Neanderthals, according to NeverTrump.

Max Boot got the shtick rolling in late 2017 in a self-flagellating article where he confessed that he is a beneficiary of "white privilege." Boot's introspection, oddly, coincided with his rising star as a Trump detractor and his new gig as a regular columnist at the *Washington Post*.

"Whether I realize it or not, I have benefitted from my skin color and my gender and those of a different gender or sexuality or skin color have suffered because of it," Boot confessed in *Foreign Affairs* magazine in December 2017.[42]

Immigrants, Bill Kristol observed, work harder than native—meaning, white—Americans. David French, in a quasi-defense of Rep. Ilhan Omar's contemptible anti-American rhetoric, referred to native-born Americans as "ingrates." He claimed he could not take "pride" in his birth here in America in the same way that immigrants take pride in obtaining American citizenship. "Native-born Americans by the countless millions don't trouble themselves to be educated enough about their own country to pass the basic citizenship test that we give to prospective citizen immigrants," he wrote.[43] French's message was clear: Just like the Left tells us, immigrants are better than US citizens.

After Charlottesville, Jennifer Rubin wrote that anyone who "continue[d] to support the president is continuing to deny he is unfit for office and to make excuses for his verbiage makes one complicit in his racial divisiveness and his determination to provide aid and comfort to neo-Nazis and white nationalists."[44]

The Charlottesville riot occurred two months after a Bernie Sanders supporter attempted to murder several Republican congressmen on a baseball field outside of Washington, D.C. Rep. Steve Scalise sustained life-threatening injuries that later required him to use a cane. Media outrage was brief and scant.

David French, in a frantic piece the night of the Charlottesville melee, when facts were still emerging, attempted to equate an attempted assassination with the events in Charlottesville:

> America is at a dangerous crossroads. I know full well that I could
> have supplemented my list of violent white supremacist acts with a
> list of vicious killings and riots from left-wing extremists—including
> the recent act of lone-wolf progressive terror directed at GOP mem-
> bers of the House and Senate. There is a bloodlust at the political
> extremes. Now is the time for moral clarity, specific condemnations
> of vile American movements—no matter how many MAGA hats its
> members wear—and for actions that back up those appropriately
> strong words.[45]

The wanna-be mass murderer hoping to kill a dozen Republican House members was a "lone-wolf progressive." The alt-right protestor who drove his car through a crowd of counter-protestors and killed one young woman, however, is associated with MAGA-hat-wearing Trump supporters. French's comparison is a craven example of the sort of false equivalency routinely employed by NeverTrump whenever it is convenient. The outrage about what happened at Charlottesville did not involve Trump. But French and his NeverTrump collaborators could not resist the chance to attack. (French also said Trump's comments after the riot "hurt the nation he leads.")

Bill Kristol called Trump's post-Charlottesville statement "depressing" and said that it made him sick. (Kristol made no known public statement about the near-murder of Representative Scalise.)

"The president's refusal to name the evil in our midst is the behavior of a man whose moral sense is stunted—if he has a moral sense at all," sneered John Podhoretz in the *New York Post*. "This is what I feared would be the case when he became president. Perhaps those who say I have an obligation as a conservative to support Trump should wonder what their moral obligations require."[46]

NeverTrump also would continue to repeat the Left's inaccurate trope that Trump commended neo-Nazis when he said there were "good people on both sides." Stephen Hayes fumed that Trump wouldn't criticize white supremacists; therefore, Hayes wrote in the *Weekly Standard*, "white supremacists are convinced that President Trump is more than just open to them."[47] Absurd.

Just as the Left twists any Trump taunt or criticism into an example of his bigotry, so too does NeverTrump. Trump's criticism of the "Squad"—which includes Rep. Rashida Tlaib, who screamed "we're gonna impeach the motherfucker" the night she was sworn in—is another example of Trump's racism and sexism, according to Mona Charen. "Every Republican who is reflexively defensive of Trump's blatant nativism and racism should put him or herself in the shoes of immigrants and minorities. How can they not feel frightened when he is willing to stoke such ugly flames?"[48]

"The idea that it's merely 'impolite' to stoke racial tensions is ignorant and dangerous," Seth Mandel, then an editor for the *New York Post*, lectured in early 2018. "Trump's playing with matches whether or not he starts a wildfire, and it's not a distraction to start fireproofing the house."[49] (Mandel provided little evidence for his accusation. Several months later, Trump hosted thousands of young black conservatives at the White House as his approval numbers among minorities continued to rise.)

The problem with NeverTrump's narrative is that Trump is an equal-opportunity insulter. He's as quick with a harsh jab toward white men, including former cabinet officials and aides, as he is with minority congresswomen or NFL players. NeverTrump knows this; they choose to ignore it.

VOTE DEMOCRAT

For the duration of Barack Obama's presidency, Bill Kristol remained a harsh critic, particularly on foreign policy, health care, and racial politics. "President Obama and Eric Holder have done damage to race relations," Kristol told radio host Hugh Hewitt in 2014. "I think they were actually getting pretty good in America, honestly, after Bush. I thought maybe President Obama would kind of complete that movement, and he set it back and that's bad for the country."[50]

By 2018, Kristol was praising the former president, concluding that Obama was a better American than Donald Trump and encouraging

Michelle Obama—who is even further to the left than her husband—to "crush" Trump in 2020.[51]

So this was NeverTrump's campaign slogan during the president's first term: Vote Democrat.

In the off-year elections of 2017, NeverTrump actively campaigned for Democrats. Kristol and McMullin endorsed Ralph Northam, the Democrat running for governor of Virginia, over Republican Ed Gillespie; Kristol and his wife donated $200 to Northam's campaign. Calling Gillespie, a longtime Republican establishment consultant, a "xenophobe" and a "right-wing cultural warrior," Jennifer Rubin urged a vote for Northam.[52] McMullin accused Gillespie of being a white nationalist.[53]

Northam won. Kristol said he was pleased with Northam's victory.[54] Northam later explained how to kill a baby after delivery.

The Senate race in Alabama, however, gave NeverTrump its first chance to burn a Trump associate in a pivotal race. The state's December 2017 special election would determine who would fill the remaining term of Jeff Sessions, Trump's sidelined attorney general. Republican Roy Moore squared off against Democrat Doug Jones in an election scheduled for a few weeks before Christmas.

"Doug Jones would be a better U.S. senator than Roy Moore," Kristol tweeted in October 2017. "Moore as a senator would be a constant embarrassment to the GOP."[55] Kristol qualified his support for Jones, adding that his election would not give Democrats control of the Senate.

Then, allegations that Moore sexually assaulted young teens more than 30 years ago emerged right before Election Day; NeverTrump had all the ammo it needed to demand that Alabamians vote for Jones, a decidedly nonconservative who opposes any restrictions on abortion.

Now, Moore is a kooky guy and the allegations against him may or may not be true. (Conservatives, those guardians of the rule of law, the Constitution, and democratic norms, now contend that stuff like evidence and due process are just legal conveniences that don't apply in the Trump era.)

Republican voters in Alabama were forced to make the same character calibration that many conservatives did in 2016 about Trump: Is the alternative worse? Despite misgivings about Moore's character or past behavior, would he best represent their policy preferences and political interests? Even if some version of the accusations against Moore were true, should they matter more than 30 years later? (Conservatives would again confront this question in the Brett Kavanaugh smear campaign the following year.)

Republicans lost two Senate seats in 2016; the GOP held a slim 52-seat majority with enough squishy Republicans who would acquiesce to the Democrats on any issue under modest pressure. Three Republicans—John McCain, Susan Collins, and Lisa Murkowski—had sided with the Democrats in July to defeat the repeal of Obamacare.[56]

Giving up a Republican vote in the US Senate would be a partial-suicide mission.

Regardless, NeverTrump lined up against Moore. Nebraska senator Ben Sasse, a two-year novice in the Senate, preened that he "believe[d] the women" and threatened to abandon the National Republican Senatorial Committee for backing Moore. "If the political committee that I'm a part of decides to contribute here, I will no longer be a donor to or fund-raiser for it."[57]

The *Weekly Standard* had a Moore-bashing binge for weeks, calling the candidate a constitutional and biblical "illiterate." The magazine implored the Senate to investigate the allegations if Moore won.[58] Gov. John Kasich said Moore should step aside. "I'm the father of two twin daughters and I think it's inappropriate," Kasich told ABC News after the *Washington Post* published the claims.[59]

David French not only argued in favor of Jones's election but shamed evangelicals in Alabama who voted for Moore. "I'm sorry Evangelicals, but your lack of faith is far more dangerous to the Church than any senator, any president, or any justice of the Supreme Court," French lectured. "Do you really have so little trust in God that you believe it's justifiable—no, necessary—to ally with, defend, and even embrace corrupt men if it you think it will save the Church?"[60]

His fire-and-brimstone fury continued. "Our failures will come back to haunt us. There will be woe to those who've compromised with evil through lack of faith. A reckoning is coming. May God have mercy on us all." Then he parted the Potomac.

Jones won. He has since voted against every Trump judicial nominee, including Brett Kavanaugh, but he did vote in favor of the Born Alive Abortion Survivors Act, which protects babies after they're born.[61] (It failed to pass.)

But NeverTrump's pro-Democrat activism in 2017 was just a warm-up for 2018.

"Republican elected officials, from Congress to the state houses, have chosen to become little more than enablers for an out of control executive branch," Tom Nichols wrote in the *Washington Post* in September 2018 in a column that encouraged voters to vote for Democrats in the upcoming midterm elections to rebuke Trump. "The only way to put a stop to this is to vote against the GOP in every race, at every level in 2018. It's tough medicine."[62] Nichols then penned a lengthy piece in the *Atlantic* explaining why he would leave the GOP—again.[63]

Nichols bragged on Twitter how he upbraided a local GOP candidate who had the misfortune of knocking on Nichols's door to ask for his vote.[64] Nichols has never had the guts to run for office himself, of course.

Kristol predicted that there was a "good chance" both the House and Senate would flip blue in 2018.[65] Jonah Goldberg wondered whether the Russians might interfere in the 2018 elections to help Democrats win the House.[66]

At a NeverTrump roundtable in the summer of 2018 with liberal commentator E.J. Dionne, Jennifer Rubin said she wanted "the Democrats, overwhelmingly, absolutely," to win the November elections.[67] Peter Wehner, an evangelical Christian and Bush administration staffer, also wanted Democrats back in power as payback for supporting the president. "The best way to do that is for Republicans to lose because they've been associated with Trump." David Frum's dream for 2018 was that "Adam Schiff replaces Devin Nunes as chairman of the House Intelligence Committee."

He got his wish.

CNN contributor and foul-mouthed Trump-hater Ana Navarro defended her vote for Democrat Andrew Gillum over Republican Ron DeSantis for Florida governor even though she opposed most of Gillum's views. "The 2018 election is a referendum on Trump and his attacks on his shared values," she explained without describing the values conservatives allegedly share with her. "But more than that, it's a battle for the heart and soul of America."[68]

George Will said, "Congressional Republican caucuses must be substantially reduced," and accused retiring House Speaker Paul Ryan of acting as Trump's "poodle," an egregious miscalculation of Ryan's role during Trump's first two years in office.[69]

"It is essential that Republicans pay a price at the ballot box for [supporting Trump]," Boot pleaded on MSNBC in October 2018. "That's why I ... am urging everyone to vote straight-ticket Democrat in November. The Republican Party ... needs to be razed to the ground, it needs to be destroyed, it needs to be burned."[70]

So here were Trump's biggest critics on the Right—people who at first denounced Trump's scant conservative credentials, then his lifestyle, then his alleged racism, sexism, xenophobia, etc.—imploring the electorate to put in power lawmakers who would go to any extreme to crush everything these self-proclaimed "conservatives" purported to cherish.

Identity politics, not principles, would rule the day. Wealth-seizing, abortion-loving, gun-confiscating climate crackpots would assume control of powerful congressional committees. And that future had the full-throated endorsement by alleged conservatives populating the NeverTrump movement.

But again, NeverTrumpers were too cowardly to confess the real reason they wanted Democrats to take over. It had nothing to do with restoring order or even reining in Donald Trump. They knew Democrats would spend every ounce of their political capital to try to oust Trump from office—which they have.

The Democrats picked up 41 seats in the House; Nancy Pelosi reclaimed her Speaker's gavel. Just like every other midterm election, the out-of-power party capitalized on the frustration of its impotent constituency; a little ballot harvesting in California helped, too.

Newcomers such as Alexandria Ocasio-Cortez, Ilhan Omar, and Rashida Tlaib, thanks to NeverTrump's backing, dominate the political discourse and policy priorities of the 116th Congress. (Republicans, however, picked up two seats in the Senate.) The far-left agenda of the Democratic Party would come into full view, right as the 2020 presidential campaign got underway.

In some ways, NeverTrump did Republicans a favor.

THANKS, NEVERTRUMP!

Fealty to the Green New Deal, open borders, Medicare for all including illegal immigrants, and free college tuition became a litmus test for each 2020 Democratic presidential candidate. No one, it seemed, could reach far enough left to satisfy the ruling "Squad," the nickname (and not an affectionate one) given to Ocasio-Cortez and her Democratic acolytes by House Speaker Nancy Pelosi.

Leading Democrats—even rank-and-file voters—started to openly embrace socialism. Articles touting the benefits of socialism blanketed news outlets and opinion websites. Commentators derided Trump for condemning socialism. "Trump is trying to make it sound scary again," complained *Washington Post*'s Glenn Kessler, as if the word wasn't scary before.[71]

Vermont senator Bernie Sanders delivered a lengthy speech, defending the "S" word: "We must recognize that in the 21st century, in the wealthiest country in the history of the world, economic rights are human rights," he told a crowd at George Washington University in June 2019. "That is what I mean by democratic socialism."[72] (Ocasio-Cortez endorsed Sanders in October.)

A Pew poll that same month revealed an astonishing 65 percent of self-identified Democrats had a favorable view of socialism. At the same time, only 55 percent of Democrats held a favorable view of capitalism.[73]

But their extreme ideas alarmed most Americans—including the same NeverTrumpers who urged voters to elect Democrats in 2018. Tom Nichols, who left the Republican Party (again) over Trump and instructed Americans to elect Democrats up and down the ballot in the midterms, penned a "Dear John" letter to his new pals on the Left. After Democratic presidential candidates participated in a disastrous CNN town hall on LGBTQ issues, Nichols fumed that they would blow the chance to boot Trump from the White House in 2020.

"We pledged over two years ago to join hands on this one issue," Nichols wrote in October 2019. "But now I worry that in your zeal to win the Woke Twitter and college campus primary, you will simply make the same mistakes you made in 2016. Your nominee will crush it in the bicoastal race to be the Honorary Governor of the New Californiork Republic. Blue cities everywhere will welcome you as liberators. And Trump will laugh at you every day from Washington."[74]

Charlie Sykes begged Democrats to stop talking about their radical agenda, including eliminating private health care, paying out reparations, and imposing new taxes.[75]

NeverTrump helped create a socialist monster, but it was too late to slay it. The useful idiots for the Left had elevated bigger idiots to control

Congress and run for president. Their buyer's remorse is delicious to watch—they would become more pathetic and desperate as the Democratic presidential field looked more and more like a clown car that couldn't drive down the middle of any political road, let alone beat Donald Trump.

CHAPTER 4

BUT GORSUCH!

The Senate will continue to observe the Biden Rule so the
American people have a voice in this momentous decision.
Give the people a voice in filling this vacancy.
—Senate Majority Leader Mitch McConnell,
March 2016, on the US Senate's refusal to
confirm Merrick Garland to the Supreme Court

Conservative voters reluctant to vote for Donald Trump ultimately punched their card for the political interloper for one reason: control of the Supreme Court.

The sudden passing of Antonin Scalia in February 2016 would be the most consequential political event that year, more pivotal than the Hillary Clinton email scandal or the release of the *Access Hollywood* tapes. His death reminded voters what was at stake on Election Day—a Republican president filling Supreme Court vacancies with conservative jurists, or at a minimum, right-of-center ones, or Hillary Clinton irrevocably shifting the court to the left.

Thankfully, despite tremendous pressure, Senate Majority Leader Mitch McConnell rejected demands to hold confirmation hearings for Merrick Garland, Obama's pick to replace Scalia. Control over the Supreme Court remained a top campaign issue that both sides leveraged for political gain.

Republicans, particularly conservatives justifiably alarmed at the image of Hillary Clinton appointing future justices—perhaps her own husband or one of the Obamas—to fill at least one seat on a tenuously balanced and aged Supreme Court, decided they trusted Trump more than Clinton with that responsibility. Trump's campaign released a list of prospective jurors in May; the move reaped the intended results as left-wing activist groups immediately condemned the candidates as "dangerous" and "extreme conservatives."[1] It played right into Trump's hands, assuring skeptical conservatives that Trump would do as promised.

After the election, exit polls confirmed that one-quarter of Trump voters said the future composition of the Supreme Court most influenced their decision.[2]

Trump nominated Neil Gorsuch in late January; Gorsuch's conservative credentials rivaled the movement's heroes, including Scalia and Clarence Thomas. The Senate confirmed Gorsuch 54–45 in April. Conservatives breathed a collective sigh of relief that Trump had fulfilled his pledge to nominate strict constitutionalists to the bench. It should have been an encouraging sign for NeverTrump, an early sign that Trump would not betray the conservatives who helped him win the White House.

After tepid plaudits from NeverTrump, they quickly figured out a way to turn the solid pick into an insult: "But Gorsuch" was a retort frequently wielded as a cudgel against Trump supporters, particularly conservatives, at every Trump misstep during the first half of his term. Conservatives sold their souls for a cheap Supreme Court seat, the meme implied.

Tom Nichols explained the motivation behind the "But Gorsuch" taunt: "The unwillingness of so many of his supporters to hold him to even a minimal standard of accountability means that a certain amount of condescension from the rest of us is unavoidable," he wrote in *USA Today* after Gorsuch's confirmation.[3] (Trump had been president for three months at that point.)

By summer, "But Gorsuch" ranked as an "evergreen meme" according to David French, who tweeted a photo of the two-word rejoinder on a road sign sinking under water.[4]

The mockery of the Gorsuch appointment signaled that NeverTrump would not be sincere in its role as the conservative hall monitor of the Trump presidency. How could conservatives possibly justify diminishing the importance of keeping a very slim conservative tilt to the Supreme Court at a time when the executive and legislative branches are abdicating their power to the judiciary? Why would so-called conservatives downplay such a significant win for their own cause, one of the few barricades between the conservative movement and the Left?

The increasing dominance of the judiciary, often undermining the will of the people and their elected representatives, has put conservatives and the bipartisan working class at a disadvantage. Michael Lind described the judiciary as "an unelected superdelegation" populated with overeducated elites who rule in favor of policies hostile to Middle America.[5] This power shift, only too happily embraced by cowardly politicians in Washington and beyond, has resulted in a "juristocracy," a constitutional imbalance that continued to play out during Trump's first term, particularly in the area of illegal immigration.

NeverTrump's diminution of the need to recalibrate this imbalance demonstrated either their tone deafness to the problem or their complicity in it. On this score, Middle America has been far more in touch with the real threat of this "juristocracy" than the self-proclaimed erudite NeverTrumpers.

The silliness of "But Gorsuch" started to grate even on Trump skeptics. Writing in *National Review* toward the end of Trump's first year in office, editor Rich Lowry suggested it was time to retire the "But Gorsuch" meme. "Trump has governed so far as more of a Republican and conservative than I expected," Lowry wrote in December 2017. "Also, it's simply not true that all we have to show from the Trump administration is Gorsuch."[6] Lowry ticked off a list of Trump's conservative accomplishments, such as the tax cut bill, elimination of Obamacare's individual mandate, and deregulation, to name a few.

Lowry's point, however, revealed NeverTrump's approach moving forward. Not only would most reverse their positions on key policies, as described in the previous chapter, but NeverTrump planned to frustrate Trump's progress on three signature MAGA issues: troops, trade, and the border.

THANKS, OBAMA

In a documentary covering the activities of Barack Obama's national security team as his term came to an end in 2016, Samantha Power, former US ambassador to the United Nations, said this: "[Our] world is a world where we have 65 million displaced, Yemen and Syria and Iraq...Nigeria, Cameroon, Chad, Central Africa Republic...South Sudan, Darfur. Afghanistan, of course. Venezuela imploding." She confessed in the 2018 HBO film, *The Final Year*, "There are concerns about terrorism...and where all the other trendlines on democracy, right now at least, are going in the wrong direction."[7]

Her colleague, Obama's "mind meld" Ben Rhodes, claimed that the administration's top international achievements were signing the Paris Climate Accord, normalizing relations with Cuba, and negotiating the Iran nuclear deal. Rhodes admitted that the White House repeatedly misjudged Russian president Vladimir Putin. Obama failed to take stronger action in Syria despite repeated promises to enforce a "red line," Rhodes explained, because it would have jeopardized both the climate and the Iran nuclear deals.[8]

In 2011, Obama assured the world that Syrian president Bashir al-Assad's days were numbered. When Trump took office, Assad was still there.

In other words, Barack Obama bequeathed to Donald Trump a dangerous world on fire.

But every time President Trump attempted to clean up one of the messes left behind by his predecessor—or his predecessor's predecessor—NeverTrump warned that the president would lead us into World War III. Our alliances would shred, they roared, and Americans would be exposed to all sorts of danger while Trump watched Fox News, ate McDonalds, and wrote mean tweets.

Official Washington objects to Trump's approach on nearly every issue, but particularly on foreign policy. This stems from their hard-wired case of FOMO—fear of missing out. It's about money and influence. A president is not to make random campaign pledges during an election year, then attempt to fulfill those promises on his own without the help of Beltway experts, according to all Beltway experts.

Any decision abroad, no matter how miniscule or irrelevant in the eyes of the American people who have actual work to do, requires massive amounts of input from professionals with advanced degrees in international relations. Working groups must convene; think tanks must host a series of seminars to debate the choice at hand; mission statements must be prepared; and harshly worded letters must be signed by all the right people and delivered to lawmakers on Capitol Hill. Former bureaucrats must proffer their expertise on the pages of the *New York Times* and on *Meet the Press*. (Their anger spilled over during the impeachment hearings when many Foggy Bottom bureaucrats whined about Trump's go-it-alone method and use of "irregular channels" of diplomacy.)

The danger in Trump's almost solitary approach to such matters poses a menace not to world security but to the power structure of the entitled diplomatic corps. But they can't say that out loud (although by 2019, they were getting close) so they instead made Trump the bad guy.

This includes, of course, NeverTrump, which paints President Trump as the greatest threat to global peace and security since the Nazis (a comparison the Left and NeverTrump used with abandon).

"America...will enter 2019 as a superpower in decline, trying to slink off the world stage. The world's jackals and hyenas already sense our weakness and are circling closer. Our national security has never—not even during the Cold War—been in this much sustained danger."[9] That hysteria, courtesy of security "expert" Tom Nichols, was prompted by the resignation of former defense secretary James Mattis, who quit in December 2018 to protest Trump's approach to international affairs.

Now, there wasn't a shred of evidence to support Nichols's hyperbole. (That warning, like all of his prophecies related to Trump, didn't come to pass.) But Nichols's motive, shared by his NeverTrump cohort, is to needlessly alarm Americans about the unstable genius in the White House in order to satiate his own contempt for the president. It is pernicious; fabricating imaginary threats by using faulty analogies isn't just dumb and lazy; it's dangerous.

The resignation of one defense secretary posed the same amount of potential harm to the world and the nation as the nuclear arsenal possessed by the Soviet Union in the 1980s? This is not the appraisal of a sober, serious person.

But, luckily for Nichols, he has the company of fools in his unhinged rants about Trump's foreign policy. "Now is the time for Republicans in Congress to declare their independence from the Republican in the White House and refuse once and for all to rubber-stamp Donald Trump's whims and desires," David French demanded in *National Review* online following Mattis's resignation. "General Mattis has performed a profoundly important public service. He has served his country in combat. He has now served it well with his resignation. Will the nation heed the warning he delivered today?"[10]

French's admonition followed a similar pattern: Whenever someone left the White House, especially a man of the military, NeverTrump insisted that the official's parting words sent a message to the republic that

Donald Trump must be ousted from office. Once upon a time, a top-level resignation coupled with a grudge-airing letter would have instead been greeted with either the usual musings about intra-administration squabbles or, worse, declared an act of insubordination by a government official, no matter how high his military rank.

But in the Trump era, everyone—congressional Republicans, the US military, Trump-supporting Americans—is required to subvert the elected president's wishes in fealty to the actual power in Washington: the unelected ruling class. NeverTrump, inexplicably, considered this wholly in line with "conservative" principles.

Trump's overtures to Kim Jong Un, the despotic leader of North Korea (another rogue nation that Barack Obama failed to tame), will lead America into war. Calling Trump's Singapore summit with Kim "arguably the worst summit outcome since Yalta," Mona Charen berated the president for acting as Kim's public relations rep. "Trump did far more than overlook Kim's atrocious human-rights abuses," Charen wrote in *National Review* in June 2018. "We've put ourselves on the same moral plane as North Korea."[11] (Reviewing some of Charen's past work, I believe she is arguably one who has taken the most precipitous slide from serious, intelligent analyst to foaming-at-the mouth untamed shrew.)

Democrats successfully co-opted NeverTrump into participating in one of the greatest hoaxes ever perpetrated against the American people—the idea that Donald Trump is a stooge of Vladimir Putin and conspired with the Russian dictator to help him win the Oval Office. After Trump's wobbly, erratic July 2018 press conference with Putin in Helsinki, NeverTrump ranted for days. "President Trump undermined the global world order, weakened our alliances, cast doubt on our commitments to NATO, sided with Vladimir Putin over our own intelligence agencies," Charlie Sykes bellowed.[12]

"He sat there on the stage like a whipped dog," Rick Wilson howled on MSNBC. "But it was very clear today the boss was in that room and who wears the dog collar."[13]

Trump twice recalled American troops from Syria: Both times, the action was met with pearl-clutching among the NeverTrump commentariat. "This should be called MAGA, make Assad great again," Bret Stephens said after Trump's 2018 decision to withdraw about 2,000 soldiers from northern Syria.[14] Trump, Stephens said, would be responsible for the "human tragedy" that awaited the Kurds once US troops left.

When Trump again announced a further drawdown in October 2019, David French insisted the president's move was immoral and represented a "betrayal" of our Kurdish allies; Jonah Goldberg called it a "scandalously incompetent and reckless action."[15]

From the Senate floor, Senator Romney blasted the withdrawal: "It strikes at American honor," he said on October 17, 2019. "What we have done to the Kurds will stand as a bloodstain in the annals of American history."[16] NeverTrump, and even some Trump-supporting lawmakers, warned that a retreating US military in Syria would embolden ISIS. (In 2012, as a candidate for president, Romney proposed that America should help arm Syrian rebels and expressed worry over attacks against "ally" Turkey.)[17]

Ten days later, on October 27, 2019, US special forces raided the compound of Abu Bakr al-Baghdadi, the leader of ISIS, who blew himself up as troops advanced.

Trump authorized a drone strike against Qasem Soleimani, an international terrorist parading as an Iranian general, on January 3. This prompted howls of injustice from NeverTrump quarters.

Tom Nichols lauded Iran's restraint in the face of Trump's recklessness. "The Americans hit the Iranians hard, but Iran's response on the night of January 7 was calibrated and smart, which suggests that Tehran is better at the game of deterrence than Donald Trump or his advisers," Nichols cooed in the *Atlantic*.[18] Nichols warned that Trump had created a "crisis" that the cooler heads in Tehran deescalated.

Also writing in the *Atlantic*, David Frum contemptibly blamed Trump for the deaths of 176 people aboard a passenger jet taking off in Tehran during Iran's January 7, 2020, retaliatory strike against the US compound in Baghdad.[19] After the Iranians admitted they shot down the plane by mistake, Frum defended the mullahs as being understandably "jumpy" in the face of Western aggression.[20] Even though Iran had started the latest round of attacks, Trump, according to Frum, was the real culprit because he canceled the Iran nuclear deal.

None of NeverTrump's dire predictions of doom have been realized. There is no nuclear war with North Korea; our allies have not abandoned the United States; World War III is not underway.[21] Trump has not channeled Hitler or Stalin, rounding up political prisoners and prosecuting them for speaking ill of the crown.

The American public is rethinking our various military commitments across the globe, Afghanistan chief among them after a nearly 20-year presence in that country with bleak outcomes. Trump pledged to gradually end that commitment. "It is up to the people of Afghanistan to take ownership of their future, to govern their society and to achieve an everlasting peace," he said in a speech in August 2017 while laying out the general guidelines of his administration's exit strategy.[22]

Americans are ready and, in some instances, regretful about our long-term engagements overseas. A heartbreaking Pew Research Poll in July 2019 found that 64 percent of veterans now say the Iraq War wasn't worth fighting, as does 62 percent of the civilian public. Fifty-eight percent of veterans and 59 percent of the public had a similar sentiment about Afghanistan.[23]

In December 2019, the *Washington Post* published a stunning exposé that contained hundreds of documents related to the failed war in Afghanistan.[24] Following a two-year legal battle, the paper finally obtained private interviews conducted by the Special Inspector General for Afghanistan Reconstruction, which revealed the mismanagement of the nearly two-decade conflict.

National security, military, and diplomatic officials from both the Bush and Obama administrations confessed that no one really knew how to handle the war from the start. The NATO alliance never worked properly; corruption is rampant; opiate production is at record levels; and the lives of more than 2,400 Americans and nearly $1 trillion in US tax dollars have been wasted on a war started by George W. Bush and promoted by many of those involved in the NeverTrump movement.

In his congressional testimony, John Sopko, the head of the agency, admitted he found an "odor of mendacity and hubris" that infected the war's planning and execution.[25] It turned out the same national security sector that has insisted Donald Trump is a threat to global order is itself a legitimate menace.

Another massive failure of Conservative, Inc. and another article of faith in the Republican Party—the use of American troops for vague purposes such as terrorist-hunting or democracy-spreading or nation-building—ground into dust.

TAKING ON TRADE

Trump's attempts to rectify unfair trade agreements and finally confront China after years of appeasement at the hands of both Democrats and

Republicans offend the "free trade" sensibilities of NeverTrump. As a candidate, Trump repeatedly condemned what he viewed as harmful trade deals such as Obama's proposed Trans-Pacific Partnership. "The Trans-Pacific Partnership will lead to even greater unemployment. Do not pass it," he tweeted in 2015 before he announced his candidacy.[26] His opposition to the TPP led to Hillary Clinton retracting her support of the pact.

On his fourth day in office, Trump withdrew from the TPP.

Trump's team also sought to renegotiate the outdated terms of the 1994 North American Free Trade Agreement. "Our aim is that NAFTA be modernized to include new provisions to address intellectual property rights, regulatory practices, state-owned enterprises, services, customs procedures...and small and medium enterprises," Robert Lighthizer, Trump's trade representative, wrote to congressional leaders in May 2017. "The United States seeks to support high-paying jobs in the United States and to grow the U.S. economy by improving U.S. opportunities under NAFTA."[27]

In 2018, Trump levied tariffs on steel and aluminum imported from Canada and Mexico. (Tariffs were lifted in May 2019 as negotiators progressed on the updated pact.)[28] Other tariffs were imposed on dairy, automobiles, washing machines, and solar panels.

"I am a Tariff Man," Trump announced in a December 2018 tweet. "When people or countries come in to raid the great wealth of our Nation, I want them to pay for the privilege of doing so. It will always be the best way to max out our economic power. We are right now taking in $billions in Tariffs. MAKE AMERICA RICH AGAIN."[29]

With few tools in his presidential arsenal that didn't require action by a feckless Congress, Trump weaponized tariffs to force the European Union to uphold its NATO commitments, muscle the Mexican government to halt border crossings, and confront China for a number of ongoing transgressions.

China had been on Trump's radar for years. As an international businessman, Trump was well aware of how the Chinese game the system with impunity. But Washington, on a bipartisan basis, looked the other way. This allowed China to steal hundreds of billions in American intellectual property each year. "For over a decade, the Chinese government has conducted and supported cyber intrusions into U.S. commercial networks targeting confidential business information held by U.S. firms," according to a detailed report by the White House on China's economic aggression. "Through these cyber intrusions, China's government has gained unauthorized access to a wide range of commercially valuable business information, including trade secrets, technical data, negotiating positions, and sensitive and proprietary internal communications."[30]

If only the cyber intrusion had been into the Democratic National Committee's email system, perhaps federal law enforcement would have taken notice.

FBI director Christopher Wray told the Senate in July 2019 that China's espionage operation is "deep and diverse and wide and vexing."[31] Secretary of State Mike Pompeo correctly assessed that previous administrations had "just ignored" China at great cost to the United States.[32] (The country would get a cruel lesson about China's insidious role in America's supply chain during the coronavirus outbreak in 2020. Americans learned how dependent we are on China for medical supplies and pharmaceutical ingredients.)[33]

But despite overwhelming evidence of China's economic war against the United States, NeverTrump objected to the use of tariffs or other measures to fight back. Bret Stephens, after detailing a list of China's transgressions, fretted at Trump's brinkmanship. Trump's approach must "keep [China] from becoming an enemy," Stephens wrote in the *New York Times.* "Generous accommodations in trade negotiations would help: The last thing the U.S. or the world needs is a wrecked Chinese economy or a humiliated Chinese public."[34]

Max Boot called Trump's trade and tariff policies "stupid" and predicted it could cause another Great Depression.[35] A trade war will ruin the economy, Tom Nichols concluded in 2018, but the upside is it would punish farmers and small business owners who voted for Trump. "Sure, a disastrous exchange of economic artillery between the United States and the rest of the world would drive some farms and small businesses under, but it would give the voters what they wanted," he sneered.[36]

By late 2019, China and the US began making progress on improved trade relations and protections of intellectual property, including China's commitment to purchase more American agricultural commodities.[37] On January 15, 2020, Trump and Chinese vice premier Liu

He signed the first phase of a historical trade agreement that began to confront China's bad behavior and ease some tariffs.[38] Trump's trade officials pledged to work throughout 2020 on a second phase to bring more tariff relief if China continued to open its markets to US products and services.[39]

The economy didn't collapse; our allies didn't abandon us; and for the first time, the US successfully confronted one of our greatest economic and national security threats.

The Trump White House renegotiated NAFTA under the banner of the US-Mexico-Canada Agreement (USMCA). The updated pact is supported by many Democrats but had been stymied by impeachment drama. Ironically, on the same day House Democrats issued two articles of impeachment, House Speaker Nancy Pelosi announced that Congress and the White House had reached a deal to move forward on the updated agreement.

The House and Senate ratified USMCA, and Trump signed the deal at the White House on January 29, 2020.[40] "We just ended a nightmare called NAFTA," Trump told a cheering crowd at an automotive supply company in Michigan the next day. "They took our jobs for a long time. For decades, politicians campaigned across Michigan promising to do something about NAFTA. I'm your spokesman, I'm someone who represents you."[41]

The president delivered on one of his biggest campaign promises. China caved as their economy slumped and a deadly virus swamped parts of the country.

The *Wall Street Journal* observed in January 2020 that much of the US economy had escaped "unscathed" from the two-year trade war.[42] And the devastating trade war and resultant economic depression never materialized.

Another NeverTrump fail.

OPEN BORDERS AND "KIDS IN CAGES"

In November 2019, Reuters posted an article with the damning headline "the U.S. has the highest rate of child detention," according to a recently released United Nations report.[43] The figure included more than 100,000 immigrant children housed in closed facilities.

One problem: The report collected data from 2015. Barack Obama, not

Donald Trump, was president when the record number of minors were detained. So Reuters pulled the article and notified their readers that "no replacement story will be issued."[44]

Reuters's move reflected an infuriating habit of the news media when it related to Barack Obama. Bad news was ignored, malfeasance was explained away, and anything that went wrong on his watch could be traced back to the Republicans. That's how, despite numerous scandals, not the least of which was a coordinated campaign of deceit about the Benghazi terror attacks two months before the 2012 election, Obama and Vice President Joe Biden still claim to this day that the Obama years were "scandal-free."

But Obama's lax immigration policies, and the Republicans' failure to correct the crisis despite controlling the legislative branch during Obama's last two years, would create another crisis for Donald Trump. And perhaps no other issue has rendered NeverTrump more hysterical, more hyperbolic, more angst-ridden, and more enraged than Trump's efforts to control the border. Their collective objections could occupy an entire chapter, but I'll just cover some of their greatest hits.

To begin, NeverTrump vehemently opposed Trump's slogan "Build the Wall." The chant smacked of nativism and racism: "At Trump rallies, 'Build the Wall' was the tent pole of his speeches and central to the crowd's Pavlovian call-and-response," Rick Wilson wrote in his 2018 book. "Xenophobic fury at brown people coming here to live a better life doesn't motivate every person who voted for Trump, but every single person motivated by a xenophobic fury at brown people coming here to live a better life was a Trump voter."[45]

Further, the prevailing view of anti-Trump conservatives on immigration was expressed by Kristol in February 2017. "Immigrants do have more of the old-fashioned American virtues than lots of old-fashioned Americans," Kristol said during an event for the American Enterprise Institute in February 2017.[46]

Kristol oddly compared a wall on the southern border with the Berlin Wall, recalling how "a long time ago, in a conservative movement far, far away, we all thrilled to Ronald Reagan saying, 'Mr. Gorbachev, tear down this wall.'"[47] Bret Stephens had a better idea: Deport Americans whose families have been here for a few generations because they're all lazy, entitled, irreligious, and drug-addicted. In Stephens's stuffy opinion, he has "always thought of the United States as a country that belongs first to its newcomers."[48]

Nope.

The avatar of NeverTrump's approach to illegal immigration during the Trump era is Mitt Romney. The junior senator from Utah ran as an immigration hawk during his failed presidential bid in 2012. He gave a lengthy speech in January 2012, detailing the stringent immigration policies he would impose if elected. "We will stop the illegal flow of immigration into this country," he told the Hispanic Leadership Network. Those here illegally, Romney said, should self-deport.[49]

But that was then, this is Trump. In a *Washington Post* op-ed on New Year's Day 2019, Romney warned that he would "speak out against significant statements or actions that are divisive, racist, sexist, anti-immigrant, dishonest or destructive to democratic institutions."[50] After he was sworn in as Utah's junior senator, a consolation prize for both losing the presidency and failing to land a primo spot in the Trump administration despite his tail-wagging before the new president, Romney replaced McCain as Trump's bitter bridesmaid in the Senate. The one-time immigration hardliner, as he had done so often before during his political career, changed his mind about securing the border.

Before Trump signed an emergency declaration in February 2019 to authorize funds to finish the wall—"the problem of large-scale unlawful migration through the southern border is long-standing, and despite the executive branch's exercise of existing statutory authorities, the situation has worsened in certain respects in recent years," the order read—Romney and his NeverTrump allies argued that the president lacked the authority to implement the National Emergencies Act.[51]

National Review posted several columns opposing Trump's move: David French caterwauled for the thousandth time that Trump was subverting the Constitution. "This is an attempted abuse of the constitutional order that is justified mainly by the existence of previous successful abuses of the constitutional order. Each abuse builds on the next; hypocrisy builds on hypocrisy. Congratulations, partisans. You claim you're saving our country. In reality, you're wrecking our constitution."[52] (Constitutional experts such as professor Jonathan Turley argued that yes, the president indeed had the authority to invoke the act.)[53]

National Review's editorial board urged Republicans to vote to disapprove of Trump's declaration, even though they admitted Congress had shirked its duty and most Republicans agreed with Trump's end goal of fortifying the border.[54]

NR got its wish: Romney joined 11 other Republican senators in March 2019 to overturn Trump's declaration. Romney, mimicking French, preened that his vote "is a vote for the constitution and for the balance of power that is at its core."[55]

But the next month, Romney was shocked that somehow illegals got the green-light message and flooded the border. In April 2019, Romney admitted to *Meet the Press*'s Chuck Todd that the situation had worsened since he and his colleagues shot down the president's emergency declaration. "In the past few weeks, there's been a dramatic change... We're seeing unaccompanied young people as well as families with lots of kids pouring into the border and they say the magic word, 'I'm seeking asylum,'" Romney explained. "We don't begin to have enough space in our facilities to maintain the kind of care these people deserve....and so they're just being turned out into our country... It's overwhelming our system."[56] Romney confirmed that more than 125,000 migrants had entered the country illegally in the first few months of the year.

But nothing exposed the double-standard of the news media and the willingness of NeverTrump not just to oppose everything Trump attempted to do but to cover for Barack Obama in the process more than the family separation debacle. In the summer of 2018, Attorney General Jeff Sessions announced a "zero-tolerance" policy on illegal border crossings. This coincided with a surge of family units attempting to seek asylum in the United States. Rachel Bovard explained this situation in *American Greatness* in June 2018:

> President Trump has decided on full enforcement of the law against illegal border crossers, implementing a "no tolerance" policy of prosecution. In law enforcement terms, this means that when illegal aliens are apprehended crossing the border, they are put in a detention facility and separated from their families while they await processing. Their children, if they have them, are transferred to the custody of the Health and Human Services Department, who care for them in temporary shelters.[57]

Some of the facilities, Bovard noted, can be in "far-flung places."

Democrats and the media pounced; NeverTrump lost their minds.

Nationwide protests fueled public outrage. Photos of children in "cages" flooded social media—until it was discovered the pictures dated back to 2014, when the Obama administration confronted a similar situation. NeverTrumpers, taking their cue from the Left as usual, amplified the most outrageous and incendiary descriptions of the calamity.

Jennifer Rubin went on a nonstop, weeks-long tirade. Family separation was the "worst human rights abuse in decades," she claimed,[58] and evoked the Holocaust-era pledge "never again."[59] She took aim at White House press secretary Sarah Sanders for speaking on behalf of the administration, urging public harassment against the first mother to fill that role. "We're not going to let these people go through life unscathed," she warned on MSNBC in July 2018, at the height of the child separation uproar. "Sarah Huckabee has no right to live a life of no fuss, no muss after...inciting against the press. These people should be made uncomfortable and I think that's a life sentence."[60]

Tom Nichols concluded that the policy was intended to please Trump's base. "But this policy is *meant* to produce photos of terrified children. It's the goal: to traumatize kids in public as a deterrent. It's immoral. If you support it, so are you," he tweeted in June 2018.[61]

A Kristol-led nonprofit—more on that in chapter 8—produced a pro-immigration ad to run on the Fourth of July featuring a video clip of Ronald Reagan praising the US as a nation of immigrants, with the Statue of Liberty in the background. The spot ended with the chyron "immigrants have always made America great."[62]

Rick Wilson accused Trump supporters of being a "bunch of tendentious doucheholes taking pleasure in the misery and trauma the policy causes."[63] Ana Navarro blasted Ivanka Trump after she tweeted a photo of herself and her toddler. "How nice that you get to hold your child in your arms and not face the anguish of having him torn from you and left to God knows what fate."[64]

Not one to be outdone in the drama department, Evan McMullin weighed in: "The lies. The dictator adoration. The bigotry. The lawlessness. The indecency. The corruption. The forced separation of families and the caging of children. This is Trumpism and it is evil. It's destructive to people, to the Republican Party and, most importantly, to our country."[65]

Some argued Trump should stop the policy unilaterally without the aid of Congress, a position they would immediately contradict months later related to his emergency declaration. "I want the president to end his administration's family-separation policy," David French wrote in *National Review* in July 2018. "He doesn't need Congress to do the right thing."[66]

The condemnation continued for weeks. Solutions to the persistent problem, however, weren't offered, a stubborn habit practiced by Never-Trump. They opposed border security, rejected the use of tariffs to encourage Mexico to halt the flow of illegal immigrants from Central America, mocked Trump's concerns about drug and child trafficking (not to mention the influx of dangerous gang members), and failed for years to implement lasting immigration reform. Yet here they were, en masse, shrieking about human rights abuses and denouncing all Trump supporters as immoral child abusers.

On every key issue important to Trump and his base, NeverTrump failed time and again to offer anything but criticism. As I wrote in *American Greatness* at the end of 2018,

> Alarmed the president wants to pull a few thousand troops out of
> Syria? NeverTrump should convince Americans that the loss of
> one U.S. soldier is worth the risk—and use something more than
> the banal "it's in the interest of our national security" trope...Don't
> like the Tariff Man? Then what, NeverTrump, is your plan to halt
> unfair trade practices and tariffs levied on American products? How
> would NeverTrump have exacted a steep reduction in Chinese-im-
> posed tariffs on U.S. automobiles, as Trump succeeded in doing
> this year?...How would NeverTrump halt the theft of hundreds of
> billions of dollars in intellectual property by the Chinese each year?
> There is no such thing as free trade between nations no matter how
> many times NeverTrump clicks its loafers and repeats it in the CNN
> green room. Ditto for border security. If a wall won't fix anything, as
> most NeverTrumpers insist, then what will?[67]

As of the printing of this book, they still have no answers.

The "But Gorsuch" meme set the stage for NeverTrump's most flagrant betrayal of the conservative movement: aiding the Left's character assassination of Brett Kavanaugh.

When the history of Trump's first term in office is written, the Left's despicable and destructive assault against Brett Kavanaugh will stand out as its lowest moment—and that's saying something. Standing with Kavanaugh, under siege by soulless activists willing to go to any extreme to keep him off the Supreme Court, should have been a no-brainer even for the most ardent NeverTrumper.

An unsubstantiated, last-minute accusation from an activist academic who claimed Kavanaugh sexually assaulted her sometime in the early 1980s monopolized news coverage just as the Senate was poised to confirm the judge in the fall of 2018. Senate Republicans delayed the process as investigators attempted to verify Christine Blasey Ford's allegations and arrange for her testimony.

For days, Kavanaugh was ruthlessly attacked by Democrats and the news media. More accusers stepped forward, their stories even more improbable than Ford's. Even Michael Avenatti, the now-incarcerated lawyer for Stormy Daniels, made a cameo appearance, representing one accuser whose charges were so outlandish that the chairman of the Senate Judiciary Committee later referred both of them to the Justice Department for lying to Congress.

The onslaught was so craven that some NeverTrumpers temporarily abandoned their enmity toward the president to voice support. "For the first time since Donald Trump entered the political fray, I find myself grateful that he's in it," Bret Stephens admitted in October 2018, at the height of the tempest. "I'm grateful because Trump has not backed down in the face of the slipperiness, hypocrisy and dangerous standard-setting deployed by opponents of Brett Kavanaugh's nomination to the Supreme Court. I'm grateful because ferocious and even crass obstinacy has its uses in life, and never more so than in the face of sly moral bullying. I'm grateful because he's a big fat hammer fending off a razor-sharp dagger."[68]

Jonah Goldberg condemned the media's complicity in the character assassination of Kavanaugh, warning that their conduct only served to prove Trump correct that the press is the "enemy of the people," as if that were the real outrage.[69] John Podhoretz accurately observed that the same cabal of Democratic activists and interest groups that aligned against Robert Bork and Clarence Thomas were taking aim at Kavanaugh.[70]

But not all NeverTrumpers were as forthright. They jumped on the anti-Kavanaugh lynch mob just when conservatives needed every voice available to fight the outmatched battle.

After Ford's allegation prompted a wave of stories from women (irrelevantly) sharing their own accounts of sexual abuse and assault, Seth Mandel declared Kavanaugh's nomination was "donezo." Not because Kavanaugh suddenly was unqualified to serve or even proven guilty of the baseless charges. No, Mandel argued, the Kavanaugh debacle had "morphed into a cultural reckoning of sorts, representative of something we haven't dealt with as a society and this is going to be the moment we do so. He's done." He continued: "It's not about Kavanaugh anymore, at least not wholly. We just crossed the Rubicon. We can argue over whether that's fair, but it's true. It's something different now, and there's nothing Kavanaugh can say that will make it revert to what it was before."[71]

He repeatedly insisted the White House should withdraw Kavanaugh's nomination.

Mandel later commented that Ford's accusations were "credible" and her bravery "undeniable." He lamented that she was thrust into the spotlight when she wanted her allegations kept private. Further, he wrote, "Christine Blasey Ford has acted honorably, with grace and care far beyond what we should in good conscience demand of a victim of sexual assault."[72] With that statement alone, Mandel declared Brett Kavanaugh guilty.

Nancy French, wife of David French and a NeverTrumper herself, insisted that if Ford's accusations were true, Kavanaugh should be denied a spot on the nation's top court. "Pundits' comfortable political opinions and their Supreme Court idolatry is poisonous when it results in waving away the gravity of assault," French wrote in the *Washington Post*.[73] French linked to a 2016 piece detailing her own story of sexual abuse from a few decades earlier, a story she would resurrect twice: once to oppose the candidacy of Donald Trump after the *Access Hollywood* tape and once to oppose the candidacy of Alabama Senate candidate Roy Moore. (In a 2017

NPR interview, French said she had "never spoken about [it] in her life," referring to a youth pastor who repeatedly sexually assaulted her when she was young, until she told her story in the *Washington Post* a few weeks before the 2016 election.)[74]

After Kavanaugh's emotional testimony in the face of unproven accusations, which led to death threats against his family, Charlie Sykes criticized Kavanaugh's "harangue" and accused him of going "full Trump" before the Senate Judiciary Committee on September 25, 2018. (Questioning Kavanaugh's judicial temperament was another last-ditch ploy by the Left to thwart his confirmation. NeverTrump, again, eagerly played along.) "The standards for judges are not the same as the standards for cable television or politics. Kavanaugh could have presented his case with dignity and controlled anger. Instead he chose to be aggrieved and petulant, more Sean Hannity than Felix Frankfurter," Sykes sniffed.[75]

Sen. Ben Sasse choked up on the floor after the Ford-Kavanaugh showdown; he had earlier advised Trump to nominate a woman to capitulate to the #MeToo movement. In a cringeworthy and at times inappropriate speech before his committee voted to advance Kavanaugh's nomination, Sasse talked about sex from the Senate floor. "Sexuality is a gift. It is an intimacy, it is a oneness that is to be shared and given, never taken. Sex is big, not small, and you don't get to decide it for someone else," he oddly lectured to an empty Senate chamber on October 2, 2018. He claimed that women and girls have been taught to consider themselves as "meat" who are to be "consumed."[76]

Sasse also insisted that Trump, not the Democrats, was dividing the nation over the nomination. He voted to confirm Kavanaugh.

Mona Charen validated Ford's claims and accused Trump of degrading Kavanaugh's accuser. "He's mocking a woman who made very painful revelations about her experience and anyone who then gets on board with that kind of treatment of women who come forward is going to get a backlash by a lot of people who think this is an important moment in our society to change the way we treat women who have the courage to come forward," she said in an October 2018 interview.[77]

An absolutely preposterous statement. An evidence-free account from an activist academic intended to not just destroy a man's Supreme Court appointment but also ruin his reputation and career is an "important moment" for the woman? The debacle—and Charen's ludicrous comments—completely fly in the face of conservatism and the rules of common decency and fairness.

Bill Kristol, Tom Nichols, Max Boot, and Jennifer Rubin all opposed Kavanaugh's confirmation. "It's not so much that the GOP has collapsed but that anything resembling an intellectually solid conservative movement has disintegrated. These people are all about power," Jennifer Rubin raged. "Kavanaugh is not an umpire but an operative able to select facts, shade truth and evade troubling data to reach a conclusion that his side wants."[78]

When more unsubstantiated and politically motivated claims against Kavanaugh surfaced a year after he was elevated to the high court, Rubin implored Democrats to impeach the sitting Supreme Court justice.

Anyone who offered aid and comfort to the Left in their attempt not just to sabotage Kavanaugh's nomination but to destroy his career and reputation should never be considered a serious influencer in the Republican Party ever again. Remember who they are.

CHAPTER 5

WEAPONS OF MASS COLLUSION

The Clinton campaign got a bunch of dirty cops to frame and spy on their opponent, the Trump campaign. After Trump won, they rolled this dirty tricks operation, this spying campaign, into a coup.
—Lee Smith, author of *The Plot Against the President*

The biggest scandal in American political history started with Never-Trump conservatives. Desperate to tarnish Trump's viability as a candidate, anti-Trump Republicans and Democrats joined together to convince the public that Donald Trump was working with Russia to influence the outcome of the 2016 presidential election. Articles connecting Donald Trump's campaign to Russian interests started appearing on conservative websites as early as March 2016.

Just two days after then-candidate Trump announced his foreign policy team in the spring of 2016,[1] the *Washington Free Beacon* posted a 1,100-word hit piece on Dr. Carter Page: "Energy investor Carter Page, one of Donald Trump's handpicked foreign policy advisers, has heavily criticized what he considers American aggression toward Russia, even comparing U.S. policy to American slavery and high-profile police shootings," Lachlan Markay wrote on March 23, 2016. "Trump's selection of Page may indicate the reality-star-cum-politician's opposition to U.S. policies that counter Russian interests in key global theaters."[2]

Markay's piece contained arcane details about Page's views on Russia, including columns Page had written for obscure energy publications. (Page is a global energy consultant.) Even the most dogged reporter would have been hard-pressed to find so many specifics on an unknown campaign advisor, draft the article, and post it in less than

48 hours. How did Markay produce a lengthy article in such a short time—and why?

According to Fusion GPS, the opposition research firm that helped concoct the Russian collusion hoax, a Republican Party elder connected Fusion with the *Free Beacon* in the summer of 2015. Fusion chief Glenn Simpson sent an email to a "longtime Republican politico" in August 2015 to pitch their expanding file of dirt on Donald Trump.

The unnamed Republican immediately expressed interest in the project; a month later, Simpson's GOP contact informed him that the *Washington Free Beacon*, reportedly backed by hedge fund manager and onetime Trump adversary Paul Singer, would hire Fusion for $50,000 per month. Simpson referred to his client as a "Never Trump operation."[3]

The editor of the *Washington Free Beacon* at the time was Matthew Continetti—Bill Kristol's son-in-law, the same Bill Kristol who, by mid-2015, was pledging to stop Donald Trump's candidacy.

The *Free Beacon*'s March 2016 article was the first to claim Carter Page had an alleged affinity for Mother Russia. It offered a platform for other anti-Trump outlets on the Right to expand upon. *National Review* published another Page-Russia article the following month; this time, the headline and content were more brazen.

"Trump: The Kremlin's Candidate," cribbed many of the same links and talking points cited in Markay's original piece. "Carter Page is an out-and-out Putinite," declared Robert Zubrin in April 2016. "With Page providing Trump's Russia policy, it is not surprising that the Donald has also attracted the support of other prominent Putinites."[4]

According to Lee Smith's book *The Plot Against the President*, a series of protodossiers—compiled by the *Free Beacon*'s paid dirt-digger, Fusion GPS—predated the infamous Steele dossier, the centerpiece of the collusion scheme. "Fusion GPS was the Clinton campaign's shadow war room and subsequently became its dirty tricks operation center," Smith wrote.[5] The Clinton campaign and the Democratic National Committee hired Fusion GPS in April 2016; the company became the nexus of the Left and NeverTrump, an alliance that would continue throughout Trump's first term.

The *Free Beacon* posted a few more smear jobs on Carter Page into July, the month that the Democratic Party heavily spun its Trump-Russia collusion narrative to bury the damaging release of internal emails the week of the party's convention to officially nominate Hillary Clinton as its presidential candidate. By that time, Steele's first installments of his dossier had been completed; the Fusion team began pitching his work to news outlets and friendly journalists in late July at the DNC's coronation of Hillary in Philly.

On July 21, 2016, *Commentary's* Noah Rothman openly doubted Trump's loyalty to America and suggested the business tycoon favored Russia over the United States. In his article, "Trump's Great Russia and Our Expense," Rothman ticked off a number of Fusion GPS–produced talking points. Then Rothman posed this ridiculous question: "In the zero-sum game of geopolitics, it long ago became crystal clear that Russia's national interests and America's national interests are mutually exclusive. So just whose side is Donald Trump on?"[6]

A few days later, on July 24, the *Weekly Standard* posted a telling piece titled "Putin's Party?" The author explained why voters should be troubled by disturbing ties between the Kremlin and Trump campaign associates Page, Paul Manafort, and Lt. Gen. Mike Flynn. "These indications provide sufficient grounds for Trump's links to Putin to be further investigated."[7]

The author of the piece? Bill Kristol, the magazine's editor-in-chief at the time. His son-in-law still had Fusion on retainer for the *Free Beacon.* (Continetti denied any ties to the Steele dossier.)

Kristol's article mimicked accusations of Trump-Russia collusion hawked by Fusion GPS in the summer of 2016. Tom Nichols followed Kristol's report with a tweetstorm sketching Trump's fealty to Russia and questioning his patriotism.[8] Calling Trump "Putin's poodle," Mona Charen penned a lengthy column about the Trump-Putin bond: "Trump bats his eyes at Putin like a schoolgirl with a crush," she wrote on July 28, 2016.[9] At the *Washington Post* on the same day, Jennifer Rubin was vexed about why "Trump . . . is so deferential toward Russia's authoritarian bully."[10]

The ensconced, and in some instances nepotistic, fiefdom of the anti-Trump conservative commentariat acted as its own Trump-Russia collusion echo chamber; but unlike their colleagues on the Left, Never-Trump's audience was nervous Republican voters.

Fusion GPS fed its anti-Trump propaganda to conservative influencers who, in turn, warned their followers about the Putin stooge at the top of the Republican ticket. As the earliest narrators of the collusion fable, NeverTrumpers—editors and writers for the *Weekly Standard, National*

Review, Commentary, and others—were heavily invested in discouraging Republicans from voting for Trump based on the fiction that he would work in Putin's interests and not America's.

NeverTrump would remain prolific peddlers of collusion hype, helping the Democrats mislead the American public for three years that the Trump campaign was in cahoots with the Kremlin prior to Election Day.

In the process, NeverTrump abetted the biggest con job in American political history while covering up the legitimate scandal, one that will be documented as the most egregious abuse of federal power ever wielded against a US presidential campaign.

CROSSFIRE HURRICANE

The same month that Markay published his first Page hit piece in the *Free Beacon*, former FBI director James Comey met with former attorney general Loretta Lynch to discuss his "concerns" about the Trump campaign volunteer. As conservative commentators ginned up the public relations end of the scam, Comey and Obama's top national security chiefs orchestrated the inside job.

Something else consequential happened in March 2016: Florida senator Marco Rubio suspended his campaign, following in the failed footsteps of 12 other Republican candidates who had already dropped out of the race. Trump, Texas senator Ted Cruz, and Ohio governor John Kasich were the three men left standing.

And it was increasingly obvious who would prevail.

But a Trump presidency, no matter how unlikely, was unacceptable to the Obama White House.

President Barack Obama held deep animus toward Donald Trump for spreading rumors about Obama's birthplace. During the White House Correspondents' Dinner in 2011, Obama mocked Trump, in attendance at the event, for his "birther" conspiracy theory about the then-president.[11] After roasting The Donald for several minutes, Obama showed a cartoon of an imaginary Trump White House, ornamented with gold columns and bikini-clad women.

A few weeks before Election Day, Obama appeared on Jimmy Kimmel's late-night talk show to read a series of mean tweets: One tweet was from Trump, saying Obama would go down as "perhaps the worst president in the history of the United States." Obama, not amused, looked into the camera and declared, "At least I will go down as a president."[12] He then stared into the camera and dropped his cell phone.

Obama never forgave Trump for raising doubts about where the president was born. (In fact, during one of his last White House briefings, Obama's press secretary, Josh Earnest, intimated that the entire Russian collusion scheme was revenge for Trump's birtherism. "The president-elect and his team are suggesting that the accusations [about Russian collusion] that are being made are totally unfounded, that there's no basis for them. This president has been in a situation in which he has been criticized in an utterly false, baseless way. And I'm, of course, referring to the president's birthplace," Earnest said on January 11, 2017, the day after BuzzFeed published the entire dossier authored by Fusion GPS hired gun Christopher Steele.)[13]

Weaned in the cutthroat world of Chicago politics, where every public agency from the school system to the Department of Streets and Sanitation is leveraged for either maximum political gain or damage, Obama would have no qualms about using the federal government's most powerful tools against his biggest rival. The Obama administration had already been caught using the Internal Revenue Service to punish Tea Party organizers before his 2012 reelection campaign.

Further, Obama and his partisan toadies who populated key agencies needed to redirect public and internal outrage over the FBI's handling of the investigation into Hillary Clinton's illicit email server. Although Comey concluded Clinton had mishandled classified material, he announced in July 2016 he would not recommend charges against her.

That very same month, Comey's FBI opened a counterintelligence probe into four individuals connected to the Trump campaign: Page, Manafort, Flynn, and George Papadopoulos, another foreign policy advisor. The operation was called "Crossfire Hurricane," a line from the Rolling Stones song "Jumpin' Jack Flash." It involved deploying informants into the campaign and manipulating a secret court to get authorization to surveil Carter Page for a year. The CIA and State Department were in on the scheme, too.

At the same time, a media blitz bolstered the FBI's alleged suspicions about sketchy ties between Team Trump and the Kremlin. That effort was coordinated by Glenn Simpson, Fusion GPS's cofounder, and his paid operative, former British intelligence officer Christopher Steele.

His so-called dossier of unproven and outlandish accusations against Trump and others was not only cited as evidence in an application prepared by Comey's FBI and submitted to the Foreign Intelligence Surveillance Court in October 2016 to obtain a warrant against Page; it was circulated among the media and top lawmakers on Capitol Hill, both Republicans and Democrats. Dossier-sourced articles claiming senior government officials had intelligence from a former British spy that proved Trump-Russia election collusion appeared in Yahoo! News and *Mother Jones* before Election Day.

Thanks to Fusion GPS's handiwork, the Trump campaign spent the last few months of the election season fending off allegations of fealty to Russia. An official statement from Obama's intelligence community in October 2016 confirmed Russia's plans to mess with the election.[14] The trap had been set to smear Trump with Russian dirt; nearly everyone in the political universe, including NeverTrump, participated in the con.

Then Trump won. The con continued—but after the election, the stakes were much higher. Removing Trump from the Oval Office on suspicions his campaign team had helped the Russians influence the outcome of the election in his favor, and worse, that his presidency would act in service to Vladimir Putin, became the Democrats' sole crusade.

And NeverTrump played right along.

POST-ELECTION COLLUSION WITH NEVERTRUMP

During an annual security conference in Nova Scotia shortly after the 2016 election, a few high-level officials gathered privately to discuss the outcome and Russia's alleged influence. One person in the meeting had a deep-seated grudge against the incoming president: Arizona senator John McCain.

McCain huddled with former British diplomat Sir Andrew Wood and David Kramer, a McCain confidant who worked for the senator's nonprofit, on the evening of November 16 in Halifax.[15] Wood briefed McCain about accusations contained in the Steele dossier, which he described as "raw, unverified intelligence," according to McCain's 2018 autobiography, *The Restless Wave*.[16]

Wood vouched for Steele's credibility, McCain wrote, assuring the senator that the former MI6 agent had dependable Russian contacts and a solid reputation. The group began discussing the contents of the dossier.

"Our impromptu meeting felt charged with a strange intensity," McCain described. "No one wisecracked to lighten the mood. We spoke in lowered voices. I was taken aback. They were shocking allegations."[17]

One charge—that the Russians had a tape recording of Russian prostitutes urinating in front of Trump in a Moscow Ritz-Carlton in 2013—was so preposterous that it should've immediately raised a red flag about the document's veracity.

Nonetheless, McCain directed Kramer to travel to the UK to meet with Steele. But the British operative did not give Kramer a copy of the dossier at that meeting in his London home on November 28, 2016. Instead, Steele arranged for Kramer to meet with Glenn Simpson, Fusion GPS's chief, in Washington the next day; Simpson provided one of McCain's top advisors with a copy of the sketchy political propaganda. (In his book, *Crime in Progress*, coauthored with Peter Fritsch, Simpson admitted he and Kramer had a working relationship dating back nearly a decade.)[18]

After Kramer gave the dossier to McCain, the senator later handed it off to FBI director James Comey, who already had the document. Forwarding partisan dirt to the head of the nation's most powerful law enforcement agency, McCain later explained in his book, was in the country's national security interest. "I did my duty, as I've sworn an oath to do," McCain preened in his customary self-aggrandizing way. "Anyone who doesn't like it can go to hell."[19]

But McCain's imprimatur on Trump-Russia election collusion would be a crucial contribution to legitimizing the scam.[20] Embracing his long-standing act as a "maverick," McCain clearly welcomed the opportunity to work as Trump's foil from the same side of the political aisle. That gave NeverTrump pundits the backing of arguably the most influential Republican senator, one who still commanded respect from rank-and-file Republicans despite his two losing presidential bids.

As chairman of the Senate Armed Services Committee, McCain wielded his post to inflict maximum damage on the incoming administration. He wasted no time scheduling a hearing into Russia's "attack" on the 2016 election. On January 5, 2017, as the Trump transition team planned to take control of the White House, McCain's committee heard testimony from top government officials, including former director of national intelligence James Clapper, an architect of the hoax, about Putin's predations.[21]

During one exchange between McCain and Clapper, the pair implied that the Kremlin's social media skullduggery might have changed votes from Clinton to Trump. "We have no way of gauging the impact...it had on choices the electorate made," Clapper told McCain. "There's no way for us to gauge that." McCain further intimated that if Russian social media tinkering actually did change any votes, it would be an act of "war" against the United States.

The message was clear: McCain goaded Clapper into saying publicly that there was a chance that Russian Facebook memes swayed people to vote for Donald Trump. The new president had been illegitimately elected thanks to chicanery from an American adversary. Enough gullible voters in Wisconsin, Pennsylvania, and Michigan had been brainwashed by weird Russian social media posts to put Trump over the finish line. And the man hinting that might have been the case was a Republican stalwart—one whom the Trump-hating Beltway media corps adored and NeverTrump revered.

Further, the official intelligence buttressing the claim that Russia hacked the election was specious at best, sloppy and dishonest at worst. Former CIA director John Brennan and Clapper finished the report in less than 25 days in December 2016. The flimsy document hardly provided the fides to justify howls about Russia "attacking our democracy" after Election Day.

Either McCain knew the intelligence was thin gruel or he was duped again by intelligence officers with an ulterior motive.

All of it started to feel eerily familiar. Sketchy intelligence touted by powerful politicians as evidence of an imminent threat to justify action against a foreign foe for domestic political purposes. I'm referring, of course, to weapons of mass destruction. It's not a coincidence that most of the very same people, McCain in particular, pushing Russian collusion based on the thinnest trove of "evidence" also successfully convinced the American people that Iraq possessed weapons of mass destruction.

As I noted in 2019,

In between the two scandals was more than a decade of recriminations against once-trusted experts on the Right who led our nation
into battle. The Iraq war cost the lives of more than 4,400 U.S.
troops, maimed tens of thousands more and resulted in an unquan-
tifiable amount of emotional, mental, and physical pain for untold

numbers of American military families. Suicide rates for servicemen and veterans have exploded leaving thousands more dead and their families devastated. And it has cost taxpayers more than $2 trillion and counting.

So, these discredited outcasts thought they found in the Trump-Russia collusion farce a way to redeem themselves in the news media and recover their lost prestige, power, and paychecks. After all, it cannot be a mere coincidence that a group of influencers on the Right who convinced Americans 16 years ago that we must invade Iraq based on false pretenses are nearly the *identical group of people* who tried to convince Americans that Donald Trump conspired with the Russians to rig the 2016 election, an allegation also based on hearsay and specious evidence.[22]

The verbiage and tone NeverTrump used to warn the country about collusion were eerily similar to those of the WMD alarms:

Bill Kristol in 2003: "We look forward to the liberation of our own country and others from the threat of Saddam's weapons of mass destruction, and to the liberation of the Iraqi people from a brutal and sadistic tyrant."[23]

Bill Kristol in 2018: "It seems to me likely Mueller will find there was collusion between Trump associates and Putin operatives; that Trump knew about it; and that Trump sought to cover it up and obstruct its investigation. What then? Good question."[24]

John McCain in 2003: "I believe that, obviously, we will remove a threat to America's national security because we will find there are still massive amounts of weapons of mass destruction in Iraq."[25]

John McCain in 2017: "There's a lot of aspects with this whole relationship with Russia and Vladimir Putin that requires further scrutiny. In fact, I think there's a lot of shoes to drop from this centipede. This whole issue of the relationship with the Russians and who communicated with them and under what circumstances clearly cries out for an investigation."[26]

David Frum in 2002 (writing for President George W. Bush): "States like these and their terrorist allies constitute an axis of evil, arming to threaten the peace of the world."[27]

David Frum in 2016: "I never envisioned an Axis of Evil of which one of the members was the US National Security Adviser."[28]

Max Boot in 2003: "I hate to disappoint all the conspiracy-mongers out there, but I think we are going into Iraq for precisely the reasons stated by President Bush: to destroy weapons of mass destruction, to bring down an evil dictator with links to terrorism, and to enforce international law."[29]

Max Boot in 2019: "If this is what it appears to be, it is the biggest scandal in American history—an assault on the very foundations of our democracy in which the president's own campaign is deeply complicit. There is no longer any question whether collusion occurred. The only questions that remain are: What did the president know? And when did he know it?"[30]

Bush's FBI director at the time publicly testified about the looming global menace posed by Iraq's stockpile of deadly materials. "Secretary [of State Colin] Powell presented evidence last week that Baghdad has failed to disarm its weapons of mass destruction," Mueller told the Senate in 2003.[31] Those weapons, the FBI director warned, could be supplied to terrorist organizations around the world.

A report issued two years after the invasion excoriated the intelligence community. "We conclude that the Intelligence Community was dead wrong in almost all of its pre-war judgments about Iraq's weapons of mass destruction," concluded a special commission in 2005. "This was a major intelligence failure."[32] (Senator McCain served on the commission.)

The FBI director pushing the weapons of mass destruction line in 2003—Robert Mueller—would become the central figure, and arguably the most powerful man in Washington, leading the two-year investigation into whether Donald Trump colluded with the Russians before the election. History would repeat itself in an uncanny way.

IT'S MUELLER TIME

Throughout the spring of 2017, the drumbeat of Trump-Russia collusion intensified along with calls for a special counsel. Lt. Gen. Michael Flynn, Trump's first national security advisor, didn't last a month in the West Wing. Flynn resigned on February 14, 2017, amid an orchestrated campaign between Obama holdovers in the administration and the news media that portrayed Flynn's phone calls with the Russian ambassador as either traitorous or a violation of the Logan Act. That law, which has been on the books for 220 years without a single conviction, prohibits US citizens from communicating with foreign powers to "defeat the measures of the United States." The so-called "dead letter" law was exhumed before Election Day; beginning in the summer of 2016, Democrats regularly accused Trump of violating the Logan Act for various comments about Russia.[33]

McCain, breaching his own rule of not attacking military heroes, accused Flynn of "lying" to the vice president about his pre-inaugural conversations with Sergey Kislyak and said Flynn's resignation raised "further questions about the Trump administration's intentions toward Vladimir Putin."[34]

In March 2017, James Comey finally confessed to the Republican-led House Intelligence committee that he had opened a counterintelligence probe into the Trump campaign in the summer of 2016 based on suspicious activity with Russian interests. (Rep. Elise Stefanik would force Comey to admit that he violated House protocol by withholding that information from congressional leaders for eight months.) Comey's sneakiness, however, was portrayed as protecting "sensitive" law enforcement activities rather than intentional deceit.

In April, the *Washington Post* disclosed the FISA (Foreign Intelligence Surveillance Act) warrant against Carter Page; the government told the Foreign Intelligence Surveillance Court that Page was a foreign agent of Russia. (The reporting on both Flynn and Page was based on illegal leaks of classified government information, a felony for which no one has been either charged or convicted.)

McCain and other NeverTrumpers insisted that a separate, full-scale investigation would be necessary. "This whole issue with the relationship with the Russians and who communicated with them and under what circumstances clearly beg, cries out for investigation," McCain told Jake Tapper on CNN in March 2017. "We should not assume guilt until we have a thorough investigation."[35] "The situation begs for a bipartisan, transparent investigation," David French wrote.[36]

Then the coup de grace: On May 9, 2017, Trump fired Comey. The dismissal was portrayed as an attempt to stop Comey from probing Trump's ties to the Kremlin; it quickly became the Democrats' latest impeachment fodder.

Deputy Attorney General Rod Rosenstein appointed Robert Mueller, a Comey pal, as the special counsel tasked with rooting out evidence of Trump-Russia collusion.[37] (Jeff Sessions, Trump's attorney general, ill-advisedly recused himself in March 2017 from any matters related to Russia based on his own innocuous contacts with Kislyak.[38] This empowered the Obama-appointed Rosenstein to take control of the Justice Department's inquiry into Trump-Putin ties.)

NeverTrump seized the moment. Mueller, they were convinced, would doom Trump's presidency. His unfettered inquiry, commandeered by a team stacked with partisan prosecutors, surely would produce evidence of impeachable offenses that would quickly dispatch Trump from the Oval Office. No comparison designed to underscore the gravity of the situation would be considered out of bounds: Max Boot compared alleged Russian election interference to 9/11.[39]

For the next two years, NeverTrump tended to the right flank of the Trump-Russia collusion front. This primarily involved protecting Mueller's investigation.

"The investigation by special counsel Robert Mueller into Russian interference with the 2016 election is now entering a new and critical phase," a group of NeverTrumpers wrote in a November 2017 letter addressed to Paul Ryan, then Speaker of the House. "We would regard dismissal of the special counsel, or pardons issued preemptively to anyone targeted by his investigation, as a grave abuse of power that justifies initiation of impeachment proceedings. It is morally imperative that the Republican Party and the conservative movement stand as bulwarks of the rule of law, not enablers of its erosion and violation. Now is the time for choosing."[40]

It was signed by more than two dozen NeverTrumpers, including Bill Kristol, Mona Charen, Max Boot, and Evan McMullin.

As Trump regularly expressed his outrage at Mueller's spiraling "witch hunt," NeverTrump rallied around the special counsel and demanded that Republicans lawmakers "protect" Robert Mueller. Kristol formed a group called Republicans for the Rule of Law, which produced television ads touting Mueller's military valor, integrity, and legal reputation.[41] The group bought airtime on Sunday news programs and Fox News.

As the investigation progressed, it became hard to distinguish between NeverTrump and Democrat Adam Schiff, the leading collusion propagandist in the House, who promised for three years that "clear" evidence of collusion existed.

It didn't.

THE END IS NEAR

In embarrassing fashion given the final result, NeverTrump salivated at every rumor, accusation, interrogation, charge, arrest, and raid initiated by Team Mueller, confident that the special counsel would soon haul Donald Trump out of the Oval Office in handcuffs; perhaps a few of his children would be arrested, too.

Hardly a day passed when some NeverTrumper didn't chortle that Trump's days were numbered or the walls were closing in or the end was near.

After Comey's June 2017 Senate testimony to complain about his firing set the stage for impeachment based on an obstruction of justice case, Jennifer Rubin warned that it was a turning point for Republicans. "Before Comey, impeachment talk was not a real concern for Republicans. After Comey, [it] surely will be a referendum on Trump, and specifically whether he should be impeached—unless, of course, Republicans decide to cut their losses and get rid of him before the midterms."[42]

NeverTrump frequently defended the contents of the Steele dossier and assured the public that Fusion's Glenn Simpson, under increasing scrutiny throughout 2017, was the real deal. His former *Wall Street Journal* colleague Bret Stephens attested to Simpson's sterling reputation; the White House and the president, warned Stephens, should be "terrified" about Simpson's congressional testimony. "Glenn is a very serious, capable journalist. He's not a partisan...If he has politics, I'm not aware of them," Stephens said on MSNBC about the Clinton/DNC hired gun.[43] Tom Nichols continued to insist the dossier was "raw intelligence" even after everyone else acknowledged that it was nothing more than fabricated political dirt.[44]

Bill Kristol was giddy after the FBI's raid of Michael Cohen's office, home, and hotel room in the summer of 2018. He could hardly contain his glee on the set of CNN. "This is war. This shows we are very close to the end game," he assured his ecstatic CNN panelists in April 2018.[45] Kristol later would claim that "reality has changed" after Cohen's guilty plea.[46] Even though the charges had nothing to do with Russian collusion, Kristol questioned whether, deep down, it was true.

"This week was the worst of Donald Trump's presidency. But it seems likely there will be worse still," Charlie Sykes warned when Mueller snagged both Manafort and Cohen.[47]

David French claimed Mueller's December 2018 sentencing memo on Michael Cohen "may well outline the roadmap for an impeachment count against the president that is based on recent presidential precedent. Donald Trump's legal problems continue to mount."[48]

After the *New York Times* reported in July 2017 that Donald Trump Jr. and other top campaign associates met with a so-called "Russian lawyer" allegedly connected to the Kremlin a few months before the election,[49] NeverTrumpers insisted the brief confab amounted to campaign collusion.

David French concluded that the meeting met the definition of collusion. "To repeat, it now looks as if the senior campaign team of a major-party presidential candidate intended to meet with an official representative of a hostile foreign power to facilitate that foreign power's attempt to influence an American election," French wrote in *National Review* in July 2017. "Russian collusion claims are no longer the exclusive province of tinfoil-hat conspiracy theorists. No American—Democrat or Republican—should defend the expressed intent of this meeting."[50]

(Evidence would later show that the "Russian lawyer" was working with Glenn Simpson on behalf of a Russian company in trouble with the US government. Simpson and Natalia Veselnitskaya met both before and after the Trump Tower meeting. No damning information about Hillary Clinton was shared with the participants.)

NeverTrump mocked a three-star general after he accepted a plea deal with Mueller's team in December 2017. Mike Flynn's guilty plea to one process crime elicited cheers from NeverTrump. "Michael Flynn going to jail? Unlike Paul, can't make $11 Million bail. Or maybe against Trump, he'll have to wail. This whole presidency is one big fail," Ana Navarro snarked on Twitter.[51]

Even the most ludicrous, unfounded charges of collusion meant doom for the president. "Big news: Mueller reportedly has evidence that Michael Cohen did travel to Prague in 2016, lending credence to Chris Steele's reporting that Cohen secretly met a Kremlin figure there to strategize about Moscow's election assistance to President Trump," Evan McMullin tweeted in the spring of 2018.[52] Mueller concluded Cohen never traveled to Prague; it was another dossier-fabricated collusion talking point.

Jonah Goldberg erroneously claimed that Trump campaign coordinator Sam Clovis sent George Papadopoulos to Russia to get dirt on Clinton and often parroted the head fake that Papadopoulos, and not the Fusion-sourced dossier, prompted Comey's probe into the campaign.[53] (Goldberg often got key details about "collusion" flat-out wrong. As late as December 2019, Goldberg had to correct a post on *National Review* that originally claimed the FBI hired a private cybersecurity firm to determine the Russians hacked the DNC server. Only after readers pointed out his mistake did Goldberg note that the DNC, not the FBI, hired CrowdStrike.)

Conversely, anyone attempting to uncover the legitimate, provable scandal—how the world's most powerful law enforcement and intelligence apparatus was weaponized against a rival presidential campaign—was partaking in a "conspiracy theory."

The very same NeverTrumpers who regurgitated every reckless charge of collusion downplayed alarming evidence of abuse at the highest level of the federal government to target Team Trump. "It's time for partisans to ditch conspiracy theories and reach mutual agreement to follow the evidence and apply the law to the facts without regard for personal affection or policy preference. Any other approach—either by pundits or politicians—fails their audience or their constituents," lectured David French in December 2018.[54] French often defended the FBI's actions,[55] even as evidence mounted that the pretext for the probe was either phony or manufactured by the FBI itself: "The FBI wasn't abusing its power. It was fulfilling the mission the president gave it."[56]

Tom Nichols suggested that people digging into "FISAgate" were wearing "tin foil hats."[57] (NeverTrump repeatedly ridiculed Rep. Devin Nunes, the Republican chairman of the House Intelligence Committee, and his effort to expose numerous offenses related to the infiltration of and investigation into Trump's campaign. See chapter 7.)

Sen. Ben Sasse, a member of the Senate Judiciary Committee, never mentioned his concerns about the FBI's illicit probe or expressed outrage at the behind-the-scenes activities of Comey, former deputy FBI director Andrew McCabe, former counterespionage chief Peter Strzok, or his lover, FBI lawyer Lisa Page.[58] There were no questions about the role of Bruce Ohr, a twice-demoted Justice Department official, and his wife's work at Fusion GPS or both Ohrs' relationship with Christopher Steele.

Again, NeverTrump sided with the Left not only to mislead the

American people about a nonexistent collaboration between Trump and Putin, but they intentionally ignored and downplayed the real scandal as a conspiracy theory.

Defending massive abuses of federal power, which included violating the constitutional rights of private citizens, prosecuting political opponents, breaching attorney-client privilege, and illegally leaking classified information to the news media, somehow became a conservative "principle" during the Trump era. Go figure.

MUELLER REPORT BOMBS

NeverTrump speculated for two years that Robert Mueller would find evidence of collusion between the Trump campaign and the Kremlin. In March 2019, Mueller submitted his long-awaited report to the Justice Department. To avoid leaks, and since Mueller had not redacted grand jury material as he was instructed, Attorney General Bill Barr released a summary of the report's contents as it underwent the classification process.

The bottom line: Mueller's team of skilled, partisan, vengeful prosecutors found no evidence of collusion between the Trump campaign and Russian state actors. (The second half of Mueller's report outlined instances of possible obstruction of justice, but Mueller declined to make a prosecutorial recommendation.)

In April 2019, the Justice Department released a redacted copy of the 448-page Mueller Report. Its findings supported Barr's summary.

The Mueller probe, more accurately described as a "witch hunt" by the president and his supporters, was over. The crimes NeverTrump and the Left had hoped to see never materialized.

NeverTrump was wrong, once again.

Kristol, commenting on MSNBC as the new editor-in-chief of the Bulwark, the *Weekly Standard*'s stepchild, griped that Team Trump were acting like the "most sore winners in the world. They're bitter and angry and want to punish people who made the mistake of thinking there might be collusion."[59]

If only Kristol knew what it was like to be a winner, even a sore one.

Following, again, the lead of the Democrats, NeverTrump dumped collusion and quickly embraced Mueller's dubious and politically motivated allegations of obstruction of justice. Charlie Sykes, writing at the Bulwark, insisted the second volume of Mueller's report was "devastating" and constituted an "open invitation to Congress to launch impeachment proceedings."[60]

Some NeverTrumpers, however, had a hard time letting go of their collusion dream. As late as November 2019, Max Boot insisted that "collusion evidence remains strong."[61] Just as they had with faulty claims about weapons of mass destruction, NeverTrump's Iraq War promoters refused to abandon the Russian collusion narrative they helped create. And when the government produced evidence to the contrary, just as was the case with WMDs, NeverTrump refused to concede or apologize. They moved on, no penalty paid, to the next manufactured scandal while looking for new foes.

CHAPTER 6

NEVERTRUMP'S ENEMIES LIST

*The Never Trumper Republicans, though on respirators
with not many left, are in certain ways worse and more
dangerous for our Country than the Do Nothing Democrats. Watch out for them, they are human scum!*

—Donald Trump

NeverTrump's enemies list is long and—shocker!—includes few
Democrats.

Conservative opinion/news outlets, Republican lawmakers, evangelical
Christians, Trump-supporting intellectuals, and think tanks comprise the
bulk of NeverTrump's roster of foes. Rarely did NeverTrump forgo an opportunity to jump on the Left's side of the political teeter-totter, launching
anyone associated with Trump into a den of Trump-hating wolves in the
press and on social media.

As the Left's scorched earth rampage against individual liberty, free
speech, constitutional guardrails, and the boundaries of common decency
accelerated after Donald Trump's election, especially when Democrats
took control of the House of Representatives in January 2019, Never-
Trump "conservatives" assessed the political battlefield and found the real
enemies occupied their own (alleged) side. Criticism of the Left's most
egregious tactics has been sparse. Proposals to confiscate guns, halt fossil
fuel use, eliminate the Electoral College, expand the Supreme Court, or
assault Trump officials were met with tacit silence or even approval.

The real enemies lurking among us, according to NeverTrump, are
House Freedom Caucus members, God-fearing Americans, and Fox
News.

The Trump-Russian collusion hoax should have enraged every conservative, Trump supporter and detractor alike.

The sham was a crucible of nefarious forces that Republicans, particularly those on the more libertarian side of the spectrum, long have
worried about: partisan bureaucrats wielding their unchecked authority
for political purposes; the manipulation of powerful government tools
designed to hunt international terrorists instead employed against private
US citizens; unmasking the names of Americans caught up in foreign
intelligence collection; misuse of classified materials; and collaboration
between the federal government and the leftist corporate media to destroy
Republicans.

So NeverTrump's contempt toward the one Republican congressman
unraveling the most outrageous case of how the federal government,
including the Obama White House, collaborated with the news media to sabotage Donald Trump's presidential campaign showed—once
again—how NeverTrump would side with the Left to destroy not just
Trump but anyone around him. Just like their role in pumping Russian
collusion fuel to gaslight the American public, their attacks on lawmakers
and journalists who were bravely exposing the biggest political scandal
in US history acted as a cover-up for widespread government corruption
under the Obama administration and by Obama holdovers in the Trump
administration.

REP. DEVIN NUNES, REPUBLICAN LAWMAKERS

Under any other Republican president, Republican lawmakers such as
California representative Devin Nunes, Ohio representative Jim Jordan,
Florida representatives Ron DeSantis and Lee Zeldin, and North Carolina
representative Mark Meadows would have been heralded as leaders, perhaps even future presidential material, by NeverTrump pundits.

But they landed in NeverTrump crosshairs for two reasons: One, their
dogged work in uncovering the corrupt origins of the government-media
operation against the Trump campaign and presidency, which Never-
Trump helped perpetuate. Two, their overall support for Donald Trump
and his administration. It became obvious that, just like the collusion
hoax, NeverTrump still takes its marching orders from Fusion GPS as

the anti-Trump shop continues its rampage against the president and his Capitol Hill defenders.

NeverTrump's biggest target is Nunes. Ever since Nunes emerged in March 2017 as the person willing to confront the massive Beltway complex of Trump antagonists, the eight-term Republican from California's central valley has been attacked, vilified, and threatened.

So, too, have his staff and his family. Right before the release of his February 2018 memo detailing how Jim Comey's FBI misled the Foreign Intelligence Surveillance Court to get a warrant to spy on Carter Page, the orchestrated assault against the Nunes family intensified. "It was during that time that the anti-Nunes operation took an even more dangerous turn," Lee Smith wrote in his 2019 book, *The Plot Against the President.*[1]

Nunes told Smith what he suspects is an ongoing professional ambush on his career, his reputation, and even his family. "They started to target my wife and the rest of my family," Nunes told Smith. Nunes's wife, a grade school teacher, and their three daughters were under full-time security; Mrs. Nunes's school had a sheriff's deputy on campus to ensure her safety.

The operatives mimicked Nunes' phone number and called his relatives to make it sound like he had been kidnapped. "Maybe the worst was to my mother-in-law," Nunes told Smith. "It was early in the morning, multiple calls from what appeared to be my numbers, and someone on the other end is saying her son-in-law in in danger and will be harmed if he doesn't back off."[2]

NeverTrump played a complicit role in fostering a pernicious narrative about Nunes, which resulted in legitimate danger to the congressman and his young family. (Please lecture more about morality and decency.)

Kristol was in on the smear campaign early. After Nunes visited a secured facility in the Eisenhower Building in March 2017 to view classified materials that proved top Obama administration officials unmasked the identifies of hundreds of American citizens swept up in possibly illegitimate surveillance—a concern, Nunes told CNN's Wolf Blitzer, that pre-dated Trump's tweet accusing Obama of "wiretapping" his phones[3]—the culprits and their media handlers ambushed the House Intelligence Committee chairman.

Everyone realized that Nunes was on to what Comey and company, including Obama's closest national security advisors, did in the months before and after the election. As the Republican chairman of a powerful committee with access to classified information and the authority to issue subpoenas, Nunes, in conjunction with a Republican executive branch, could blow the whole thing wide open. Democrats, the media, and NeverTrump had no intention of letting that happen.

Kristol flooded Twitter and cable news for days in late March with harsh condemnation of Nunes. The narrative was that Nunes committed some nefarious offense when he viewed the documents on the White House grounds—the Eisenhower Building is adjacent to the West Wing—to meet with unnamed sources to view the evidence. (Despite requests from Nunes, a member of the Gang of Eight of legislative intelligence officials, the materials could not be moved to the House.) "I do believe the evidence is mounting up that Devin Nunes got whatever evidence he has or claims to have from the White House," Kristol said on CNN on March 27, 2017.[4]

"The whole question of the use of Nunes becomes not just Devin Nunes stumbling into something, but Devin Nunes being a pawn of the White House in an attempt to divert attention from the Russia connection," Kristol hyped on MSNBC on March 30, 2017, while downplaying the possibility that top Obama officials "had some political stuff in mind when they changed the way [unmasking requests were] processed in early January."[5]

NeverTrump lemmings took the cue from their leader. Jennifer Rubin ranted from her *Washington Post* corner about Nunes, calling his actions "disqualifying,"[6] and advised Democrats to refuse to participate in Nunes's "half-baked investigation" into the Justice Department's activities in 2016 and into early 2017.[7]

"Chairman Nunes chose to cover for Trump in a politically motivated effort to distract attention from increasing revelations of Trump's ties to the Kremlin," said failed presidential candidate Evan McMullin in a statement. "We can no longer trust Nunes to put America's best interests above those of Donald Trump."[8]

Sen. John McCain, fearful Nunes would reveal the Arizona senator's pivotal role in legitimizing the collusion hoax, also blasted Nunes, calling his behavior "very disturbing."[9] McCain then undermined Nunes and told MSNBC's Greta Van Susteren that he wanted a select committee to look into Russian election meddling. "No longer does the Congress have the credibility to handle this alone and I don't say that lightly," McCain said on March 22, 2017.[10] McCain feigned confusion about Nunes's White House trip and subsequent comments, lamenting a "chasm" between Nunes and his Democratic counterpart, Rep. Adam Schiff.

Their fury helped bolster a demand, orchestrated by MoveOn.org, to launch a House Ethics Committee investigation into Nunes. Shamefully, House Republicans signed on to the bogus probe; Nunes agreed to step aside from the Russian collusion aspect of his committee's work.

But that wasn't good enough for NeverTrump. "Just at the time when the nation desperately needs adults to step forward who can give the public confidence that they not only understand the stakes of the Russia investigation, they also can be entrusted to conduct that investigation in good faith, Nunes unnecessarily poured gasoline on an already-raging fire," David French wrote in *National Review* on March 30, 2017. "The American body politic is awash in conspiracy theories, mistrust, and wild claims of espionage and criminality. It needs leaders. It needs integrity. If Nunes steps down as chairman, he can quickly transition from part of the problem to part of the solution."[11]

The Left's full-fledged crusade to destroy Devin Nunes was on—and NeverTrump would be right alongside.

Cleared of any wrongdoing by the House Ethics Committee in December 2017, Nunes prepared his memo outlining how Obama's Justice Department abused the Foreign Intelligence Surveillance Act to mislead the secret court to spy on Carter Page. Comey was enjoying his newfound hero role as a Trump slayer after the president fired him; Comey's memos about his alleged interactions with Trump found a home in the Office of the Special Counsel. Nunes's memo would raise new questions about Comey's integrity and credibility. (Further, Comey's book, *A Higher Loyalty*, was scheduled for release in the spring of 2018. Nunes's revelations would present a whole set of uncomfortable questions for the megalomaniacal former FBI director.)

Charlie Sykes, blathering the day before the memo was issued— meaning he hadn't seen it—hyperventilated about all sorts of boundaries and norms being violated. "The willingness of the Republican leadership of the House to become willing tools of the Trump administration, in fact to become complicit in this obstruction is really rather dramatic," Sykes ranted on MSNBC on February 1, 2018. "The long-term damage this does to the institution of the FBI...is striking," he insisted, without irony.[12]

Sen. John McCain objected to the release of Nunes's memo. Never missing a chance to promote the collusion hoax he helped perpetuate, McCain feared the memo would thwart the Mueller probe. "Our nation's elected officials, including the president, must stop looking at this investigation through the warped lens of politics and manufacturing partisan sideshows. If we continue to undermine our own rule of law, we are doing Putin's job for him."[13]

On the day of its release, Bill Kristol went into full drama-queen mode: "When the history of Trump's presidency (and impeachment?) is written, the Nunes memo will be a minor footnote," Kristol tweeted on February 2, 2018. "When the history of the (temporary?) degradation of the Republican Party is written, the Nunes memo will be a significant moment."[14]

Claiming Nunes had "impugned the motives of former British spy Christopher Steele," Max Boot concluded that Nunes's effort was an attempt to persuade Trump's future Senate impeachment jury against conviction.[15] Boot, cribbing from a *Weekly Standard* piece, compared Nunes to O.J. Simpson lawyer Johnnie Cochran, dirtying up the cops in hopes of a not-guilty verdict.

Not only did David French decide that Nunes's memo justified the FBI's initial probe and the special counsel investigation, he later defended a counter memo authored by Rep. Adam Schiff, then the ranking member of the House Intelligence Committee.[16] (This view was disputed by Andrew McCarthy, French's *National Review* colleague.)

"[Schiff's memo] indicates that parts of the infamous 'Steele dossier' may now be verified, asserts that Carter Page's lies may have helped trigger the FISA application, and provides an exact quote from the FISA application that undermines GOP claims of deception," French wrote.[17]

Calling both memos "mostly useless" and "political instruments," French asserted that, contrary to the Nunes memo, the FBI did alert the secret court of the political provenance of the Steele dossier. (It did not.)

French defended the Steele dossier: "There are a lot of Republicans laboring under the impression that use of the Steele memo in any capacity is scandalous. The words 'salacious and unverified,' used by James Comey, in his congressional testimony, to describe parts of the Steele dossier, are seared into their brains...No doubt the Steele dossier is salacious, but never forget that 'unverified' is not the same thing as 'false.' Moreover, no one should think that opposition research is always inaccurate. Sometimes even partisan investigations can reveal real wrongdoing," French, a constitutional lawyer, explained.

His *National Review* colleague Andrew McCarthy, a former federal prosecutor, rebutted French's analysis. McCarthy carefully dissected French's "flawed premise" in defending the Steele dossier. "It is forbidden to use false information. That does not mean using unverified information is proper—it is irresponsible. And the more distant the information is from being verified, the more it is in the nature of rank hearsay, and the more reckless it is to use it," McCarthy wrote.[18]

Further, Schiff's memo, the one French defended, did not wear well as the truth trickled out in late 2018 and 2019. As I wrote in *American Greatness* in February 2019, "But new evidence now contradicts much of what Schiff claimed in his counter-memo, including a crucial timeline of contacts between the Justice Department and dossier author Christopher Steele, yet he has not corrected the record. Schiff's failure to correct this record amounts to lying to Congress—his counter-memo was addressed to all members of the House of Representatives."[19]

Bret Stephens personally attacked Carter Page in a column mocking the Nunes memo as a "nothingburger" while defending the FBI's abuses. Page, Stephens wrote, is "stupid," "self-important," and a "useful idiot," and he noted that Page's PhD thesis had been rejected twice.[20] (Stephens later offered a mealy-mouthed apology to Page, not for his vile insults but for failing to offer Page the presumption of innocence.)[21]

But a wide-ranging investigation conducted by the Justice Department inspector general exonerated Nunes. Michael Horowitz, in a 478-page report released in December 2019, provided damning evidence about how Barack Obama's FBI did exactly what Nunes alleged—and more. Horowitz and his team discovered 17 "significant errors," a nice way of describing it, on the initial FISA application and three subsequent referrals.[22] The inspector general found that the dossier indeed comprised nearly all the evidence cited in the FISA application on Carter Page. An FBI lawyer altered an email about Page's government service that would have acted as exculpatory evidence before the secret court.

One of the most controversial claims in Nunes's memo—that the FBI withheld from the court the partisan funders of Steele's work—was confirmed in the Horowitz report. The agency "failed to update the description of Steele after information became known to the Crossfire Hurricane team...that provided greater clarity on the political origins and connections of Steele's reporting, including that Simpson was hired by someone associated with the Democratic Party and/or the DNC," Horowitz wrote.[23]

During his December 11 Senate Judiciary Committee testimony, Horowitz told Sen. John Kennedy that "it's fair for people to look at all these 17 events and wonder how it could be purely incompetence." (Democrats and NeverTrump seized on one slice of the report that said the inspector general team "did not find documentary or testimonial evidence that political bias or improper motivation influenced the decisions to open the four individual investigations.")[24]

In another Senate hearing the following week, Horowitz clarified his analysis. "There are so many errors, we couldn't reach a conclusion in order to make a determination on what motivated those failures other than...the explanations we got," Horowitz told Sen. Josh Hawley on December 18, 2019.[25]

Nunes foes took another hit when the Foreign Intelligence Surveillance Court issued an order in January 2020 confirming that two of the four warrants against Page were "not valid."[26] The Justice Department had determined that there was "insufficient predication to establish probable cause to believe that [Carter] Page was acting as an agent of a foreign power," the central accusation in all four FISA applications.

NeverTrump's three-year campaign to bolster Russian collusion and ignore or justify high-level government corruption intended to destroy Donald Trump ended disastrously for all accomplices involved. Yet the very same people who daily lecture Trump supporters about integrity and decency and honesty said nothing.

None of the NeverTrumpers apologized for their smears on Nunes. In fact, when confronted on Twitter about his criticism of Nunes and his memo, the always petty David French tagged his accusers as "malicious grifters" and claimed that he *all along* wanted a full investigation into FISA abuse. "I've endorsed the investigation (and disclosure of the FISA documents themselves) for years," he scoffed.[27] French, however, did not retract his numerous attacks on Nunes, his work, and his integrity.

Neither has anyone else.

But Nunes isn't the only Republican House member reviled by Never-Trump. When several House Freedom Caucus members assembled for a press conference in May 2018 to demand a second special counsel to investigate the FBI's incursion into the Trump campaign, Jennifer Rubin declared the group, which included Reps. Jim Jordan, Mark Meadows, Andy Biggs, and Ron DeSantis, "unfit for office, [and] have violated their oaths."[28]

In 2015, Bill Kristol wanted Rep. Jim Jordan to run for Speaker of the House. By 2018, as Jordan teamed with Nunes to demand that the Justice Department stop stonewalling congressional demands for documents related to its handling of the Trump campaign probe and other scandals, Kristol called Jordan a "demagogue" for his hardline questioning of Deputy Attorney General Rod Rosenstein.[29]

Kristol's *Weekly Standard* published a quasi hit piece on Jordan in the summer of 2018, regurgitating Fusion GPS–sourced accusations related to Jordan's time as an assistant wrestling coach at Ohio State University.[30] (Those specious allegations will not be repeated here.)

When Rep. Ron DeSantis ran a pro-Trump commercial during his campaign for governor of Florida—an ad clearly meant to be humorous; in one scene, DeSantis read part of Trump's book to his toddler son—Kristol scoffed that the ad "sounded better in the original North Korean." Kristol condemned DeSantis for "using" his children. "A reasonably intelligent, responsible congressman has become a devotee or at least presents himself as a devotee of the Trump cult," he said on CNN in July 2018.[31] (DeSantis is a naval officer, Yale undergraduate, and Harvard law graduate.)

Adam Schiff, according to Jennifer Rubin, has a "calm demeanor and his exacting eye for detail."[32] Republicans such as Nunes, Mark Meadows, and Jim Jordan, on the other hand, "are so deluded or dishonest that they continue to misrepresent the facts behind the impeachment inquiry, shamelessly peddle conspiracy theories and defend the president's illegal threatening of a whistleblower."[33]

"I, too, am soul-weary and incredulous that so many Republicans...could become imitators and enablers of the most dishonest and corrupt president in U.S. history," said Max Boot. "I'm not talking about crazy conspiracy-mongers like Rep. Devin Nunes (R-CA), Rep. Jim Jordan (R-OH) or Rep. Matt Gaetz (R-FL). Given their intellect and character, you can't expect anything better from them."[34]

After some House Republicans stormed Adam Schiff's secret impeachment lair on Capitol Hill, *Washington Examiner* writer Quin Hillyer compared the group to Antifa; this included Rep. Steve Scalise, the congressman who barely survived after being shot by a Bernie Sanders supporter in 2017. The act, Hillyer raged, was "the most serious breach of House decorum I've seen in my 40 years of caring what happens on the Hill. It must not go unpunished."[35] As if he would be the guy to throw down the penalty shot.

Conversely, criticism of far-left demagogues such as Alexandria Ocasio-Cortez or Ilhan Omar, not to mention House Speaker Nancy Pelosi, is sparse.

PRO-TRUMP INTELLECTUALS

Trumpism, NeverTrump scoffs, has no substantive, intellectual mooring. According to NeverTrump, the Trump phenomenon has been embraced only by bitter clingers—to paraphrase Barack Obama—who are uneducated, racist, sexist, Islamophobic rubes. (Some use that term often. Rick Wilson once described Trump's supporters as his "rube, ten-tooth base."[36]) Deplorables, not academics or scholars or experts, define Trumpism.

"When today's conservative writers signed up in the 1980s and 1990s, they could imagine their core audience being well-off and educated people politely having dinner at the Union Club while hearing a lecture on an important subject from a [*sic*] intelligent person," Tom Nichols once whined.[37] Trump, he lamented, disrupted those clubby, halcyon days.

Trump's orbit, according to folks like Nichols, only includes Fox News hosts and talk radio celebrities; it should not have attracted erudite thinkers such as Victor Davis Hanson and Michael Anton and Roger Kimball. Nor should repositories of conservative thought such as the Claremont Institute deign to promote Trumpism.

In September 2016, more than 100 intellectuals signed a letter in support of Donald Trump. "Given our choices in the presidential election, we believe that Donald Trump is the candidate most likely to restore the promise of America, and we urge you to support him as we do," the letter read.[38] An impressive list of PhDs, credentialed conservative writers and editors, economists, and foreign policy experts endorsed the rogue Republican candidate.

R.R. Reno, an editor, author, and theologian who contributed to *National Review*'s "Against Trump" issue eight months earlier, joined the esteemed group to support Trump.

Intellectuals who not only defend Trump's politics but analyze his policies and approach based on any sort of scholarly foundation really rankle NeverTrump.

"My great sin, I think in their view, is that I'm supposed to be like them," Michael Anton, author of "The Flight 93 Election," told me about NeverTrump's enmity toward intellectuals who support Trump. "Their view of me is you got this training, you studied these things and weren't taught them in order to marshal support for Donald Trump. We didn't learn the Great Books to make arguments in favor of Donald Trump. You're using it in a disreputable cause. How dare you!"[39]

Anton, who has two master's degrees and is a lecturer at Hillsdale College (and also a fellow at the Claremont Institute), became an early target of NeverTrump after his essay gained nationwide attention in the fall of 2016, when syndicated radio show host Rush Limbaugh read the piece on air.[40] (The websites for both the *Claremont Review of Books* and *American Greatness*, where the piece was posted subsequently, crashed, Anton told me.)[41]

Anton, working in investment banking at the time, a field highly supportive of Hillary Clinton, wrote the piece using a pseudonym to protect his livelihood.

But Bill Kristol unmasked Anton on Twitter. "'The Flight 93 Election' is elegantly-written garden-variety sophistry. I presume the author is Mike Anton," Kristol tweeted in September 2016.[42] Anton had worked in the Bush administration as a speechwriter.

After the Trump White House hired Anton in early 2017 to work at the National Security Council, the *Weekly Standard* outed him again as the anonymous author of "The Flight 93 Election" and described Anton as "a traitor to his class of conservative intellectual."[43] (The piece initially accused Anton of writing President Bush's 2003 infamous statement that "the British government has learned that Saddam Hussein recently sought significant quantities of uranium from Africa." The author later corrected that claim.)

Commenting on a New York magazine hit piece on Anton in February 2017, Kristol compared him to Nazi propagandist Carl Schmitt.[44]

In a review of Anton's 2019 book, *After the Flight 93 Election*, the Bulwark (the *Weekly Standard*'s successor) ridiculed Anton's work and status as an intellectual. "Can anyone with eyes to see really question that Donald Trump is a font of lies, a paragon of depravity, a nepotistic, venal, corrupt dreg from the gutter of Fifth Avenue?" bleated Gabe Schoenfeld. "True intellectuals are seekers of truth. Anton has built an elaborate edifice on a foundational falsehood. Whatever is worthwhile in his book—and I strained to find much at all—is discredited by his Trump idolatry."[45]

Tom Nichols, speaking of sophistry, claimed Anton's Flight 93 approach demands that "trifling things like the Constitution must be pushed aside because guns and abortion and drag queens and stuff."[46]

Schoenfeld also took aim at Victor Davis Hanson. In a scathing ad hominem hit piece disguised as a book review of Hanson's book, *The Case for Trump*, Schoenfeld claimed it was "sophistry in the face of evil."[47]

After detailing his latest series of Trump-inspired grievances, Schoenfeld expressed disgust that anyone with an IQ above 90 would defend Trump: "We have Victor Davis Hanson, a respected historian of military strategy, a retired professor of classics, and now a senior fellow at the Hoover Institution, to tell us that Donald Trump is actually, despite what we see daily with our own eyes, a great American president."

Schoenfeld blasts Hanson as an unoriginal writer prone to conspiracy theories about Obama loyalists orchestrating and executing a "deep state" sabotage of the Trump campaign. (Schoenfeld, it's worth noting, has authored zero original reporting or analysis of the FBI's probe into Trump campaign associates or subsequent investigations into the president.)

Then, of course, after accusing Hanson of being a lazy writer, Schoenfeld dealt the Nazi card. "As a part of a larger phenomenon, [Hanson's book] is instructive in its way. Anyone with an iota of historical awareness is familiar with the fact that intellectuals in Europe and the United States lauded Joseph Stalin even as he sent millions to the Gulag and their death. By the same token, Adolf Hitler, one of the 20th century's other mega-mass murderers, also found his share of admirers in the academy, among them such brilliant minds as Carl Schmitt and Martin Heidegger."

In response to widespread criticism about his smear job, Schoenfeld backed off his comparison. (Schoenfeld was up to his old tricks; in October 2016, he attacked Encounter Books publisher Roger Kimball in the same way: "As we watch intellectuals who are supposed truth-seekers and truth-tellers become allies of and apologists for those who would spread [anti-Semitism], it is past time to be alarmed.")[48]

Tom Nichols often condemns Hanson on Twitter. "But [Hanson] is also a tragic case, as this shows, of an intellectual selling his soul for pennies on the dollar," Nichols tweeted on February 2019.[49] Nichols called Hanson's support of Trump "heartbreaking" and predicted that "the sad decline of Victor Davis Hanson accelerates, like an asteroid that can't wait to make its first and only crater."[50] (Irony alert!)

After Hanson outlined why the Democrats' case for impeachment is illegitimate, Max Boot offered an ineffective rebuttal and concluded with this: "All that is left is the tribal loyalty that Republicans, including Republican intellectuals, feel toward a Republican president."[51]

David French, at his new gig at the *Dispatch*, a new collaboration with Jonah Goldberg, also took issue with Hanson's use of the word "coup" to describe the nonstop campaign to oust Trump from office. "While people expect hyperbole from Sean Hannity or any other screaming Trump defender on talk radio, the same ideas from the pen of a respected historian sends a message that 'this really is a coup.' It's not. It's not even close."[52] (French, again worth noting, defended Comey's unfounded and politically motivated probe into the Trump campaign as well as the multiple investigations into never-found "collusion." It's unfortunate French never seems to apply his own exacting standards to himself.)

French accused Hanson of concocting a "word salad" and "despoiling his expertise."

Now, imagine being wrong about basically everything for the better part of three years and having the audacity to call someone else, a scholar who actually gets it right, an idiot. What NeverTrump lacks in integrity, class, and political instincts they make up for in hubris.

Hanson responded: "French's modus operandi has been to deplore incivility and to call for an end to ad hominem attacks—and yet sometimes as *praeteritio* in order to liberate himself to do the opposite...French resorts to a concocted parody rather than any actual quotation of what he believes are frequent boneheaded references to idiots like me: 'Akshually (sic), a Hoover Institution senior fellow and esteemed historian recognizes impeachment as a coup.'"[53]

When the Claremont Institute, a conservative think tank, announced its 2019 fellows, the list very much disappointed NeverTrump's in-house church lady, Mona Charen. Concluding that the recipients were people beneath her, Charen lamented how "many conservative institutions and individuals have adjusted their standards and long-proclaimed principles to accommodate Trump and Trumpism. Some have become almost unrecognizable. But Claremont stands out for beclowning itself with this embrace of the smarmy underside of American politics," she wrote in *National Review*.[54]

She continued her denunciation of Claremont in a podcast interview with Charlie Sykes, editor of the Bulwark. Sykes called Jack Posobiec, a journalist and naval intelligence officer, a "troll" and wondered aloud why Claremont would associate itself with someone who is so "radioactive" based on his alleged penchant for pushing "conspiracies" such as Pizzagate. (This from the same folks who peddled phony tales of Russian collusion for three years.)

"He is very faithful to the God Trump so I guess that must be Claremont's rationale," Charen said. "I don't know how any can take Claremont seriously ever again."[55]

While NeverTrump continues to bash everything and everyone, including intellectuals, associated with Trump, Anton has a warning: "They no longer have a place in the party or the movement, considering where both are going. Some of them know that, but many don't and think they can get it all back. Well, if they do, they'll kill it," he told me. "They can have it; go to your Chamber of Commerce roundtables to an audience of twelve. We will go off and do something else."

NeverTrumpers are "temporarily useful to the Left now," but in reality, their schtick is tied to Donald Trump. "As soon as Trump is gone, their expiration date is here. Then what? If they don't realize they're being used, they're even dumber than I thought they were."[56]

A strong possibility.

FOX NEWS

"Who needs RT [Russia Today] when you have Sean Hannity," David French, attempting to humor his MSNBC host, remarked on the network in May 2018.[57] At the time, French was mocking as conspiracy theorists anyone questioning the veracity of the FBI's investigation into the Trump campaign.

When, and if, a fair accounting of the Trump era ever is conducted, the news media will fare worse than even the administrative state and the Democratic Party in terms of institutions that disgraced themselves in service of taking down Donald Trump. No accusation against Trump is too outlandish, no slur against his cabinet or supporters is too vulgar, no prediction of pending doom is too farfetched—unnamed sources with unverified claims made it to the front page or top story without hesitation.

Corrections, retractions, and embarrassing moments litter the media's Trump coverage. But, as a part of the Trump-hating elite media, Never-Trump has no words of condemnation for their new journo-pals. No, the real "fake news" came from the cable news network founded by Rupert Murdoch and Roger Ailes in 1996.

Fox News promotes a cult-like following of ignorant Trump supporters, decry NeverTrumpers. Commending Nancy Pelosi for all the "wonderful things" she's done as a leader of the Democratic Party, Charlie Sykes told Bill Maher in 2017 that Fox presented an "alternative reality" of political events. Had Fox News existed in the Watergate era, Sykes continued, Nixon would have survived impeachment efforts. "You would have had Sean Hannity talking about a witch hunt, you would have had all that air cover that would have allowed him to get away with the cover."[58]

Of course, none of this commentary is original or thought-provoking or even true. NeverTrump simply is repeating the Left's well-worn tropes about Fox News, or any conservative news/opinion outlet for that matter.

After Michael Bloomberg announced his run for president, Jennifer Rubin said he should instead spend his billions to buy Fox News, "a journalistic toxic-waste dump that has misinformed millions of Americans, damaged our civic culture, spread xenophobia and insulated an unfit president from scrutiny," concluded the contributor to a newspaper that purposely endangered the lives of pro-life teenagers.[59] (In January 2020, the *Washington Post* settled a libel lawsuit filed by Nicholas Sandmann, the Covington Catholic High School student the paper repeatedly targeted in its inflammatory coverage of the teenagers' encounter with a self-described "native elder" during the March for Life in 2019. Press coverage led to threats of violence and death against the teens and their families.)[60]

Any tragic event is fodder for a NeverTrump diatribe against Fox. After a horrific synagogue shooting at a Pittsburgh synagogue in October

2018, Max Boot blamed the network for fostering a climate of "hate" and warned that the network should be shut down until it cleaned up its act. "Advertisers and investors need to boycott Fox News until they pull back from their promotion of extremism and hate," Boot said on CNN. "This is not acceptable."[61]

Boot made those remarks on a network that doxed a Florida grand-mother for voting for Trump,[62] employs journalists who publicly harass female Trump aides, held an on-air forum that blamed gun control op-ponents for the deaths of high schools students after the Parkland high school massacre, and bullied Catholic teenagers at the March for Life.

Fox News, Tom Nichols concluded after an alleged conversation with someone whose father is "addicted" to the cable channel, manipulates the elderly. Admitting he rarely watches Fox, Nichols nonetheless said that the network is "pure, stupid, unvarnished rage for the old and the ignorant."[63] The anecdotal expert.

The very same Republican Party mouthpieces who relied on Fox News to promote the Iraq War now accuse the network of acting as a "reflex-ive" arm of the GOP, a criticism astoundingly made by David Frum, the infamous "axis of evil" author.[64]

But nighttime host Tucker Carlson is on the receiving end of some of the most blistering criticism from NeverTrump, including from his onetime friend and editor Bill Kristol. Carlson admits to many Trump-in-spired epiphanies—one of his funniest confessions is that he started re-considering the existence of UFOs after November 2016. "If Trump can be elected, what else is real?"[65]

The fact that Carlson, with the right Beltway pedigree and résumé, jumped even half-heartedly onto the Trump Train infuriates Never-Trump. Kristol, Carlson's former boss at the *Weekly Standard*, accused his protégé on Twitter of "defending slavery" and anti-Semitism after Carl-son's post-Charlottesville monologue on Fox.[66] Carlson rejected Kristol's ad hominem, shaming his ex-boss for his social media addiction: "[Kristol] goes on Twitter and stays on Twitter all day every day. Dashing off little thoughts and impressions, scoring tiny little points against strangers in cyberspace, keeping obsessive track of his likes and re-tweets. At an age when he could be playing with his grandchildren, Kristol is glued to social media like a slot machine junkie in Reno."[67]

Carlson's rebuke, however, didn't stop Kristol. In 2018, Kristol said

Carlson's view "is close now to racism...I don't know if it's racism exactly but ethno-nationalism of some kind, let's call it. A combination of dumbing down...and stirring people's emotions in a very unhealthy way."[68]

Max Boot did the same during a fiery exchange with Carlson on Fox News in 2017. Boot accused Carlson of lacking morality because he didn't share Boot's outsized outrage about Russia's meddling in the 2016 election—an act, it's worth underscoring, that occurred on Barack Obama's watch—that it was "an assault on our democracy."[69]

Carlson's more populist view offends the nuanced sensibilities of NeverTrump. In a thought-provoking 15-minute monologue to kick off 2019, Carlson blasted Mitt Romney's New Year's Day attack against Donald Trump disguised as defense of the "conservative" status quo; Carlson unleashed a powerful denunciation of the ruling class's antipathy toward most Americans. He noted, accurately, that a populist uprising against tone-deaf, self-interested elites is happening around the world.[70]

Carlson, the father of four, pondered aloud about the condition of the country his children would inherit. "Anyone who thinks the health of a nation can be summed up in GDP is an idiot," slammed Carlson. He ticked off a list of maladies widely suffered by tens of millions of Americans, including suicide, out-of-wedlock birth rates, and drug addiction. Rural white America now looks "a lot like Detroit."

But the leaders of both parties, Carlson said, not only don't have answers but don't care. It is a spot-on diagnosis, endorsed by even the most reluctant Trump supporters but denied by NeverTrump. Carlson's analysis elicited mockery and derision from NeverTrump; David French insisted that Carlson's portrayal of large swaths of desperate Americans is essentially nonexistent, and to the extent that it is accurate on an individual basis, it is their own fault.

Setting up a number of strawmen—a French specialty—he urged Americans to reject Carlson's populism: We must not create a victim class of angry citizens. "We must not tell them falsehoods about the power of governments or banks or elites over their personal destinies. We must not make them feel helpless when they are not helpless."[71]

In a December 2019 profile on Carlson in the *Atlantic*, French accused Carlson of promoting racism. "Carlson has radically reinvented himself and one would hope he'd reinvent himself again, grant the reality of right-wing populism's race problem, and do something determined and intentional to overcome it."[72] (Carlson responded: "David French is a buffoon, one of the least impressive people I've ever met. Only in nonprofit conservatism could he have a paying job.")[73]

NeverTrump's smugness, coupled with a shoulder-shrug and eye-roll about the plight of tens of millions of American families while falsely defaming people as racists, defines the chasm between Conservative, Inc. and more Trumpified conservatives. It's Carlson versus Kristol, Trump versus Romney, and French versus the flock.

EVANGELICALS

Nowhere is NeverTrump's contempt for white, working-class Americans who voted for Donald Trump more evident than in their appalling condemnation of Trump-supporting evangelicals. If their collective scorn had been repeatedly aimed at any other religious group, they would have been called out, and rightly so, as bigots. But since their target is faithful Christians who dared to vote for someone who is on his third marriage and said naughty things about women in private conversations, NeverTrump not only gets a pass but is egged on by their Christian-hating buddies on the Left.

Evangelical leaders who endorsed Trump and continue to support the president because they rightly view him as someone who will fight to defend the unborn, protect religious liberty, and appoint conservative jurists to the federal courts, including the Supreme Court, are excoriated by NeverTrump. "It's a disgrace," John Podhoretz, who is not Christian, said of Jerry Falwell Jr.'s and Franklin Graham's backing of Trump after allegations about Trump's 2003 dalliance with Stormy Daniels were made public. "These guys are supposed to be moral leaders, you give people a mulligan?"[74] Not only is Podhoretz a political ignoramus, but he is uninformed about Christian tenets such as forgiveness and redemption.

Evangelicals who defend Trump are under a swoon of "religious fervor immune to reason," says Jennifer Rubin.[75] (Irony alert!) In a tweetstorm in early 2019, Tom Nichols finally said the quiet parts of NeverTrump out loud: They have never been comfortable with faithful conservatives, Nichols admitted, but tolerated them as part of the Republican coalition. He should have stopped them from assuming power within the party—as if he from his academic perch on the East Coast could have done so—and now regrets he didn't purge evangelicals from the GOP. "I knew the political evangelicals were hypocrites; I didn't realize they would go to the wall" for Trump.[76]

CNN's Ana Navarro mocked social-value Christian conservatives as "pearl clutchers" who need to "look at themselves in the mirror" for not criticizing comments made on Fox News.[77]

In his profane anti-Trump tirade disguised as a book, Rick Wilson repeatedly taunts evangelicals. Admitting he's not one himself, Wilson reminded the flock that "being a goddamned degenerate pussy-grabber with a lifetime of adultery, venality, and dishonesty is not, to my knowledge, one of the core tenets of the Christian faith." Wilson, whose claim to fame is the infamous Reverend Wright commercial he produced during the 2008 McCain presidential campaign and serving as a "strategist" for Evan McMullin, downplayed evangelicals' legitimate worry about the Left's infestation of every American institution. Evangelicals are the "dead-enders of the Trump World" who "continue to feel as if they're under attack from secular culture, the media, and the government."[78]

Wilson, rather than admit that reality, stupidly questions its legitimacy.

One of the best shticks in politics, as NeverTrump figured out, is to blast your own side. To that end, David French has the martyr role down pat. Nothing gratifies the Left more than religious conservatives using biblical phrases to pound the political pulpit about the sins committed by other religious conservatives. French (who attends a Presbyterian church, a denomination hardly considered on the evangelical side of Christianity) uses any Trump scandal to question the faith of Trump-supporting evangelicals; their unholy alliance with Trump, the Frenches warn, will despoil the church for kingdom come.

It's a form of political Munchausen syndrome by proxy: assigning a malady to people allegedly under your same tent to get attention for yourself.

In response to the accusations about Stormy Daniels and alleged hush money, French denounced his fellow Christians for not abandoning their Orange God. After Trump leaves the political scene, French warned, "you'll stand in the wreckage of your own reputation and ask yourself, 'Was it worth it?' The answer will be as clear then as it should be clear now. It's not, and it never was."[79]

In May 2019, French took to the pages of that guardian of piety, *Time* magazine, to explain that evangelicals back Trump over "fear." While giving lip service to their valid worries, French nonetheless preached that "the church is acting as if it needs Trump to protect it. That's not courageous. It's repulsive. And so long as this fear continues, expect the church's witness to degrade further. In seeking protection from its perceived enemies, the church has lost its way."[80]

Evangelical leaders, French insisted, have "seared the conscience of the church, and granted the nation reason to question our sincerity as believers."[81]

Now, think about that. French, in the most incendiary terms, is giving the Left license to mock the faith of millions of Christians because they back Trump. It is the sort of judgment that not only defies the core of Christianity but that can only be explained as religious bigotry. Switch out "evangelicals" for Muslims or Jews or even Catholics. Would not French be widely denounced as a bigot? Would *National Review* continue to publish that garbage? Would French still be allotted time on MSNBC? The answer, of course, is no.

Faithful Christians finally had enough of French's holier-than-thou antics. After the writer's scorching criticism of Franklin Graham, the American Family Association launched a petition drive against French's "yellow journalism" and asked signers to protest the "character assassination by David French."[82] It has more than 66,000 endorsers.

Chris Buskirk, the publisher of *American Greatness* and a devout Christian, took to task both French and his wife, Nancy, a political writer who follows in her husband's evangelical-bashing footsteps.[83] (She even sided with the Left in its evil and unholy campaign against Supreme Court nominee Brett Kavanaugh.)

Buskirk accused both Frenches of misusing the gospel in service of wrapping their political preferences in a Christian robe. Further, Buskirk argued, there is no biblical basis that sin should disqualify someone from public life.

"The Frenches and others wrap themselves in just such pious, Christianist rhetorical flourishes and scriptural references. But by conflating the role of the secular and the sacred, by attempting to immanentize the world which is to come, they misrepresent orthodox Christian teaching about the role of Church and the practice of secular politics to the detriment of both."

But the Frenches found some backup to their fire-and-brimstone fury when the editor of *Christianity Today* posted an editorial right before Christmas 2019 calling for Trump's removal from office. Editor Mark Galli argued that the impeachment case against Trump was "unambiguous" and "immoral."[84] David and Nancy French leveraged the column for maximum media attention: Mrs. French opined on two news outlets openly hostile to Christians—the *Washington Post* and CNN—about the decency of the *Christianity Today* editorial.[85]

"There is a part of the Christian church that will not tolerate any longer what Donald Trump has been doing," French said in a CNN interview on December 22, 2019.[86] She whined that evangelical support of Trump was disappointing to her "as a Presbyterian," a denomination she mocked in the memoir co-written with her husband: "If a Presbyterian skips church it has less to do with the workings of Satan and more to do with the golf schedule at the country club."[87]

In a blog post, David French claimed that Trump's "unique presidency is placing more strain on theologically serious Evangelicals than most Americans perceive."[88] In a follow-up column, French suggested Trump-supporting Christians were flouting commands from Jesus, Paul, and Micah by not being nice to their Christian-hating political foes. "Time and again, we see Christians in public life shed even the pretense of upholding those values," he wrote, without evidence.[89] The debate over whether evangelicals are justified in supporting Trump despite his moral failings is one more example of the widening chasm between NeverTrump "conservatives" and the movement's rank-and-file. In fact, as Trump fortified his conservative credentials and the Left's rampage intensified during his first term, some NeverTrumpers had second thoughts about their previous opposition to the president.

CHAPTER 7

NEVERTRUMP SPLITS UP

The decency of being scandalized is what being Never-Trump is centrally about, and why the movement remains important. It's the opposite of the opportunism required to go along with the president because you might get something out of him.

—Bret Stephens, November 2019

The break-up of NeverTrump was inevitable, leaving the remaining detractors more isolated and more desperate for attention. Like Stephens's comment above implies, the holdouts insisted they held the morally superior ground. But as they displayed more alarming and irrational behavior, even original NeverTrumpers took notice. They turned on each other.

"Since Donald Trump burst onto the political scene, Rubin has become precisely what she dislikes in others: a monomaniac and a bore, whose visceral dislike of her opponents has prompted her to drop the keys to her conscience into a well."[1]

That comment refers to Jennifer Rubin, the Trump-hating pundit once marketed as a "conservative" by the *Washington Post*. But the author of that quote is not from MAGA world; it is Charles Cooke, editor of *National Review* online. A frequent critic of Donald Trump and his most rabid defenders, Cooke nonetheless recognized by the end of 2017 that some NeverTrumpers were exhibiting the same pathologies they assigned to the president.

Cooke continued: "How, I have long wondered, could Trump's un-principled acolytes do what they do and still sleep at night? How can Jen Rubin?" The answer, of course, is simple—in no other political era would Jennifer Rubin, a wholly unappealing person inside and out, earn unlimited airtime on cable news and column inches in the pages of the *Washington Post*. Like an aging call girl willing to perform any contortions to titillate unimaginative clientele, Rubin became a parody of herself with her over-the-top diatribes against Trump and reversal of nearly every view she held prior to 2016.

But Cooke's column prompted a strong reaction from diehard NeverTrumpers; it stung because they considered Cooke one of them. In a post-election article, Cooke reiterated that "during primary season, I tried to convince my readers that Donald Trump was a terrible choice for a nominee. During the general election I gave my honest and unfiltered view of the proceedings, which was that I could neither back nor vote for either of the major nominees."[2] (Cooke, a British native who came to America in 2011 and became a US citizen in 2018, could not vote in the 2016 presidential election.)

So his takedown of Jennifer Rubin was viewed as an "et tu, Brute" moment in the wobbly NeverTrump movement. The *Atlantic*'s David Frum accused Cooke of falling in line with Team Trump for craven economic reasons. Referring to Cooke's critique as a "savagely personal attack," Frum defended NeverTrump as the noble outliers picking up the pieces of a conservative movement gone awry, protecting a country at risk, and fighting a president endangering every facet of American life.

Frum glumly assessed his tribe's shrinking ranks: "Twenty-one prominent conservatives signed individual statements of opposition to Trump's candidacy. Of those 21, only six continue to speak publicly against his actions," Frum observed about *National Review*'s January 2016 "Against Trump" issue. "Almost as many have become passionate defenders of the Trump presidency, most visibly the Media Research Center's Brent Bozell and the National Rifle Association's Dana Loesch."[3]

By the end of Trump's first year in office, the majority of NeverTrump conservatives aligned, in varying degrees, with the president. Ben Domenech, co-founder of the *Federalist*, contributed to the "Against Trump" missive. His website would become, and remain, one of the few reliable pro-Trump websites during the president's first term. Townhall.com's Katie Pavlich, blogger Erick Erickson, and broadcaster Glenn Beck evolved into backers of Trump.

Even those who still occupied a spot along the NeverTrump spectrum, such as Cooke, began calling out the antics of their most extreme colleagues. In a response to Frum, Cooke noted that NeverTrumpism is a good gig: "We all know, in advance, what Rubin will write, as we know in advance what Frum will write. She—and [Frum]—now have in-built networks, and, judging by the number of Frum's Twitter followers, they are thriving in them."[4]

Others from inside the NeverTrump bunker started to admit defeat. "A lot of us never-Trumpers assumed momentum would be on our side as his scandals and incompetences mounted," confessed *New York Times* columnist David Brooks. "It hasn't turned out that way. I almost never meet a Trump supporter who has become disillusioned. I often meet Republicans who were once ambivalent but who have now joined the Trump train."[5]

By early 2018, Rich Lowry, editor of the magazine that spawned the NeverTrump movement, accused the movement's thinning ranks of being delusional about the political realities of Trump's first term.[6] That prompted a heated response from Lowry's colleagues at *National Review*. Jonah Goldberg and Ramesh Ponnuru argued, "Most Republican voters did not vote to affirm the entire Trump package. They wanted someone other than Hillary Clinton, and conservative judges. Pretending otherwise is to give license to the president's worst instincts."[7]

But any internecine disapproval emboldened NeverTrump's self-imposed victim/martyr status. They considered themselves not just political patriots but heroes in the same league as history's bravest dissidents.

Bret Stephens compared the group to post–World War II freedom fighters living in Soviet-occupied countries in Eastern Europe fighting Joseph Stalin. "NeverTrumpers haunt the conservative movement the way Polish or Czech dissident intellectuals such as Czeslaw Milosz and Vaclav Havel haunted that segment of Central European intelligentsia that made its peace with Stalinism after World War II," Stephens wrote. "The Trumpers (and Stalinists) traded conscience for power; the NeverTrumpers and dissidents chose the reverse."[8]

Stephens freely—and safely—posting his political opinions in the pages of one of the world's most widely read newspapers, often met with massive approbation by the ruling class, in his mind, makes him as courageous as a Czech artist intermittently imprisoned by Communists for years. Now, one might be inclined to laugh at such absurdity, or at least entertain the thought that the writer needs a very long vacation. (A year later, Stephens, the self-proclaimed equal of Vaclav Havel, became unhinged when a random Twitter user compared him to a bedbug.[9] The fearless columnist emailed the Twitter harasser, a university professor, and the professor's boss to complain; the use of the word *bedbug*, Stephens explained, was "dehumanizing."[10] In protest, just like Havel would have, Stephens deactivated his Twitter account.)

But Stephens's self-aggrandizement, risible comparisons, nonexistent alternative agenda, and touchy ego, a toxic combination shared by the remaining NeverTrumpers, prompted further isolation from more objective Trump critics on the Right.[11]

As their diehard opposition to Trump started to look less like valid analysis about policy and more like the airing of personal grudges, NeverTrump lost its footing. Some struggled to design a game plan to keep the loose claque unified.

Blaming Trump voters for buying "into white-grievance politics on a massive scale," Seth Mandel, near the one-year anniversary of Trump's inauguration, wrote that NeverTrump's mission is to make sure no one like Trump ever is nominated or elected again.[12] (Mandel failed to provide any ideas about how the Republican Party can recruit anti-Trump candidates or a policy agenda to defend free trade, more immigration, and extended American troop presence in foreign countries.)

A devastating blow to NeverTrump came in September 2018: the death of John McCain.

THE LOSS OF NEVERTRUMP'S TOP SENATE ALLY

McCain gave NeverTrump a veneer of valor; he was NeverTrump's most influential ally on Capitol Hill. He validated the bogus collusion ruse from the start, then unyieldingly backed the Mueller probe. McCain acted as a shield between Republican senators, such as his close friend Lindsey Graham, who might otherwise have been more powerful supporters of the president during Trump's crucial first months.

NeverTrump heralded McCain as everything Trump wasn't, even though McCain's personal life included tales of infidelity and a second marriage to a much younger woman. McCain was part of the Keating Five; and his unrelenting push for war in Iraq resulted in the deaths of more than 4,000 US soldiers for a dubious outcome.

But McCain's biggest failure was running a facile campaign against Barack Obama in 2008, essentially handing the White House to a political neophyte whose damaging legacy survives today.

Before McCain died on August 25, 2018, after a protracted battle with brain cancer, the senator planned his own funeral. Barack Obama, the Clintons, and George W. Bush made the guest list. President Trump did not. (Obama and Bush delivered eulogies.)

In his farewell statement, McCain took a few jabs at the sitting president, commenting that the nation is weaker when we "hide between walls."[13] (In a 2010 campaign ad, McCain blamed illegal immigrants for "drug and human smuggling, home invasion, [and] murder" and promised to "complete the danged fence.")[14]

McCain asked his Trump-hating allies to "not despair of our present difficulties but believe always in the promise and greatness of America, because nothing is inevitable here."

The week between his death and final goodbye was filled with recriminations for Trump's past comments about McCain and overinflated contrasts between the two. "The death of Sen. John McCain has elicited an enormous amount of commentary about the differences between the former Navy pilot and POW and the current president of the United States, who received five draft deferments, one of them for 'bone spurs,' and who once remarked that avoiding getting a sexually transmitted disease was his 'personal Vietnam,'" Jonah Goldberg wrote on August 31, 2018.[15]

On the day of McCain's death, Bill Kristol noted that he had thrice voted for the Arizona president and never for Donald Trump.[16] A few days later, Kristol tweeted that McCain's death invited two options for the country: "McCain points to some of what is best in America, Trump to much of what is worst. It's up to us to decide which man to emulate, whose path to follow."[17] (The senator's death triggered a contest among NeverTrump for who could be the most dramatic.)

Not only should Trump have been barred from the services, Vice President Mike Flynn, Senate Majority Leader Mitch McConnell, and House Speaker Paul Ryan should not have spoken of McCain's death, either, according to Jennifer Rubin.[18] Rick Wilson tweeted that "history will record John McCain as a hero, a legend and a man in full. @realDonaldTrump will go down as a coward, cheat, weakling, failure, and traitor."[19]

Max Boot echoed Wilson: "As he showed again this week, [Trump] is petty, vindictive, insecure, self-centered and utterly bereft of dignity, honor or grace. McCain, by contrast, was a larger-than-life figure, a paragon of integrity who represented the best of America."[20] (There was a kerfuffle about lowering the flags at the White House; despite McCain's snub, Trump issued a proclamation after his death and provided a US military transport of McCain's remains between Arizona and Washington, D.C.)[21]

But McCain's parting shots would set the tone for a more than three-hour memorial service on September 1, 2018, at the Washington National Cathedral. In a eulogy that veered from grief to pride to bitterness, Meghan McCain occasionally drew parallels between her father and Trump. "The America of John McCain has no need to be made great again because America was always great," she said with a flip of the page of her prepared speech as she waited for applause from the packed church.[22]

The distasteful politicization of McCain's passing did nothing to endear NeverTrump to the Republican base; McCain's anti-Trump antics during Trump's first two years in office eroded his support in the GOP. (The year before he died, McCain had a higher approval rating among Democrats than Republicans.)[23] Just like everything else they did, NeverTrump's exploitation of McCain's death to score cheap political points against Donald Trump backfired.

But that wouldn't represent NeverTrump's rock bottom. Trump continued to fortify his support among Republicans and conservatives; NeverTrump became more desperate and more hysterical. Their anti-Trump myopia blinded them from seeing in real time perhaps the Left's most despicable attack during Trump's first term: the social media–fueled mob against pro-life teenagers attending the March for Life in January 2019. The teens' only crime? Wearing MAGA hats. And NeverTrump not only failed to realize the rampage was manufactured and dangerous, they piled on. In the process, so-called conservatives betrayed an innocent group of young people devoted to the morals and principles the conservative movement professed to defend.

It would mark the lowest of many lows for NeverTrump.

THE COVINGTON HIGH SCHOOL CRACK-UP

As events rapidly unfolded in the early evening of January 19, 2019, I wrote this on Twitter: "Don't forget. The Left doesn't just want to destroy you. They want to humiliate, disgrace and banish your children forever."[24] I subtweeted a comment from a blue-checkmark Twitter account that, among other treacheries, demanded that the Covington Catholic High School student purportedly "smirking" at a Native Elder steps from the Lincoln Memorial in Washington, D.C., never be forgiven.[25]

It was clear to anyone mildly cognizant of the Left's uninhibited venality, especially a few months removed from the attempted political assassination of Brett Kavanaugh, what was going down that Martin Luther King holiday weekend. The plotline had all the hallmarks of a hit job from the Left: White, male, conservative, Trump-supporter as the villain. Person of color from disenfranchised community as the victim. A spontaneous-looking frenzy on social media, cable news, and press corps. Immediate outrage from political pundits, celebrities, and Democrat Party leaders. Demands for nationwide reflections about "who we are" in the Trump era. Threats of violence against the evil perpetrators, offers of love and solidarity for the innocent victim.

The incident, like other events such as Charlottesville, could not be taken at face value; because Donald Trump occupies the White House, any confrontation, no matter how isolated or random, must be viewed in the wider context of the Bad Orange Man ripping the country to shreds.

One of the quickest and harshest analyses seethed that the students' actions were akin to defiling the cross. The writer struggled to come up with a term that would convey the "full extent of the evil on display here."[26] (Never mind that the teenagers had boarded buses from Kentucky in the dead of winter to rally for a cause at the heart of the conservative movement.)

Not only should the teens' faith be questioned, the author raged, so too should their devotion to the unborn over their fealty to Donald Trump: "In its heart the pro-life movement in the United States in 2019 is less concerned to advocate for human rights than to cheer for one of the two major political parties."

But the commentator does not work for the *New York Times* or CNN, although his account was indistinguishable from the depiction offered by Trump-hating, corporate Left media that weekend. No, the condemnation was posted at *National Review* online and written by Nick Frankovich, one of its editors.

Rich Lowry, *National Review*'s editor, also condemned the teens' behavior on Twitter. When Covington's principal hastily apologized on behalf of the school before the facts were known, Lowry said the mea culpa was "appropriate." After conservatives on social media pointed out the discrepancies in the narrative, Lowry still accused the teens of "obnoxious, dumb, and disrespectful behavior."[27] (Not from teenage boys!)

Lowry's tweets were retweeted by other conservatives, including Ben Shapiro.[28] Ana Navarro tweeted, "Native-American elder taunted by racist MAGA-hat wearing teens, speaks and cries for America, the country he defended and sacrificed and wore the uniform for. It is people like Nathan Phillips who make America great. Thank you for your dignity, sir."[29]

Bill Kristol wrote, "The contrast between the calm dignity and quiet strength of Mr. Phillips and the behavior of #MAGA brats who have absorbed the spirit of Trumpism—this spectacle is a lesson which all Americans can learn."[30] Dozens of other anti-Trump "conservatives" posted similar tirades against the Kentucky high schoolers, but they won't be named here because they are unworthy of mention.

The Right's betrayal of conservative Christian kids, as I later noted, occurred on the third anniversary of *National Review*'s "Against Trump" issue. The boy they targeted, Nick Sandmann, was a 15-year-old attending a rally in support of unborn children, a core cause of the conservative movement.

Once the facts were out, NeverTrump was backed into a corner amid harsh criticism from myself and others on social media; the unconvincing mea culpas began. Lowry deleted his tweets and issued an explanation for his misfire. He had fallen, he explained, for a "hoax," which sounded better than fessing up to emboldening a leftist hit job against innocent conservative kids. "If not a hoax, this at the very least was not what it initially seemed. I deleted my original tweet and we also took down a strongly worded post by my colleague Nick Frankovich that relied on the incomplete video. It's another reminder—even for an old hand like me—that it's best not to make snap judgments and to wait for all sides of a controversy to have a chance to be heard."[31]

Calling his article "preachy and rhetorically excessive," Frankovich offered a brief apology nearly 24 hours later. *National Review* removed his post.

Lowry, Kristol, and others deleted their original, incriminating tweets. On *The View* later that week, Meghan McCain defended her snap judgment about the situation; growing up in Arizona, she explained, made her instantly sympathetic to Phillips over the children. (She said the attack on Phillips was her "worst nightmare come to life" and accused the kids of being bigots.)

"These are kids, I hope their lives aren't ruined over this and I felt really guilty that I had somehow been a part of ruining Nick Sandmann's life in one way or another," she admitted. To her credit, McCain's confession was more heartfelt than the others.[32]

But the damage had been done. Here's what I wrote for *American Greatness* two days after the initial incident:

> These weren't just any group of random high schoolers. These are boys who were attending an event to support a cause that conservatives have championed—despite immense cultural opposition—for the past four decades. Young boys who attend a religious school and presumably are from faithful families trying to instill traditional values in their children despite the Left's continued assault on those values. Young boys who probably represent everything that the modern-day conservative movement has claimed to promote since its inception. Young boys who probably view their MAGA hats as a sign of patriotism and respect for the president, not a symbol of Racist Rube Nation. Young boys who we now know acted in a polite and deferential manner even while they were under attack by grown men taunting them and hurling hateful epithets at them. But what did Trump-hating "conservatives" do? They betrayed boys who, by all appearances, are the progeny of conservatism. They aided the Left in the virtual thrashing that prompted death threats against the children and their families. They acted in the same way—worse!— they accuse the president of behaving. They sided with the enemy.[33]

NeverTrump had learned nothing. Keep in mind, these are the same folks who insist any off-color remark from Donald Trump, including comments made during private conversations about pussy-grabbing or "shithole" countries, resulted in the degradation of the presidency and the culture in general. Yet here they were, en masse, making horrible accusations without evidence against children who, from all accounts, represent the best of American youth.

NEVERTRUMP TURNS ON EACH OTHER

The split in NeverTrump hastened during 2019. Rank-and-file conservatives continued to support the president in record numbers; no viable primary challenger emerged to take on the president in 2020. Kristol, Boot, Rubin, Wilson, and Nichols continued to beclown themselves with tiresome tirades that Trump skeptics could no longer tolerate. No one took Evan McMullin seriously; NeverTrumpers expressed regret for voting for him as he continued to embarrass himself on social media.

Even family ties weren't enough to bond NeverTrump. In an April 2019 interview, Norman Podhoretz, founder of neoconservatism along with Irving Kristol, the father of Bill Kristol, explained how he got aboard the Trump Train—and lost friends in the process.[34] Like so many reluctant Trump supporters, Norman Podhoretz admits that Trump's presidency forced him to rethink his views on many issues, trade and immigration in particular. He admires Trump's instinct to fight and his "blue collar sensibility."

Conversely, Podhoretz detests how NeverTrump looks down on not just Trump but his supporters as well. Of his former friends, Podhoretz concludes,

> Some of them have gone so far as to make me wonder whether they've lost their minds altogether. I mean, I've known Bill Kristol all his life, and I like him. But I must say I'm shocked by his saying that if it comes to the deep state versus Trump, he'll take the deep state. I think the first thing in the world you defend is your own, especially when it's under siege both from without and within. So the conservative elite has allowed its worst features—its sense of superiority— to overcome its intellectual powers, let's put it that way.

Podhoretz's son, John, remains a NeverTrumper; in late 2019, Podhoretz was making the case for Trump's impeachment.

NeverTrump's race-baiting, in some cases, exceeded that of the Left. Max Boot, referring to Trump as "President Archie Bunker" in yet another failed attempt at humor, rambled on about Trump's racism and his supporters' attachment to white supremacy. "White people can be pretty clueless. (I know, I'm one myself.) Get a grip, folks. We're not the victims here," he wrote for about the hundredth time in August 2019. "Thinking that we are is not just wrong. It's dangerous."[35]

Boot's preposterous diatribe, in which he compared the United States to apartheid-era South Africa, provoked justified scorn from commentators on the Right. "Like most white authors in this genre, Boot's self-hatred is boutique and performative," John Hirschauer wrote in *National Review* in response to Boot's column. "Max Boot can claim all he wants that President Trump is stoking the flames of race hatred, but if he really believes that, he ought to stop fanning them himself."[36]

Boot, who might be the touchiest and most easily triggered of the NeverTrump lunatic fringe—and that's saying something—unloaded on *National Review*. He accused some of its writers of succumbing to white nationalism based on their views of illegal immigration.[37] After warning whites not to be victims, Boot fully embraced the role of the victim, appearing on CNN to whine about *National Review*'s "attack" on him.[38] He claimed the magazine accused him of "race treason," whatever that means.[39]

"Boot's full-on Chernobyl meltdown is here, and it is quite a thing to watch," tweeted Seth Mandel, a NeverTrumper. "The saddest part is the embrace of this paranoid anti-intellectualism by the McCarthyite hangers-on rushing to link arms with him."[40]

Tom Nichols rushed to the aid of his wounded compatriot. In a tweetstorm, Nichols, per his habit, instead of addressing the legitimate criticism of Boot, launched his own ad hominem rant. Nichols accused the Trump-supporting Right of having a "nervous breakdown." Their collective future is imperiled: "They now know, without a doubt, that they're in a shrinking minority, dead-ended, and stranded with no way back."[41]

But Trump skeptics are getting weary of Nichols's shtick, too. In a parody piece posted at *National Review* in September 2019, Kyle Smith lampooned Nichols's Boot-like tendencies. The "insufferable" self-professed expert who spends most of his time on Twitter churning out predictable taunts about Trump supporters—Nichols often refers to Trump voters as "rubes"—had morphed into a lesser version of the Trumpified caricatures he imagined in his mind. "You may have noticed that I have many times urged Democrats not to compare Trump to Hitler, when I haven't myself been comparing Trump to Hitler, saying he's borrowing Hitler's tactics, calling his voters Hitler lovers, saying Hitler would be pleased by Trump rallies, or predicting that the GOP will nominate Hitler next," Smith mocked.[42] Nichols was not amused.

A movement that began as a reasonable if misguided opposition to an outlier Republican candidate amid fears he wasn't conservative enough had deteriorated into a race-baiting, name-calling, grudge-airing claque of humorless scolds appeasing the Left and doing whatever is required to extend the coda of their fading chorus.

This is why, as Trump geared up for reelection, NeverTrump hangers-on embarrassingly groveled for their continued alliance with the Left. Alarmed at the aged, radical, and batty field of Democratic presidential candidates, NeverTrump offered some unwelcome advice to Democrats: Stop acting like Democrats.

The existential threat posed by Donald Trump, NeverTrump warned, will not be averted by promises of universal health care, open borders, free college tuition, slavery reparations, and jacked income tax rates. NeverTrump begged for mercy in a spasm of "Dear Democrat" letters and columns.

Charlie Sykes wrote in June 2019, "Trump could still win reelection, because he has one essential dynamic working in his favor: You. He doesn't need to win this thing; he needs for you to lose it. There are millions of swing voters who regard Trump as an abomination but might vote for him again if they think you are scarier, more extreme, dangerous, or just annoyingly out of touch."[43]

In July 2019, Tom Nichols said, "If Democrats cannot be 'energized' or 'motivated' unless the candidate…is committed to policies that have almost no chance of winning in the areas Democrats need to recapture in 2020, then this is already a coalition going into electoral battle with a fundamental disagreement about why we're all even bothering in the first place."[44]

"Democratic friends, if you go on like this, you're going to lose the elections. And you'll deserve it," wrote Bret Stephens in June 2019,[45] and the same month, from David Brooks, "I could never in a million years vote for Donald Trump. So my question to Democrats is: Will there be a candidate I can vote for? The party is moving toward all sorts of positions that drive away moderates and make it more likely the nominee will be unelectable."[46]

In a cringeworthy column that was part-scolding, part-groveling, Mona Charen informed Democrats that, yes, they do need NeverTrump Republicans to win in 2020 because they helped Democratic candidates win in 2018.[47]

Charen ticked off a list of extreme policies promoted by the leading Democratic presidential candidates—such as eliminating the Electoral College and abolishing the Immigration and Customs Enforcement agency—then pleaded for more "moderation" to earn her support. "But this cycle, other Trump-disgusted Republicans and I can contemplate voting Democrat. We could do so not because we've become progressives, but because we think it's in the long-term interests of conservatism and the country to be rid of Trump. Still, much will depend upon whether the Democratic Party can resist its own drift toward Trumpiness."

Their entreaties, however, were met with the same level of scorn and ridicule that NeverTrump has heaped on the Right for more than three years. Nichols was gobsmacked at the "hostile" reaction to NeverTrump's advice by the Left; his Twitter mentions were filled with angry progressives accusing "The Expert" of being a racist and sexist. Some of the language used in the comments to their articles, Nichols whined, couldn't be "printed in a family newspaper."[48]

MSNBC's Chris Hayes mocked NeverTrump's attempted meddling in Democratic politics: "We should just ditch this whole primary thing and just have a small panel of Never Trump Republicans solomonically decide which Democrat would make them most comfortable." he tweeted.[49] Some Democratic activists wondered why NeverTrump pundits who have been wrong about everything felt their advice merited any consideration.[50] They've had their day, one columnist noted.[51] Go back to the GOP.

It was a pathetic display of political prostration. NeverTrump's role as the Left's useful idiots only extended to its dependable browbeating of the president and his acolytes. Once NeverTrump ventured beyond its mandate, the Left pummeled it back in line. The political refugees gave up their homeland only to be abused by their adopted countrymen.

To make matters worse, NeverTrump lost its mothership publication: As 2018 came to a close, the owners of the *Weekly Standard* shut down the magazine. Its gambit of serving as Trump's biggest critic from the Right had failed. Further, disclosures that Kristol was on the dole of a leftist billionaire hostile to every conservative principle that NeverTrump claimed to cherish and protect hastened the publication's demise.

It also signaled a major reconfiguration of the conservative media space; new online publications with a more Trumpian edge would thrive while stale legacy outlets would struggle to survive.

Some did not.

CHAPTER 8

THE DEATH OF THE *WEEKLY STANDARD*

But the life and death of The Weekly Standard is really the story of the death and rebirth of American conservatism, which is nothing more than the modern political expression of America's founding principles. The final years of The Weekly Standard, and of neoconservatism generally have been a sad coda on what had been an intellectually vibrant political initiative and ensure that its best-known legacy will be cheerleading endless, winless wars in the Middle East and carrying water for #TheResistance.

—Chris Buskirk, *American Greatness*, December 2018

On December 17, 2018, the *Weekly Standard* published its final issue. Rumors about the publication's pending demise had swirled for weeks. Efforts to sell the outlet before its owners decided to close up shop were futile. The brand had been damaged beyond salvation; its anti-Trump gambit had failed, and spectacularly so. According to one report, the *Standard*'s print circulation dropped 30 percent between 2013 and 2017.[1]

When the news finally was confirmed, it resonated throughout the political commentariat, both Left and Right. In an announcement on Twitter, editor-in-chief Stephen Hayes reacted with defiance and hubris, the same combination that precipitated his publication's rapid slide into irrelevance. "I am profoundly disappointed in the decision to close the Weekly Standard," Hayes tweeted. "For nearly a quarter century, TWS has provided an unapologetically conservative and fiercely independent voice on American culture and public affairs. That voice is needed now more than at anytime in our previous 23 years."[2]

(Hayes moved his family to Spain in mid-2018 while still attempting to run a political magazine based in Washington, D.C.)[3]

Not only was Hayes's message bitter and self-serving, it was dead wrong. For the first two years of Trump's presidency, the *Weekly Standard* was far from an independent voice—it served as an organ for the Resistance. The publication did little to advance "conservative" ideas or offer conservative alternatives to Trump's policy agenda; in fact, the magazine and its top editors, including Hayes and editor-at-large Bill Kristol, repeatedly took cheap shots not only at Trump and his administration but at Republican lawmakers who supported the president.

Further, there is no proof the *Standard* was needed "more" during the Trump years rather than, say, Obama's eight-year reign of terror against conservatives. The fact Hayes truly believed that the *Standard* was more vital during the mostly conservative presidency of Donald Trump instead of the far-left rule of Barack Obama pretty much says it all.

The death of the *Weekly Standard* evoked much pearl-clutching and finger-pointing from longtime pals on the Right and new allies on the Left. Like most obituaries, details about how the decedent's bad habits might have contributed to its death were overlooked and the outlet's value overblown.

The *Standard* was shuttered, we were told, not because it alienated its audience to gratify their personal grudge against Donald Trump, but because its employees were better than the rest of us and wouldn't "sell out" to the Bad Orange Man. "The Weekly Standard's editors and writers refused to prostitute themselves to the Trumpists," Jennifer Rubin, a former *Weekly Standard* contributor, blathered in the *Washington Post*. "In doing so, they stood as a continuing rebuke to those who jettisoned integrity for access and traded ideals for fame."[4]

NeverTrumpers who ignore the plight of unemployed steelworkers or sneer at people who don't know how to order a fancy lunch on the Upper East Side—David Brooks once mocked a friend (safe to assume now an ex-friend) with "only a high school degree" who didn't understand the menu items at a "gourmet sandwich shop"[5]—were outraged at the abrupt firing of *Standard* employees. NeverTrump, the "principled" crowd that defends free markets and the invisible hand, channeled Bernie Sanders when one of their own was under the ax.

Phil Anschutz, the *Standard*'s owner, was "a run-of-the-mill arrogant billionaire," wrote sandwich snob David Brooks in the *New York Times.* "He was used to people courting him and he addressed them condescendingly from the lofty height of his own wealth."[6] (But I bet he knows what soppressata is!)

The owner "murdered" the *Standard,* according to Brooks, a one-time *Standard* contributor, out of "greed and vengeance."

John Podhoretz, who helped create the magazine in 1995 with Bill Kristol, erupted over the magazine's collapse.[7] He, too, compared it to homicide. Even though Podhoretz admitted that the magazine never made money, Anschutz was required to keep funding his losing enterprise because, well, because John Podhoretz said so. Any financial loss Anschutz suffered, Podhoretz sniffed, was merely a "rounding error" on the billionaire's profit and loss statement.

Then he went full into drama-queen mode: "[If] Anschutz had been motivated by an unwillingness to bear the cost any longer, he could have sold the Standard. He chose not to. He chose to kill it," Podhoretz fumed. "The cessation of the Standard is an intellectual and political crime." In a craven corporatist move, he advised *Standard* readers to subscribe to *Commentary.*

But at least one man refused to mourn the end of the *Weekly Standard*: President Trump cheered the news on Twitter. "The pathetic and dishonest Weekly Standard, run by failed prognosticator Bill Kristol (who, like many others, never had a clue), is flat broke and out of business. Too bad. May it rest in peace!"[8]

Contrary to what Podhoretz or Brooks or other defenders believed, the *Standard* wasn't killed or murdered. It committed suicide.

In print, on its website, and on various cable news shows, writers and editors affiliated with the *Standard* kept up a steady drumbeat of anti-Trump sentiment. Rather than embrace the rarity of a Republican White House, a Republican House of Representatives, and a Republican Senate—a political jackpot that had eluded the GOP for a decade—the *Standard* instead worked to undermine that power trove.

The outlet offered a bleak outlook when it should have formulated a plan of action to capitalize on what would surely be a small window of opportunity. In his first column after Trump's inauguration, Bill Kristol wallowed in despair rather than triumph. (So much for country over party.) He wrote in the *Standard* on January 27, 2017: "Every party wants to claim that when the chips are down, it can and will act on behalf of the country. For the Republican party to stand successfully, where fitting and proper, both in private and if need be in public, against a Republican president would be an impressive accomplishment. It would be one not inferior to the Grand Old Party's previous achievements."[9]

That is the talk not just of a defeatist or a sore loser but of a saboteur. From the beginning of the very rocky start to Trump's presidency, Kristol and the *Standard* signaled they would antagonize, not aid or even fairly assess, the Trump administration. Republican lawmakers who did not subscribe to the *Standard*'s dim view of Donald Trump would be ostracized—and they were.

When the *Standard* questioned Trump's firing of FBI director James Comey, its editors wondered aloud why more Republicans weren't standing up to the president for his completely justified and lawful dismissal of the corrupt G-man. "Where are the senior statesmen among congressional Republicans?" the *Standard* asked.[10]

Before Trump's first year in office ended, the *Standard* was bemoaning his "capture" of the Republican Party. An unhinged editorial in October 2017 decried how "the great bulk of elected Republicans have surrendered to the forces of Donald J. Trump. And they didn't even put up much of a fight. Has a hostile takeover of a historic institution ever been accomplished with less resistance?"[11] What exactly Republicans should have resisted about Trump's pending tax cut proposal, aggressive deregulatory agenda, vow for greater energy exploration, and the appointment of Neil Gorsuch to the Supreme Court—all as the president fought a suffocating special counsel investigation—the *Standard* did not specify.

The magazine did, however, reiterate its approach under the Trump era: "Readers of this magazine won't be surprised to find that we think going along to get along is not in the interest of Republicans, conservatives, or the country. Robert Frost famously described a liberal as someone unwilling to take his own side in a fight. Will that be what is said of conservatives and Republicans? That they stood on the sidelines and watched as the party of Lincoln and Teddy Roosevelt and Reagan was destroyed?"

Nothing of the sort was underway; the destruction of the GOP existed only in the polluted, high-minded imagination of NeverTrump. The economy hummed along; consumer confidence had just hit a 17-year high.[12] The Republican House passed a bill to ban abortions after 20 weeks.[13]

Conservative groups heralded Trump's unapologetic pro-life agenda. "Who knew that a billionaire playboy from Manhattan would be the most pro-life president in history?" commented the head of Concerned Women for America.[14]

Not only did the *Standard* continue to peddle a phony depiction of a nonconservative president, but the publication hypocritically echoed Democratic talking points about Republicans.

The editors backed the resignation of former EPA administrator Scott Pruitt, a longtime enemy of the environmental Left.[15] Activists funded by wealthy benefactors declared war on Pruitt from the moment Trump nominated the former Oklahoma attorney general to run the agency.[16] (*National Review* also capitulated to the anti-Pruitt mob and demanded his ouster.) Charlie Sykes authored a separate hit piece on Pruitt, gratuitously linking articles from the *Washington Post* and *Slate*, to insist that Pruitt represented the "sleaze" of Trump world.[17]

Sen. Rand Paul, according to Stephen Hayes, was a "Russian stooge."[18] The *Standard* mourned the transformation of Sen. Lindsey Graham from a NeverTrumper to a "Neo-Trumper."[19] Meanwhile, the publication boosted Trump detractors such as Sen. Ben Sasse—he diplomatically offered a "civics lesson" as Brett Kavanaugh was ravaged by left-wing lunatics during his confirmation process, the *Standard* cooed[20]—and the clownish Sen. Jeff Flake.[21]

A cover article on Rep. Devin Nunes, the Republican under siege from the Left for his pursuit to expose a massive scandal that should have outraged every conservative, smeared the California congressman as a conspiracy theorist after the Justice Department released a redacted version of the FISA warrant against Trump campaign aide Carter Page: Nunes's committee first alerted the nation about the disturbing surveillance in February 2018.

The hit piece wasn't authored by a Republican or a conservative but by a Democratic operative who worked for the Senate Intelligence Committee investigating the phony "collusion" scheme. The FBI's intentional manipulation of a secret court intended to catch foreign terrorists isn't as bad, April Doss wrote, as "the damage done by Devin Nunes's actions, and the hype surrounding them. This time, it isn't the executive branch whose actions need to be checked. It's Congress that needs to rein itself in."[22]

Haley Bird, a writer for the *Standard*, accused Rep. James Jordan (largely considered, like Nunes, a hero by rank-and-file conservatives) of "carrying water" for Nunes.[23] Rep. Ron DeSantis and Rep. Matt Gaetz were portrayed as Trump sycophants.[24]

In May 2018, the *Standard* declared the southern border "safe and secure" and explained that the only problem was the number of desperate people trying to come to America to find work. The reporter claimed that "on the Mexican side, people understood the need for border security but were sick of the way Donald Trump belittles their country." The wall, the *Standard* insisted, was a "waste of time and money."[25]

The decline in support among Republicans for free trade was a "distressing trend," and it betrayed the legacy of Ronald Reagan.[26] Withdrawing from Syria would be a mistake.[27] So would leaving Afghanistan.[28]

Up and down the line, the *Weekly Standard*, partially responsible for creating the domestic and international messes Trump needed to clean up, criticized his efforts. The outlet condemned Republican lawmakers while handling Democrats with kid gloves. A "conservative" magazine devoted its resources and influence to thwart a president governing in a mostly conservative way.

And they paid the price.

"The Standard was in an absolutely perfect position to cover the Trump presidency," author Lee Smith told me. Smith contributed to the *Standard* for seven years before he was fired in October 2017. "They had everything at their disposal, real talent, people with decades of political experience. But their post-election strategy was rage and revenge. And they took it out on Trump supporters."[29]

Smith, a foreign policy expert who supports many of Trump's national security initiatives, is unsure what caused his dismissal from the publication; he is one of the handful of reporters who reported on the Trump-Russia collusion hoax, a scandal that the *Standard* largely ignored. "If you are a political analyst and you're not able to read Russiagate clearly then either you're corrupt or witless," Smith said. "In any case you are not an analyst or pundit to be trusted."[30]

But there were more reasons to doubt the integrity of the folks running the show at the *Weekly Standard*. As I reported in late 2018, Kristol and most of his NeverTrump cohorts are on the dole of a left-wing philanthropist generously underwriting any cause or influencer committed to ending the Trump presidency. This billionaire benefactor has tried to stop

Trump since 2016; he's buying off so-called conservatives to create the illusion of broad intra-party disgust with Donald Trump, an illusion that does not exist but that NeverTrump is paid—handsomely—to represent.

RESCUED BY A TRUMP-HATING TECH TITAN

Pierre Omidyar is a very rich man.

He started eBay, the online auction site, in 1995; a few years later, Omidyar became a billionaire at age 31 after the company's initial public offering. With a net worth of more than $12 billion, he ranks number 36 on the Forbes list of the wealthiest people in America.[31] (Born in Paris to Iranian parents, Omidyar is a naturalized US citizen.)

The tech titan runs an extensive operation of nonprofits through the Omidyar Network, based in Silicon Valley. In 2017 alone, his foundation donated roughly $85 million to a variety of causes around the world.[32] As one would expect from a Bay-area billionaire, Omidyar is anything but conservative. He, along with like-minded tycoons such as George Soros and Tom Steyer, promotes a far-left radical agenda. "As George Soros retires more and more from the political funding spotlight, liberal bankrollers like [Warren] Buffett, [Michael] Bloomberg, Steyer, Omidyar and the younger Soros were vying to take his place," according to a media watchdog group. "Together, they have contributed at least $2.7 billion since 2000 to groups pushing abortion, gun control, climate change alarmism and liberal candidates."[33]

In 2009, Omidyar donated $30 million to the Clinton Global Initiative.[34]

One of Omidyar's pet projects since 2016, however, has been to take out Donald Trump. Omidyar contributed $250,000 to the Never Trump PAC;[35] after Trump won, Omidyar directed his largesse at destroying Trump's presidency. Like everyone on the Left and the NeverTrump Right, Omidyar views Donald Trump as an existential threat not just to the country but to the world.

The president of Democracy Fund, Omidyar's most politically active foundation, detailed in 2018 why his boss planned to commit nine figures to various causes in the Trump era. "Over the past two years, I have seen alarming and sometimes unprecedented violations of our country's democratic norms," wrote Joe Goldman, who, like all hysterics who make such a claim, offered no detail about Trump's norm-destroying assault on the Constitution. "For an organization committed to strengthening democracy on behalf of the American people, this isn't just disturbing—it's humbling."[36]

Well, it must be hard to be humble when you have one-tenth of a billion dollars to burn buying off friends on the Trump-hating Left and Right; that summer, Goldman announced that Democracy Fund was in the process of awarding $100 million in grants to organizations devoted to "strengthening U.S. democracy." An odd statement for a well-funded and orchestrated attempt to destroy the duly elected president of the United States, but when you hobnob with the some of the world's richest men, details and facts aren't really that important.

Some of Omidyar's grant recipients include well-known havens of Democratic activism, such as the League of Women Voters, the Brookings Institute, and Common Cause. Omidyar also owns *The Intercept*, an online magazine that touts its "adversarial journalism."

But Omidyar discovered new allies on the Right after Election Day 2016: NeverTrump.

In late 2018, I researched Omidyar's financial ties to several organizations either operated or populated by NeverTrumpers. Nearly every outspoken Trump foe on the Right is somehow connected to Omidyar's largesse through the Democracy Fund and its "sister organization," Democracy Fund Voice.[37]

STAND UP REPUBLIC

This outfit is headed by the losing presidential ticket of Evan McMullin and Mindy Finn; board members include former Florida congressman David Jolly, another NeverTrumper, and Charles Sykes. (Sykes also served on of the national advisory committee for the Democracy Fund. In February 2020, Sykes said his term had expired.)[38]

Like a lot of NeverTrump claques, Stand Up Republic attempts to disguise its contempt for Trump and his supporters behind a lot of patriotic gobbledygook: "America has always thrived under the promise of liberty for all. But that promise is threatened when we ourselves are not committed to the principle of equality, or when ethno-nationalists stoke division and hatred."[39]

The nonprofit received more than a million dollars from Democracy Fund in 2017 and 2018.[40] Stand Up Republic spent $500,000 on ads against

Roy Moore, the Republican Senate candidate in Alabama.[41] After the Senate acquitted Trump, Stand Up Republican vowed to take action against the senators who "put their seal of approval on a lawless presidency and a coordinated cover-up."[42]

The group claims to be nonpartisan but of course condemns only Trump and the Republican Party.

PROTECT DEMOCRACY

"While Donald Trump poses an immediate, acute, and extreme threat to our democracy that must be blunted, he is not the sole cause of the problem and is a symptom of political forces that are eroding support for democracy at home and abroad," its website blares.[43] Protect Democracy maintains a "threat index" that calculates the alleged threat to American democracy based on input from "democracy experts."[44] (In February 2020, the threat was a 47, defined as a "substantial erosion" to our democracy. Science!)

McMullin and Finn are advisors to this group, along with several NeverTrumpers: *National Review* author Mona Charen, ABC News contributor Matthew Dowd, and writer Linda Chavez are also advisors.

Democracy Fund committed $2 million to Protect Democracy between 2017 and 2019.[45] The group organized a letter signed by roughly 2,000 former Justice Department officials demanding the resignation of Attorney General Bill Barr in February 2020.[46]

ALLIANCE FOR SECURING DEMOCRACY

This group features a star-studded list of NeverTrumpers on the Left and Right, including Kristol, McCain associate David Kramer, former Homeland Security secretary Michael Chertoff, and former Clinton campaign chairman John Podesta.[47] ASD rings a nonstop alarm about prospective election interference; it also operates Hamilton 68, a dashboard that claims to track Twitter accounts tied to the Russians, but the site has been criticized for its methodology.[48] Democracy Fund invested $1.2 million in ASD between 2017 and 2019.[49]

NISKANEN CENTER

A think tank named after a Reagan economic advisor, the Niskanen Center received $500,000 from Democracy Fund in 2017 and 2018.[50] (Another contributor is George Soros; his Open Society Foundation donated $300,000 to Niskanen in 2018.)[51] It's billed as a "libertarian" group,[52] but Niskanen promotes left-wing causes such as climate change, refugee resettlement, and universal health care.

Niskanen houses a who's who of NeverTrumpers. Gabe Schoenfeld, author of the hit piece on Victor Davis Hanson, and writer Linda Chavez are senior fellows. Its advisory board includes McMullin, Finn, David Frum, and Tom Nichols. In December 2018, Niskanen hosted a daylong seminar entitled "Starting Over: The Center-Right After Trump."[53] Panelists included conservatives-turned-lefties Jennifer Rubin, David Frum, and Bill Kristol.

DEFENDING DEMOCRACY TOGETHER

Kristol, in fact, is the biggest recipient of Omidyar's political grudge money. In 2018, Kristol formed Defending Democracy Together, an advocacy group that targets the president, his policies, and his Republican backers in Congress. "Defending Democracy Together is…created by lifelong conservatives and Republicans—many of whom have served in Republican administrations and write for conservative publications. We are dedicated to defending America's democratic norms, values, and institutions and fighting for consistent conservative principles like rule of law, free trade, and expanding legal immigration."[54] (The Trump era has been a boon not only for groups seeking nonprofit status, but also for unimaginative public relations flacks who just recycle "norms" and "values" over and over.)

Kristol and Mona Charen are listed as directors for Defending Democracy Together; other NeverTrumpers include Linda Chavez and former Republican governor Christine Todd Whitman.

One of Defending Democracy Together's pet projects was the Mueller investigation. The group produced several ads demanding that Republicans protect the special counsel from interference by the president.[55] DDT bought airtime on Fox News and during Sunday morning network shows. After the Mueller report was released, devastating NeverTrump collusion truthers with its failure to find any evidence of collusion between the Trump campaign and the Russians to sway the election, Defending Democracy Together produced more ads accusing the president of obstructing justice and imploring Republicans to hold him accountable.

Senate Majority Leader Mitch McConnell and South Carolina senator Lindsey Graham have been just two of the targets of Defending Democracy Together's ad campaign. The group also opposes Trump's tariffs and plans to limit illegal immigration, including opposing Trump's national emergency declaration to secure the border. When Trump announced he would recall US troops from Syria, Defending Democracy Together blasted the president for "abandoning" our Kurdish allies.

Ironically, as Democrats continue to legitimately violate constitutional boundaries and democratic norms in their unrelenting crusade to destroy Donald Trump, Defending Democracy Together remains silent.

But producing television commercials and buying airtime to attack the president and his allies don't come cheap: That's where Omidyar has been very helpful.

In 2017 and 2018, Omidyar's Democracy Fund Voice contributed $1.6 million to Kristol's nonprofit.[56] In less than two years, the "conservative" who vows to uphold conservative principles and values against the Bad Orange Man was on the take from a progressive Silicon Valley tycoon opposed to every policy the conservative movement has promoted for the past three decades.

As I wrote in November 2018 when I exposed Kristol's extensive financial ties to Omidyar, "It's one thing for a political pundit like Kristol to brand himself as a Trump-hating 'conservative' to earn hits on cable news shows and get fawning coverage in elite media publications. It's quite another to partner up with the sworn enemies of the very principles one has claimed not only to champion, but of which he has insisted he is the last, best defender."[57]

After *American Greatness* published my column, Kristol responded on Twitter with a link to the piece. "Grateful to all—left, right, and center—who are willing to step up to defend liberal democracy and the rule of law. Nothing would make me happier if such impressive examples of public-spiritedness on the left inspired more public-spiritedness on the right!"[58]

He tweeted that on November 14, 2018. Exactly one month later, the owners of the *Weekly Standard* shut down the magazine Bill Kristol had founded 23 years earlier.

Kristol destroyed his brand, humiliated his funders, and betrayed his loyal subscribers. "The Weekly Standard's leadership led an institution off a cliff, led several dozen people off a cliff," Smith told me. "These are people who had families, some in their 50s and 60s who would have a tough time finding another job. I've worked in media for a long time and I have never seen anything like the top editors of a magazine turning on their own readers."[59]

But Kristol wouldn't be homeless for long. Some *Weekly Standard* writers went to work for the *Washington Examiner*, another Anschutz-funded media outlet, which would employ several NeverTrump writers and take on a more anti-Trump tone as the 2020 election approached. (Never-Trumper Seth Mandel is the editor of the site's print magazine.)

But Kristol and Charlie Sykes quickly formed another anti-Trump website: The Bulwark launched in January 2019. Its primary benefactor? Defending Democracy Together, the nonprofit supported by $1.6 million of Pierre Omidyar's money. (Figures for 2019 are not publicly available.) Sykes is both the president of the Defending Democracy Together Institute and a former member of the national advisory committee of Omidyar's Democracy Fund.[60]

Falsely advertised as "home for rational, principled, fact-based center-right voices who were not cowed by Trumpism," the Bulwark hired Trump-hating writers and editors to continue what the *Standard* could not finish. Defending Democracy Together directors Mona Charen and Sarah Longwell joined the staff. It even published work by Molly Jong-Fast, a liberal Trump-hater who generated outraged when she mocked a cancer-stricken and beloved conservative journalist at a conservative event in March 2019.

"We also intend to have fun and name names," Sykes told Jennifer Rubin in an interview after the outlet's launch on January 8. "One of our core missions will be to call out the grifters and trolls who've done so much to corrupt conservatism. We will also report on and chronicle the ongoing political and intellectual struggle for the soul of conservatism. We know it's uphill, but most of us have a thing for lost causes."[61]

Obviously.

The Bulwark provides a daily platform for all sorts of invective about Donald Trump, his family, his administration, his backers in Congress, and his supporters across the country. In its first week, the Bulwark published a puff piece on Rep. Alexandria Ocasio-Cortez—"she's fresh and genuine"[62]—and warned that the real crisis was in the White House, not at the southern border.[63] (That same month, nearly 60,000 illegals were apprehended at the border.[64] In April, as illegal crossings surged into six figures, contributor Linda Chavez admitted there was indeed an immigration crisis.[65] The cause of the crisis? Donald Trump, of course.)

The site spun fantasies about a GOP primary challenger to Trump—it found one in former Massachusetts governor and non-conservative William Weld. "The fact is, if Weld plays his cards right, he could come out of New Hampshire with a not-insignificant percentage of the vote," one writer predicted.[66] Another article referred to Weld, disgraced congressman Mark Sanford, and clownish former congressman Joe Walsh as the "three horsemen" who could damage Trump in the primaries.[67] (Sanford and Walsh dropped out.)

The hyperbolic headlines about Trump rival those at the *New York Times* or Vox. Trump is an imperial president, a traitor, a racist, a Putin puppet (still!), an obstructer of justice, a war criminal apologist, a danger to democracy, a lover of dictators, and a betrayer of allies. Republican lawmakers who don't view Trump the same way are cowards and sycophants. After the Mueller report was released, Attorney General William Barr became public enemy #1 at the Bulwark as the Left worked feverishly to discredit the hard-charging prosecutor who pledged to get to the bottom of the FBI's corrupt activities in 2016 and early 2017.

Trump doesn't understand the law or the Constitution or even the Fourth of July. (Yes, that was a real article.)[68] He's unwell. A recession is likely to begin before Election Day 2020.[69]

Nancy Pelosi, on the other hand, is the "grown up in the room." Joe Biden is a swell guy, and there is nothing wrong with the fact he threatened a Ukrainian prosecutor investigating a company paying his son at least $50,000 per month for five years. Pete Buttigieg is cool, too.

A discussion about reparations should be "taken seriously," according to one Bulwark contributor. So, too, should policies to mitigate climate change.[70]

The last few months of 2019 featured dozens of articles about the manufactured Ukraine controversy, with the Bulwark offering full support for Trump's impeachment.

In other words, the *Weekly Standard*'s castaways had learned nothing. The Bulwark was the *Weekly Standard* 2.0 with fewer intelligent writers, less wit, and far less influence. "The final years of The Weekly Standard, and of neoconservatism generally have been a sad coda on what had been an intellectually vibrant political initiative and ensure that its best-known legacy will be cheerleading endless, winless wars in the Middle East and carrying water for #TheResistance," my publisher, Chris Buskirk, wrote in December 2018.[71]

The Bulwark is poised to carry on that shameful legacy. How long it will last, however, is anyone's guess.

Donald Trump has hastened both a reckoning in Republican Party politics and a major reconfiguration of conservative media. The *Weekly Standard* is gone; *National Review* may never restore its once vaunted place among the conservative commentariat.

In late 2019, David French and Jonah Goldberg left *National Review* to join Stephen Hayes, former editor of the shuttered *Weekly Standard*, to form yet another "conservative" news and opinion outlet. The *Dispatch* is a subscription-based website that promises to provide "engaged citizens with fact-based reporting and commentary on politics, policy and culture—informed by conservative principles. It is a community for thoughtful discussion and a forum for civil disagreement."[72] Early submissions, however, sound much like the trio's previous rantings about the Bad Orange Man instead of offering anything thoughtful, illuminating, or even original.

Fox News and the *Wall Street Journal*, once reliable organs of conservative thought, increasingly offer more hostile commentary and news about the Trump administration. The Drudge Report, a news aggregator and longtime go-to for conservatives, turned on Trump, too.

Pundits for the *Washington Examiner* published columns supporting Trump's impeachment based on the orchestrated Ukrainian "scandal." Seth Mandel, the print magazine's editor, suggested Republicans were conspiracy theorists (of course!) for questioning how the controversy unfolded literally one day after Robert Mueller's disastrous testimony on Capitol Hill. "The instinct to see a conspiracy everywhere is eating Trump and his supporters alive right now," Mandel tweeted in October 2019. "It's like 2016 all over again. Watching the right devolve into the hunt for moles and turncoats and saboteurs. What happened to arguing in good faith over the substance?"[73]

One *Washington Examiner* contributor explained in December 2019 how Republicans could benefit from "evicting Trump" from the White House.[74] A young reporter published the text of an off-the-record phone conversation with Kellyanne Conway, one of Trump's closest advisors.

But the Trump era has cultivated fertile ground for the rising influence of newcomers and established outlets that understand politics in the Trump era. As Seb Gorka, a former White House advisor and current host of a popular daily radio show, points out, these organizations have replaced Conservative, Inc., probably for good. "These are outlets that cover a wide array of topics, from politics and culture to entertainment and history," Gorka explains in his book, *The War for America's Soul*.[75]

He lists 13 prominent online journals where political junkies can get their fix. Toward the top of the list is my home, *American Greatness*, which published the "Flight 93 Election" essay; we also feature marquee writers including Gorka, Victor Davis Hanson, and Conrad Black. The *Federalist* offered some of the best reporting on Russiagate and top-notch coverage of the crisis at the border; editor Mollie Hemingway often tangled with NeverTrump collusion truthers as a Fox News contributor.

Townhall, Breitbart, and the Daily Caller feature prominent conservative influencers and reporters. Human Events has been resurrected in a more Trumpian mold.

Mark Levin commands a massive following on Twitter, on radio, and for his own television show; Levin is one of the key media figures exposing Russiagate. Ditto for Dan Bongino; he produces a popular podcast and launched his own news aggregator site to challenge the Drudge Report. Stalwarts such as Sean Hannity, Rush Limbaugh, and Dennis Prager continue to dominate talk radio. One America News Network gained White House access and influence; viewers displeased with Fox News's anti-Trump slant flocked to OANN.

Conservative media's landscape is forever changed. Neoconservatism, the reigning ideology of the post-Reagan Republican Party, has been buried. Republican public officials and candidates will be forced to address old canards about free trade, immigration, intervention in global disputes, and oversight of monopolistic tech companies. The government's role in promoting strong families and communities while confronting cultural ills such as easily accessible online pornography and deviant behavior aimed at sexualizing children will be a key part in future Republican party platforms. And the new conservative media will promote this reform agenda as its laggards insist on ignoring insidious issues under the guise of "individual liberty" and unfettered capitalism.

Anti-Trump conservative media spends most of its time talking to each other—that is, when they're not venting on MSNBC or authoring columns for the *Washington Post*. Podcast hosts and guests are recycled. Editors of the Bulwark interview editors from the *Dispatch*; the next week, the roles are reversed. They are little more than vanity projects, intended only to maintain their spot in the Trump-hating commentariat while changing few minds and making no impact in either political party.

As one anti-Trump writer at the Bulwark admitted shortly after it launched, "Where is someone like me going to go?"

As Trump's 2020 reelection campaign heats up, the new conservative influencers will play a critical role in promoting "Trumpism" and warning Republicans about returning power to the old guard Republican establishment. On the flip side, as Election Day approaches, NeverTrump is scrambling to resurrect its lost prestige in another attempt to keep Donald Trump out of the White House.

CHAPTER 9

TRUMP 2020

In the wider world of conservative Trump opponents,
William Kristol, editor at large of The Weekly Standard,
said he had begun informal conversations about creating
a "Committee Not to Renominate the President."
—Jonathan Martin and Alexander Burns, August 2017

This wasn't supposed to happen.

According to NeverTrump, Donald Trump wasn't supposed to win nearly all of the Republican primaries. Nor was he supposed to clinch the nomination for president. He wasn't supposed to win the White House.

He wasn't supposed to last the first year. He wasn't supposed to survive the Mueller investigation. He wasn't supposed to prevail over impeachment.

The economy, NeverTrump warned, would crash. The stock market would tank. Trade wars would alienate our allies and tariffs would punish consumers. War with North Korea was imminent. America's global standing in the world, whatever that means, would falter.

Republicans would flee the party. A serious primary challenger would emerge to replace Donald Trump at the top of the ticket if Trump didn't decide to abandon a reelection bid amid dismal approval numbers and widespread dissatisfaction among rank-and-file GOP voters.

In 2018, Kristol bragged that he was building a "war machine" to take on Trump in the 2020 primaries.[1] Potential candidates included Sen. Ben Sasse, former Ohio governor John Kasich, and Maryland governor Larry Hogan. NeverTrump speculated that, by the time primary season rolled around in early 2020, Republicans weary of their party's leader and Democrats regretful they had voted to put Trump in the White House would be open to another option. Kristol, ever the attention seeker, even floated the idea of running himself.

Longtime Republican strategist Mike Murphy—best known for burning through $150 million of Meg Whitman's fortune to have her lose the California governor's race, shortly followed by burning through $115 million of Jeb Bush contributions before he exited the Republican presidential primary in March 2016—also promised to create a "war room" to prepare a battle plan to oust Trump.[2]

Murphy said that after Charlottesville, he didn't know a "single highly experienced GOP operative who is not deeply concerned about 2018 and the damage Trump is doing to our party." Did you hear that, Trumpified hoi polloi? *Highly experienced* operatives were very, very concerned. Murphy also predicted Trump would leave office in early 2019 after being humiliated by a Democratic wipeout in the 2018 midterm elections. "A resignation is far from impossible," Murphy mused.[3] Highly experienced, you say?

But, of course, none of it happened. Just like after November 8, 2016, NeverTrump once again stands amid the ruins of its own scorched predictions of disaster and doom. The economy continues to notch record numbers; unemployment, especially among minorities, is at record lows. Wages are up, consumer confidence is up. On the same day House Democrats introduced two articles of impeachment against the president, Trump and his accusers signed an updated pact to replace NAFTA, a cornerstone of Trump's 2016 campaign platform.

One year before American voters would decide whether to reelect Donald Trump, polls in key battleground states showed Trump running dead-even with the leading Democratic contenders. "Democrats would probably need to win three of the six states to win the White House, assuming other states voted as they did in 2016—an outcome that is not at all assured," mourned the *New York Times* when it published the poll results in November 2019.[4]

Most voters, when asked, predicted Trump would win reelection.

There were no war rooms or political machines. No disgruntled base preparing to flee their president in favor of a more moderate and modest alternative. Trump's rallies were sold-out events where people began standing in long lines the day before to secure a seat. The strategy by the Left and NeverTrump Right to demonize Donald Trump for his every move was having the opposite effect. Just as in 2016, Trump was a proxy; behind their hatred for the president lurked a contempt for every American, especially working-class whites, who dared to support Donald Trump against the elite's wishes.

They weren't even hiding it any longer. NeverTrump routinely dismissed Trump supporters as "rubes" and "Bubbas." They were unthinking members of a "cult." On November 4, 2019, exactly one year before Election Day 2020, Tom Nichols unloaded his contempt for Trump backers in a lengthy tweetstorm (his signature move).[5] The GOP, Nichols raged, is "a party of opportunists manipulating an ignorant mass of propaganda-addled people." Trump is a "sociopath" who remained in power and was "getting rich by scaring rubes and old people," a reference to Fox News viewers. If you were stupid enough to have a friend or family member who was a Trump backer, that person should be "shunned." And by the way, if you still support Trump, Nichols considers you "morally flawed."

Nichols's diatribe revealed the collective frustration of NeverTrump that, unless some political miracle occurred, Donald Trump would be reelected in 2020, perhaps by a wider margin than in 2016.

THE MUELLER SEQUEL

That prospect left NeverTrump with one more Hail Mary: to support impeachment of the president based on a brief phone call to the newly elected president of Ukraine. After all their previous efforts failed—from the firing of James Comey and the Mueller investigation to Stormy Daniels pay-off accusations and Michael Cohen's testimony—a 30-minute conversation between Trump and a foreign leader would be their last chance to boot Trump from the Oval Office before the 2020 primary season got underway.

NeverTrump had been betting on Trump's impeachment since early 2017. Bill Kristol posted dozens of tweets pondering if, when, where, why, and how Trump would face impeachment. "Here's a question that's increasingly been pre-occupying me: If Mueller doesn't find grounds to impeach, what then?" he tweeted in August 2017.[6]

"Ukrainegate," the ruse's shorthand, might have been the worst justification for impeachment of all. After Robert Mueller's cringeworthy testimony on July 24 dealt a death blow to the bogus collusion hoax, Democrats desperately needed a new ruse. House Intelligence Committee chairman Adam Schiff hastily masterminded a new scheme: an alleged "quid pro quo" demand by Donald Trump to the newly elected president of Ukraine that he investigate not just Ukrainian interference in the 2016 election but also Hunter Biden's $50,000-per-month spot on the board of Burisma, a Ukrainian energy company widely suspected of various crimes including money laundering and tax evasion. (The call, unironically, occurred one day after Mueller's disastrous appearance on Capitol Hill.)

When reports that an anonymous "whistleblower" in the intelligence community had the goods on the president, Democrats and NeverTrump smelled blood. Kristol's Omidyar-funded group, Republicans for the Rule of Law, quickly produced a commercial to express panic over the anonymous complaint, which consisted entirely of hearsay evidence. "The president crossed the line by engaging a foreign leader's help to investigate a political rival," the ad blared.[7] Trump, the ad continued, was attempting to hide his "abuse of power" by refusing to release both the complaint and a transcript of the call. (The White House shortly did both.)

Kristol urged Republican senators including Mitt Romney and Ben Sasse to "stand up for themselves" against the president.

In a dramatic tweetstorm attached to the ad, Kristol cited quotes from the Federalist Papers, Thomas Paine, and Edmund Burke to give intellectual weight to his latest impeachment frenzy.[8] (Keep in mind, no one had yet read the report or had any details outside of what the leftist media was reporting.)

Like the old soft shoe, Kristol hoped his worn routine of overwrought hyperbole, solemn reminders about the founders, stern warnings about the rule of law, and condescending taunts of Republican lawmakers and, of course, the Bad Orange Man would finally wow the crowd.

"Looks pretty bad!" Seth Mandel tweeted after the White House released the call's transcript.[9] (Mandel, like most of the media, gave an inaccurate summary of the call.)

Jennifer Rubin cackled that the call's transcript would seal Trump's fate—really and truly this time.[10]

Jonah Goldberg was aghast at the allegations: "I mean, my God, the day after Robert S. Mueller III testified to Congress about his report investigating whether the Trump campaign had colluded with one foreign power, Russia, the president got on the horn and encouraged another foreign power, Ukraine, to help with his reelection."[11]

But the Schiff-produced story quickly fell apart when Trump released the transcript, which contradicted NeverTrump's treasonous claims. The aid was released without the alleged "quid pro quo" and Ukrainian officials, including President Volodymyr Zelensky, said they were never pressured to investigate anything. Further, Schiff had to confess that, despite protestations to the contrary, his staff met with the "whistleblower" before he filed an official complaint.

Further, a video from 2016 showed Biden, as vice president, threatening to withhold $1 billion in US aid unless the Ukrainian prosecutor investigating Burisma was fired. The Democrats' impeachment ploy began to backfire on Uncle Joe, the Democratic candidate most voters believed was the only one who can beat Donald Trump.

House hearings throughout November and December repeatedly highlighted Hunter Biden's multi-million-dollar ghost-payrolling gig for a shady company based in one of the most corrupt nations on the planet. Nearly every impeachment witness for the Democrats agreed that Hunter Biden's role on the Burisma board represented a conflict of interest.

One State Department official testified that he would support reopening Ukraine's investigation into the company, a probe that Joe Biden demanded shut down if Ukrainians wanted US aid. (So basically the same thing, if not worse than, the Democrats accused Trump of doing.)

As the process dragged on and the Bidens remained as much as a part of the narrative as Donald Trump, the media finally started asking questions. The scrutiny could not have come at a worse time for Biden, or for NeverTrump, many of whom had signaled their support for Biden.

In an impressive feat of rhetorical gymnastics, NeverTrump defended Joe Biden's threat as a legitimate attempt to halt corruption in Ukraine (ha ha) while unintentionally arguing that Biden and his son should be shielded from any investigation because the elder Biden was running for president. Trump, on the other hand, was a criminal for doing far less. This subterfuge was designed to protect their preferred Democratic candidate.

Both Cindy and Meghan McCain indicated they might support Biden over Trump. "I love [Joe Biden] dearly and I think he is a truly decent, wonderful human being that could be very healing for the country," Meghan McCain gushed in September 2019. "I hope he stays true to the politician he has always been."[12]

The Bulwark published several puff pieces on Biden, offering unsolicited campaign advice. One writer defended Biden's icky touchy-feely habit even with children. "Biden's public touchiness looks much more rooted in the need for emotional connections—to both find comfort in and give support to others," Tim Miller explained. "Because if Joe Biden is expert in anything, he is expert in the management of grief. He knows on a deep, personal level the primal human need for connection."[13] A healer, you see. Not a creeper.

Bill Kristol, Jennifer Rubin, and Tom Nichols all cooed over Biden.[14] "It's possible that in the end I could be a reluctant Biden voter," Charlie Sykes, editor of the Bulwark, admitted.[15] "I loved it," squealed Ana Navarro on *The View* after Biden mocked an Iowa farmer in December for asking a question about his son's patronage post. "I'm glad he's getting some practice in calling out damn lies because if he wins the primary, he's going to be running against a damn liar."[16]

Biden strong-arming a country to halt an investigation into the firm paying his son millions of dollars—a gig the junior Biden only surrendered the month dad announced his third run for the presidency in spring 2019—was copacetic to NeverTrump. The president's phone call, however, caused a constitutional crisis, NeverTrump insisted.

"This level of flagrant norm-shattering and proud lawbreaking demands more than tut-tutting," Mona Charen tut-tutted. "Along with the shakedown of foreign countries to get dirt on opponents, Trump is demonstrating that he truly believes he is above the law. A nation of laws cannot tolerate that."[17] (As Trump continued to evade their headhunting, NeverTrump's harangues became more and more bombastic.)

While declaring Trump guilty as charged, Jonah Goldberg proposed that Trump should just fess up and apologize for the nonexistent quid pro quo.[18] David French told Goldberg in a podcast interview that the president was "running an independent diplomatic operation" based on a "conspiracy theory" about Ukraine's meddling in the 2016 election.[19] French, writing in *Time* magazine, wailed that Trump's brief hold on aid to Ukraine jeopardized national security. "It's not just the nature of Trump's abuse of power that argues for his impeachment, it's the gravity of harm that he risked with his reckless malice."[20]

Stephen Hayes said Republicans' defenses of Trump "didn't even pass the laugh test" and that there was clear evidence of a "quid pro quo."[21]

It was as if NeverTrump, after wearing much egg on their collective face for promoting phony Russian collusion for nearly three years, learned nothing. Their conduct was like a song stuck on repeat: Once again, NeverTrump either wittingly or unwittingly followed like lemmings the Democrats' carefully constructed fabricated plot to ruin Donald Trump.

Either too lazy, too arrogant, or, quite frankly, too dumb to be bothered with the details of how the latest scheme was hatched, NeverTrump regurgitated every Democratic talking point, including that Barack Obama and Joe Biden were very worried about corruption in Ukraine. (While at the same time, sending billions in US tax dollars to the rogue country to spend on who knows what.)

The Democrats and NeverTrump accused Trump of all sorts of criminality, including bribery, extortion, abuse of power, and inviting a foreign power to interfere in an election. Tough stuff. But on December 11, the House Judiciary committee approved only two articles of impeachment: abuse of power and obstruction of Congress.[22]

After the vote, however, House Speaker Nancy Pelosi refused to send the impeachment case to the Republican-led Senate. Republicans in the Senate started calling her bluff. Historians and experts argued that if the case wasn't forwarded to the Senate, it might not count as impeachment after all.

While NeverTrump and the Democrats stumbled to make sense of the impeachment debacle, the year-end economic news couldn't have been worse for Trump haters. The stock market closed at a record high; wage growth, especially among minorities, continued to surge, beating all expert projections. "The unemployment gaps between both blacks and whites as well as Hispanics and whites have reached all-time lows," Bloomberg News reported in November 2019. "It's not just that the job market has been good: For minorities, it has been historically good."[23] Wages and income were up across the board while unemployment hit another record low.

Housing starts hit a 12-year high in 2019.[24] And as Washington roiled with impeachment drama before the holidays, American consumers rang up the biggest shopping day of all time, buying more than $34 billion in stocking stuffers on December 21.[25] In December 2019, Senate Majority Leader Mitch McConnell confirmed Trump's 50th circuit court judge; in addition to Trump's two Supreme Court justices and 120 district court justices, Trump's imprimatur on the judiciary "will reverberate for years regardless of the next elections, as right-leaning courts scrutinize progressive laws passed by Congress and the states," worried *Politico*'s Burgess Everett.[26]

Polls indicated Trump held a strong position headed into the election year: A credible survey conducted in Virginia, a state rapidly trending blue, showed Trump beating every Democratic candidate except Joe Biden.

Amid every insidious, immoral, and corrupt attempt to thwart his presidency, Trump entered 2020 looking as presidential as ever; his Democratic contenders, on the other hand, started 2020 defending a murderous terrorist, accusing Trump of committing war crimes, and backpedaling on impeachment.

It was not how NeverTrump envisioned 2019 would end, or how 2020 would begin.

EPILOGUE

On February 1, 2020, Bill Kristol tweeted this declaration of party loyalty: "Not presumably forever; not perhaps for a day after Nov. 3, 2020; not on every issue or in every way until then. But for the time being one has to say: We are all Democrats now."[1]

His statement was intended to be the preamble to a week that would feature the acquittal of the president by Senate Republicans, another show of solidarity for the party whose futile impeachment crusade was about to end.

Kristol's alliance with a political party touting taxpayer-funded abortion-on-demand, open borders, college loan forgiveness, free health care for all including illegal immigrants, slavery reparations, and other outlandish proposals inimical to conservatism indicated that his transition to full-fledged leftist was complete.

But, as usual, Kristol's reverse political Midas touch kicked in. The Democratic Party proceeded to have its worst week since November 2016, while President Trump enjoyed one of his best.[2] NeverTrumpers who had aligned themselves with Democrats since well before the 2018 midterm elections would be forced to own up to their new allegiance to a party completely imploding just months before their convention in Milwaukee to officially nominate Trump's Democratic opponent.

THE DEMOCRATIC PARTY FALLS APART

The weekend before the Iowa caucus, the *Des Moines Register* refused to release its traditional poll amid protests from Pete Buttigieg's campaign that his name had not been listed in the survey.[3] This prompted widespread suspicion, particularly from Bernie Sanders's team, that the Democratic Party was up to its old tricks, burying results that many speculated would show Sanders in the lead and Biden badly trailing other front-runners.

But that dustup was nothing compared to the party's disastrous caucus on February 4. A failed app was blamed for disrupting the vote count, leading to inconsistencies in the final tallies and mass confusion for days.[4] South Bend mayor Pete Buttigieg prematurely declared victory, a claim disputed by the media and his primary opponents. Under fire, Tom Perez, chairman of the Democratic National Committee, demanded a recanvassing of the votes from each caucus site;[5] some party stalwarts, such as former Clinton confidant James Carville, called for Perez's ouster.

Nearly a week later, Iowa Democrats were still recounting votes. Sanders and Buttigieg essentially tied the contest; Biden came in a dismal fourth place.

While Democrats fumed over the bad optics of the Iowa catastrophe—how could a party that wants to run the economy and the health care system mishandle a small election in a small state—Donald Trump delivered his State of the Union address the night before the Senate impeachment vote.

In an uncharacteristically low-key fashion, Trump articulated his administration's achievements, including record economic growth, low unemployment, and wage increases across every demographic. But when Trump introduced several American heroes, House Speaker Nancy Pelosi and her petulant caucus remained seated. Not only did they refuse to cheer Trump's good news on the economy, Democratic lawmakers snubbed military heroes, the mother of a child who had survived a very premature birth, and the brother of a California man killed by an illegal immigrant.

And after Trump finished his speech, with great dramatic flair, Pelosi ripped in half the copy of the speech Trump had handed to her before he began. Her childish act reflected the frustration of a party defeated, whose three-year pummeling of Donald Trump was backfiring in all sorts of ways.

There was more bad news for Democrats and their NeverTrump boosters. A Gallup poll showed Trump with his highest job approval rating ever, at 49 percent, higher than Obama's at the same time in his presidency.[6] Voters overwhelmingly approved of the way Trump was handling the economy. Overall optimism was at record levels; 90 percent of

Americans said they were satisfied with their personal lives, a four-decade high.[7] Three-quarters of respondents said they believed their financial situation would improve in the following year.[8]

Fifty-one percent held a favorable view of the Republican Party, compared to 45 percent for the Democratic Party. The GOP held a slim lead in party preference for the first time in years. Ninety-four percent of Republicans approved of the president.

Just as Democrats struggled to digest the positive news for the president and the GOP, a separate job report delivered another blow. The US economy produced 225,000 jobs in January, blowing away expectations.[9]

House Speaker Pelosi held an incoherent press conference on February 6 where she suggested the president was "sedated" during his State of the Union address.[10] Recriminations about the Iowa fiasco spilled onto the campaign trail in New Hampshire as the party prepared for the primary on February 11. Biden produced an attack ad against Buttigieg, signaling how far the former vice president had fallen as his aides scrambled to salvage his flailing campaign and deteriorating faculties on the stump.[11]

A grief-stricken article in the *Washington Post* that week gauged the party's mood. "The developments have generated convulsions of angst among Democrats, who watched their first-in-the-nation Iowa presidential caucuses conclude in a chaotic fiasco and deliver an inconclusive result," wrote Robert Costa and Philip Rucker on February 8. "Many in the party are now sounding the alarm that denying Trump a second term could be far more difficult than they had calculated."[12]

TRIUMPHANT TRUMP

Trump, on the other hand, was buoyed by the week's events. In what was part victory lap, part rhetorical stick-in-the-eye, and part warning, the president held a celebration in the White House with a standing-room-only crowd of cheering supporters. Trump acknowledged what everyone had been through for three years: "It was evil, it was corrupt, it was dirty cops," Trump said. "It was leakers and liars. Had I not fired James Comey, who was a disaster by the way, it's possible I wouldn't even be standing here right now."[13]

The president thanked his legal team, his family, and a lengthy roster of supportive Republican lawmakers in the House and Senate. In an act that must have agitated NeverTrump even more than Trump's acquittal, when the president identified Rep. Devin Nunes as the first person to uncover the Russiagate scandal, everyone in the room stood for a lengthy ovation.[14]

Trump hinted that the plotters of the soft coup against him would soon face a reckoning. "When I fired that sleazebag [Comey], all hell broke out," Trump said toward the end of his remarks. "They were ratting on each other, they were runnin' for the hills. Let's see what happens. It's in the hands of some very talented people."

The president was referring to the criminal investigations into the origins of the FBI's counterintelligence probe of his 2016 presidential campaign and the suspicious activities of Obama operatives still in power between Election Day and Inauguration Day attempting to derail his presidency.

The worst, it appeared, was still ahead for the Left and their Never-Trump useful idiots. The corrupt sleazebags, as the president called them, who had been defended and protected by NeverTrump might finally get their legal comeuppance. If and when the investigation resulted in long-awaited charges against Comey and company, it would be the most indelible black mark on the collective reputation of the onetime "conservative" thought leaders, influencers, and pundits populating NeverTrump.

Meanwhile, panic infiltrated NeverTrump quarters about the presumptive Democratic nominee. Polls showed Sanders with a comfortable lead and the Iowa debacle energized his fervent base of supporters.

DESPERATION AND DEFEAT

Kristol, who once threatened to set up a "war machine" to promote a Republican primary challenger to Donald Trump,[15] was in New Hampshire in February 2020, but not to back a Republican because no legitimate candidate had emerged. (Joe Walsh, a former Illinois congressman, ended his campaign that week after being booed out of a Republican campaign event in Iowa.)

No, Kristol campaigned in New Hampshire days before the primary to urge Republicans and independents to pull a *Democratic ballot* and vote for anyone besides Bernie Sanders. "I'm happy to have joined with some others to help remind New Hampshire independents, who might be accustomed to voting in the Republican primary, that this year, they may be able to make more of a difference by voting for a responsible and electable candidate in the Democratic primary," Kristol confirmed to a local newspaper. "We're trying to save the nation from a choice between Trumpism and socialism."[16]

It was one more act of desperation in Kristol's humiliating and failed attempt to destroy Donald Trump. Without a viable third-party candidate, Kristol and NeverTrump were again campaigning for a Democratic presidential nominee. (After Buttigieg, Minnesota senator Amy Klobuchar, and billionaire Mike Bloomberg exited the race in early March, the once-doomed candidacy of Joe Biden was resurrected).

The betrayal to the party that once served as their meal ticket would come full circle. NeverTrump—after pimping for a phony Russian collusion hoax, defending bureaucratic saboteurs who had trampled the law and the Constitution in their crazed mission against Donald Trump, boosting impeachment, harassing pro-life teenagers, and aligning with the worst political schemers, such as Adam Schiff—also would be unwelcome to Trump's foes on the Left. As NeverTrump urged Democrats to elect Joe Biden instead of Bernie Sanders, their fair-weather allies rejected NeverTrump's involvement. "When Trump won, there was still the chance that he would face opposition from his own party as president, and these pundits could help provide insight into what the non-Trump portion of the party thought," Parker Molloy wrote for Media Matters for America on February 23. "Instead, we exist in a world where their views are utterly irrelevant, and they're just taking up time that could be better spent with people who represent actual political constituencies."

Molloy specifically referred to anti-Sanders comments made by Rick Wilson, Jennifer Rubin, Bret Stephens, and David Frum: "The continued elevation of 'Never Trumpers' hasn't seemed to have had much of an effect on Republicans, leaving them to armchair quarterback their way through the Democratic primary."[17]

And that was NeverTrump's status as the Democratic presidential primary field narrowed to two elderly men: scorned by the Right, mocked by the Left, and unjustifiably elevated by the Trump-hating corporate media. No one wants them. NeverTrump lives in a political no-man's-land.

NeverTrump's disloyal opposition to Donald Trump, his administration, his supporters, and the Republican Party failed to take down the president. And it won't ever be forgiven or forgotten. One day, Donald Trump will leave the national political scene and new Republican leaders will take over. But the traitorous conduct of NeverTrump should automatically disqualify any of them from holding a position of influence again. NeverTrump should be a cautionary tale about the fate of the "disloyal opposition" during one of the most volatile and consequential periods in American political history.

ACKNOWLEDGMENTS

Despite my best efforts, I can't think of a pithy story or clever anecdote to start this part of my book so let's just get down to business.

To my husband, John Kelly, who has urged me to write a book since the *Wall Street Journal* published my first guest op-ed in 2014. We met at a Republican Party event in suburban Chicago in August 1994, both working for Republican officeholders at the time. Politics has been a big part of our lives ever since, even though he went to the dark side and is a registered Democrat. We come at politics from two different angles, but he's taught me more about this business than anyone. I want to thank him first for his love, advice, and encouragement on this project and my unexpected career as a political writer. He has (mostly) tolerated my rants about everyone in this book, in addition to James Comey, John Brennan, and Adam Schiff. Thanks for a great life, babe.

To my daughters, Victoria and Josie, the loves of my life. On my deathbed, I will look back at my years as a stay-at-home mom as the very best time of my life. I could fill this book with everything I've learned from both of you, but you already know. And thanks for choosing mommy's side of the political aisle.

To my brother, Jason Copeland, a political junkie like me who always makes me laugh. Thanks, bro.

To my late father, Jack Copeland, and my late grandparents, John and Lois Copeland, the two best people I've ever known. My dad and grandma would have loved the Trump era. My grandfather, a gentleman to his core, would not.

I'm blessed with lots of friends but want to give a special shout-out to Kathy Scott (who sat with me drinking wine on the fateful day when I opened my Twitter account), Renee Poppie, Jill Stefan, and Colleen Rotkis.

To my team at *American Greatness*. When Chris Buskirk, the publisher, called me in early 2018 and asked me to write exclusively for *American Greatness*, I asked what I could write about. "Whatever you want"—a reply he undoubtedly regrets at times. I am forever grateful he invited me to be an early part of what is quickly becoming one of the most influential outlets in politics. Thanks to Ben Boychuk and Julie Ponzi for their solid editing work; to Liz Sheld, my occasional sounding board and podcast partner; and to Deb Heine, who churns out an impressive amount of work while raising six kids.

To Roger Kimball and Encounter Books for taking a risk on a first-time book author. I think Roger has enjoyed this project as much as I have. Also thanks to Sam Schneider, Amanda DeMatto, and Lauren Miklos. Barbie Halaby at Monocle Editing did a superb job and I appreciate her patience with a first-time book author.

To Victor Davis Hanson, a national treasure, who also encouraged me to write this book.

To Sebastian Gorka, Larry O'Connor, Dan Proft and Amy Jacobson, Ed Martin, and Steve Cortes for hosting me regularly on their radio shows.

To the fighters at the *Federalist* (which published some of my earlier work), especially Sean Davis, Mollie Hemingway, and Margot Cleveland for their groundbreaking coverage of the biggest political scandal of all time and challenging NeverTrump's complicity in the Russiagate hoax.

To Lee Smith, the toughest and smartest journalist I know, and to Michael Anton, for their interviews included in this book.

Thanks to the following people who have promoted my work on social media, coauthored columns with me or been helpful in some important way: Dr. Henry Miller, Kurt Schlichter, David Reaboi, Ned Ryun, Emerald Robinson, Jack Posobiec, Ace, Julie Gunlock, Jeff Stier, and Nick Short.

Bucket list: Write a book.

Done.

NOTES

PREFACE

1   Peter Wehner, "The Trump Presidency Is Over," *Atlantic*, March 13, 2020, https://www.theatlantic.com/ideas/archive/2020/03/peter-wehner -trump-presidency-over/607969.

2   Bill Kristol (@BillKristol), "This new ad from @ForTheRuleOfLaw will run Friday morning on Fox and Friends," Twitter, March 19, 2020, https://twitter.com/billkristol/status/1240716869729783808.

3   William Kristol, "Trump Could Still Win," Bulwark, March 19, 2020, https://thebulwark.com/trump-could-still-win.

4   David French (@DavidAFrench), "A quick thought on this 'China virus' controversy," Twitter, March 18, 2020, https://twitter.com/davidafrench /status/1240345189820051459.

5   Scott Morefield, "Jennifer Rubin: More Republicans Will Die from Coronavirus Than Democrats," Daily Caller, March 15, 2020, https:// dailycaller.com/2020/03/15/jennifer-rubin-republicans-coronavirus -deaths.

6   Rick Wilson (@TheRickWilson), "President Kevorkian's followers are going to die from taking taking an unproven drug," Twitter, March 24, 2020, https://twitter.com/TheRickWilson/status/1242302300582010882.

INTRODUCTION

1   Julie Kelly, "Why I've Decided to Break-Up with Bill Kristol," *Federalist*, February 27, 2017, https://thefederalist.com/2017/02/27/ive-decided -break-bill-kristol.

2   Kurt Schlichter, *Militant Normals: How Regular Americans Are Rebelling Against the Elite to Reclaim Our Democracy* (New York: Center Street, 2018), 21.

3   Schlichter, *Militant Normals*, 218.

CHAPTER 1: THE BIRTH OF NEVERTRUMP

1   Callum Borchers, "'You're Practically Crying!' Joe Scarborough and Bill Kristol Get Heated," *Washington Post*, October 20, 2016, https://www

.washingtonpost.com/news/the-fix/wp/2016/10/20/youre-practically
-crying-joe-scarborough-and-bill-kristol-get-heated.

2   "William Kristol: Defeating President Clinton's Health Care Proposal,"
March 3, 2009, Brad Delong's Egregious Moderation blog, https://
delong.typepad.com/egregious_moderation/2009/03/william-kristol
-defeating-president-clintons-health-care-proposal.html.

3   Michael Crowley, "Last Man Standing," *Politico Magazine*, July/August
2016, https://www.politico.com/magazine/story/2016/07/2016-bill
-kristol-republicans-conservative-movement-donald-trump-politics
-214025.

4   Eric Levitz, "The Donald's Debate Boycott Officially Pays Off, As Bill
Kristol Predicts Trump Has Peaked," *Intelligencer*, January 29, 2016,
http://nymag.com/intelligencer/2016/01/bill-kristol-declares-peak
-trump-again.html.

5   Levitz, "The Donald's Debate Boycott."

6   NR Symposium, "Conservatives Against Trump," *National Review*,
January 22, 2016, https://www.nationalreview.com/2016/01/donald
-trump-conservatives-oppose-nomination.

7   "Trump: 'It's Possible' I Gave Money to Planned Parenthood," *Meet the
Press*, August 16, 2015, https://www.nbcnews.com/meet
-the-press/video/trump--its-possible-i-gave-money-to-planned
-parenthood-506206787896.

8   Michele Gorman, "A Brief History of Donald Trump's Stance on Gun
Rights," *Newsweek*, May 20, 2016, https://www.newsweek.com/brief
-history-donald-trumps-stance-gun-rights-461705.

9   NR Symposium, "Conservatives Against Trump."

10   NR Symposium, "Conservatives Against Trump."

11   CNNPresentsVideo, "CNN Talks with John McCain About His Marital
Infidelity," YouTube video, 03:57, https://www.youtube.com/watch
?v=of53-j7QKR0.

12   Dan Riehl, "After Getting Everything Wrong in 2016, Stephen Hayes
Elevated to Editor-in-Chief at the Weekly Standard," Breitbart, December
18, 2016, https://www.breitbart.com/the-media/2016/12/18/after-getting
-everything-wrong-in-2016-stephen-hayes-elevated-to-editor-in-chief
-at-the-weekly-standard.

13   Mark Steyn, "Witless Ape: The Director's Cut," Steyn Online, January 22,
2016, https://www.steynonline.com/7433/witless-ape-the-director-cut.

14   Donald J. Trump (@realDonaldTrump), "The late, great, William F.
Buckley would be ashamed of what had happened to his prize, the dying
National Review!," Twitter, January 21, 2016, https://twitter.com
/realDonaldTrump/status/690382722162913280.

15   Jack Fowler, "Houston, We Have a Problem," *National Review*, January
22, 2016, https://www.nationalreview.com/corner/houston-we-have
-problem.

16   Jeremy W. Peters, "The 'Never Trump' Coalition That Decided Eh, Never Mind, He's Fine," *New York Times*, October 5, 2019, https://www.nytimes.com/2019/10/05/us/politics/never-trumper-republicans.html.

17   Peters, "The 'Never Trump' Coalition."

18   CBSN, "Full CBS News South Carolina Republican Debate," YouTube video, 1:39:20, February 15, 2016, https://www.youtube.com/watch?v=Un3OhYs-tCE.

19   Fox News, "Trump: All Smart People Know the Iraq War Was a Huge Mistake," YouTube video, 08:45, February 14, 2016, https://www.youtube.com/watch?v=NllVMluog1Y.

20   Quinnipiac University, "Five Leaders in 2016 Republican White House Race, Quinnipiac University National Poll Finds," May 28, 2015, https://poll.qu.edu/national/release-detail?ReleaseID=2228.

21   J. Baxter Oliphant, "The Iraq War Continues to Divide the U.S. Public, 15 Years After It Began," Pew Research Center, March 19, 2018, https://www.pewresearch.org/fact-tank/2018/03/19/iraq-war-continues-to-divide-u-s-public-15-years-after-it-began.

22   George W. Bush Administration, "National Security Strategy 2002," National Security Strategy Archive, September 17, 2002, http://nssarchive.us/national-security-strategy-2002.

23   Nicholas Ballasy, "George Will: I Left the Republican Party (Exclusive Interview with Nicholas Ballasy)," YouTube video, 43:48, November 5, 2013, https://www.youtube.com/watch?v=iGsSrH6v7ro.

24   Viewing Liberty, "George Will Responds to Trump's Tweet on Him Leaving the Republican Party," YouTube video, 01:30, June 26, 2016, https://www.youtube.com/watch?v=OkIaA9TsNiU.

25   Donald J. Trump (@realDonaldTrump), "If dummy Bill Kristol actually does get a spoiler to run as an Independent, say good bye to the Supreme Court!," Twitter, May 29, 2016, https://twitter.com/realDonaldTrump/status/737056428452630528.

26   Dylan Matthews, "Meet David French: The Random Dude Off the Street That Bill Kristol Decided Will Save America from Trump," Vox, May 31, 2016, https://www.vox.com/2016/5/31/11824280/david-french-bill-kristol.

27   Jack Moore, "Who Is David French? The Third-Party Conservative Who Might Be Running for President?," *GQ*, June 1, 2016, https://www.gq.com/story/who-is-david-french-explained; Kathryn Jean Lopez, "Avoiding Cain's Pain," *National Review*, December 12, 2011, https://www.nationalreview.com/2011/12/avoiding-cains-pain-kathryn-jean-lopez.

28   David French, "Why I'm Not Running for President," *National Review*, June 6, 2016, https://www.nationalreview.com/2016/06/david-french-not-running-president.

29   Delegates Unbound, "TV Ad: Follow Your Conscience," YouTube video, 0:30, June 26, 2016, https://www.youtube.com/watch?v=tFlgP1hnU1o.

30 John Fun, "What's Next for the Never Trump Camp?," *National Review*,
    July 10, 2016, https://www.nationalreview.com/2016/07/never-trump
    -delegates-not-bound-convention.

31 William Kristol, "As Convention Approaches, Will Romney or Kasich
    Step Up?," *Washington Examiner*, July 10, 2016, https://www
    .washingtonexaminer.com/weekly-standard/as-convention-approaches
    -will-romney-or-kasich-step-up.

32 Russell Berman, "Never Trump Almost Succeeds," *Atlantic*, July 18, 2016,
    https://www.theatlantic.com/politics/archive/2016/07/never-trump
    -almost-succeeds/491885.

33 Susan Collins, "GOP Senator Susan Collins: Why I Cannot Support
    Trump," *Washington Post*, August 8, 2016, https://www
    .washingtonpost.com/opinions/gop-senator-why-i-cannot-support
    -trump/2016/08/08/821095be-5d7e-11e6-9d2f-b1a3564181a1_story.html.

34 Eric Black, "GOP Insider Vin Weber: We Have Never Before Nominated
    Someone So 'Fundamentally Unqualified' As Trump," *Minnesota Post*,
    August 5, 2016, https://www.minnpost.com/eric-black-ink/2016/08
    /gop-insider-vin-weber-we-have-never-nominated-someone-so
    -fundamentally-unqual.

35 Kevin Bohn and Caroline Kelly, "Influential GOP Consultant with Ties
    to Manfort Resigns from Major DC Consulting Firm," CNN, August 30,
    2019, https://www.cnn.com/2019/08/30/politics/vin-weber-lobbyist
    -resigns-mercury-mueller/index.html.

36 Donald B. Ayer et al., "Statement by Former National Security Officials,"
    n.d., https://assets.documentcloud.org/documents/3007589
    /Nationalsecurityletter.pdf.

37 Alex Altman and Zeke J. Miller, "Why Donald Trump Picked Kellyanne
    Conway to Manage His Campaign," *Time*, August 23, 2016, https://time
    .com/4462283/donald-trump-kellyanne-conway-campaign-manager.

38 Josh Rogin, "The Story Behind Evan McMullin's Run for President,"
    Washington Post, August 22, 2016, https://www.washingtonpost.com
    /news/josh-rogin/wp/2016/08/22/the-story-behind-evan-mcmullins
    -run-for-president.

39 David A. Fahrenthold, "Trump Recorded Having Extremely Lewd
    Conversation About Women in 2005," *Washington Post*, October 8, 2016,
    https://www.washingtonpost.com/politics/trump-recorded-having
    -extremely-lewd-conversation-about-women-in-2005/2016/10/07
    /3b9ce776-8cb4-11e6-bf8a-3d26847eeed4_story.html.

40 Donald J. Trump (@realDonaldTrump), "Paul Ryan should spend more
    time on balancing the budget, jobs and illegal immigration and not waste
    his time on fighting Republican nominee," Twitter, October 10, 2016,
    https://twitter.com/realDonaldTrump/status/785530928256933888.

41 Deb Fischer (@DebFischerNE), "It would be wise for him to step aside
    and allow Mike Pence to serve as our party's nominee. (2/2)," Twitter,

October 8, 2016, https://twitter.com/DebFischerNE/status
/784824577415340032.

42 Jenna Portnoy, "Republican Rep. Barbara Comstock of Virginia Urges
Trump to Drop Out of Race," *Washington Post*, October 8, 2016, https://
www.washingtonpost.com/local/virginia-politics/republican-rep-
barbara-comstock-of-virginia-urges-trump-to-drop-out-of-race
/2016/10/07/79119406-8d06-11e6-bff0-d53f592f176e_story.html.

43 Alex Isenstadt, "John Kasich's Anger Management," *Politico*, July 20,
2015, https://www.politico.com/story/2015/07/john-kasichs-anger-
management-120345.

44 Eli Stokols, "Kasich: I Told You So," *Politico*, October 8, 2016, https://
www.politico.com/story/2016/10/john-kasich-donald-trump-229362.

45 David French, "Trump Supporters Have No One to Blame Now But
Themselves," *National Review*, October 13, 2016, https://www
.nationalreview.com/2016/10/donald-trump-sexual-assault-allegations
-accusers-stories-match-access-hollywood-tape.

46 Calvin Freiburger (@CalFreiburger), "Never forget how many of our
supposed betters in the righty commentariat supported this guy," Twitter,
October 19, 2019, https://twitter.com/calfreiburger/status
/1185569112082321409.

47 Emily Schultheis, "Nebraska Senator Re-endorses Trump After Tape
Scandal," CBS News, October 11, 2016, https://www.cbsnews.com/news
/nebraska-senator-deb-fischer-re-endorses-donald-trump-after-tape
-scandal.

48 Jonathan Martin, "Some in GOP Who Deserted Donald Trump Over
Lewd Tape Are Returning," *New York Times*, October 12, 2016, https://
www.nytimes.com/2016/10/13/us/politics/gop-reaction-donald-trump
.html.

49 Jeremy W. Peters, "Trump Campaign Tried to Seat Bill Clinton's
Accusers in V.I.P. Box," *New York Times*, October 10, 2016, https://www
.nytimes.com/2016/10/11/us/politics/bill-clinton-accusers-debate.html.

50 "Presidential Debate—DT: Bc You'd Be in Jail!—Hillary Clinton vs.
Donald Trump," YouTube video, 0:36, October 9, 2016, https://www
.youtube.com/watch?v=Hbh2qXBMjuY.

51 CNN, "Obama, Romney Get Heated Over Libya," YouTube video, 2:59,
October 16, 2012, https://www.youtube.com/watch?v=NXkLYIZabWE.

52 Ipsos, "Ipsos Poll Conducted for Reuters: Core Political Daily Tracker,"
November 7, 2016, https://www.ipsos.com/sites/default/files/news_and
_polls/2016-11/7468-results.pdf.

53 ABC News, "Clinton, Trump at Campaign's End: Still Close—and Still
Unpopular," Langer Research, November 7, 2016, https://www
.langerresearch.com/wp-content/uploads/1184a162016Election
TrackingNo16.pdf.

54 "The Republicans Opposing Donald Trump—And Voting for Hillary

Clinton," NBC News, November 6, 2016, https://www.nbcnews .com/politics/2016-election/meet-republicans-speaking-out-against -trump-n530696.

55 David French, "No, God Doesn't Want You to Vote for Donald Trump," *National Review*, October 18, 2016, https://www.nationalreview.com /corner/no-god-doesnt-want-you-vote-donald-trump.

56 Darren Samuelsohn, "George H.W. Bush to Vote for Hillary Clinton," *Politico*, September 19, 2016, https://www.politico.com/story/2016/09 /exclusive-george-hw-bush-to-vote-for-hillary-228395.

57 Publius Decius Mus, "The Flight 93 Election," *Claremont Review of Books*, September 5, 2016, https://claremontreviewofbooks.com/digital/the -flight-93-election.

58 Jonah Goldberg, "Is This a 'Flight 93' Election?," *National Review*, September 10, 2016, https://www.nationalreview.com/g-file/flight-93 -election-hillary-clinton-threat-america.

59 MSNBC, "Bill Kristol, More Hidden Voters for Hillary Clinton Than Donald Trump," YouTube video, 06:49, November 4, 2016, https://www .youtube.com/watch?v=2__ESk5cXRY.

60 Bill Kristol (@BillKristol), "Basically: 2016 will be 2012, but perhaps a bit more so as voting groups move further in the direction they were already moving," Twitter, November 8, 2016, https://twitter.com/BillKristol /status/796157843997069312.

61 Weatherlover1192, "ABC News Election Night Coverage—1 am Hour," YouTube video, 47:40, December 5, 2016, https://www.youtube.com /watch?v=ZAehotRlYxA.

CHAPTER 2: TRUMP WINS, NEVERTRUMP REGROUPS

[EPIGRAPH] Victor Davis Hanson, *The Case for Trump* (New York: Basic Books, 2019), 308.

1 Stephen F. Hayes, "Editorial," *Weekly Standard*, November 21, 2016, http://s3.amazonaws.com/assets.weeklystandard.com/WStandard.v22 -11.2016-11-21.pdf, p. 7.

2 Jonah Goldberg, "The Trump Era Begins," *National Review*, November 9, 2016, https://www.nationalreview.com/corner/donald-trump-election -new-era.

3 Ross Douthat and Reihan Salam, *Grand New Party: How* Republicans *Can Win the Working Class and Save the American Dream* (New York: Anchor Books, 2018), 7.

4 Douthat and Salam, *Grand New Party*, 9–10.

5 CNN, "President: Full Results," CNN Politics, December 10, 2012, https://www.cnn.com/election/2012/results/race/president.

6 Hanson, *The Case for Trump*, 41.

7 CNN, "Exit Polls," CNN Politics, updated November 23, 2016, https:// www.cnn.com/election/2016/results/exit-polls.

8   Tucker Carlson, *Ship of Fools: How a Selfish Ruling Class Is Bringing America to the Brink of Revolution* (New York: Free Press, 2018), 3.

9   Paul Farhi, "Bill Kristol Knows His Predictions Have Been Bad But He's Going to Keep Making Them," *Washington Post*, February 17, 2016, https://www.washingtonpost.com/lifestyle/style/bill-kristol-knows -his-predictions-have-been-bad-but-hes-going-to-keep-making-them /2016/02/17/3a301680-d4d4-11e5-9823-02b905009f99_story.html.

10 Ruairí Arrieta-Kenna, "The Worst Political Predictions of 2016," *Politico*, December 28, 2016, https://www.politico.com/magazine/story/2016/12 /the-worst-political-predictions-of-2016-214555.

11 William Kristol, "#NeverTrump: A Final Word," *Washington Examiner*, November 7, 2016, https://www.washingtonexaminer.com/weekly -standard/nevertrump-a-final-word.

12 Bill Kristol (@BillKristol), "And to my fellow #NeverTrumpers: Let us be magnanimous losers," Twitter, November 9, 2016, https://twitter.com /BillKristol/status/796359464257470465.

13 David French, "Farewell," *National Review*, October 18, 2019, https:// www.nationalreview.com/corner/farewell.

14 Tom Nichols, "Why I'm Leaving the Republican Party," *Atlantic*, October 7, 2018, https://www.theatlantic.com/ideas/archive/2018/10/tom-nichols -why-im-leaving-republican-party/57241.

15 Tom Nichols (@RadioFreeTom), "In other words, Trump and his lunatics have left me with no choice. I will have to vote for Hillary Clinton. /17x," Twitter, October 21, 2016, https://twitter.com/RadioFreeTom /status/789618164971823104.

16 Ali Gharib, "Conservative Pundit Jennifer Rubin Joins the Mainstream Media," *Columbia Journalism Review*, December 7, 2010, https:// archives.cjr.org/campaign_desk/conservative_pundit_jennifer_rubin .php.

17 Tim Hains, "Jennifer Rubin: Sarah Sanders Deserves 'Life Sentence' of Harassment After Role in Trump Admin," *Real Clear Politics*, July 3, 2018, https://www.realclearpolitics.com/video/2018/07/03/jennifer _rubin_sarah_sanders_deserves_life_sentence_of_harassment_after _role_in_trump_admin.html.

18 Bret Stephens, "My Former Republican Party," *Wall Street Journal*, October 25, 2016, https://www.wsj.com/articles/my-former-republican -party-1477353852.

19 MSNBC, "CPAC Crowd Boos Conservative Columnist | Morning Joe | MSNBC," YouTube video, 4:20, February 26, 2018, https://www.youtube .com/watch?v=AtxiCq5IFe0.

20 Mona Charen, "Opinion: I'm Glad I Got Booed at CPAC," *New York Times*, February 25, 2018, https://www.nytimes.com/2018/02/25/opinion /im-glad-i-got-booed-at-cpac.html.

21 McKay Coppins, "Evan McMullin's War," *Atlantic*, July/August 2017,

https://www.theatlantic.com/magazine/archive/2017/07/the-defector
/528714.

22 Ben Shapiro, "Max Boot: '2017 Was the Year I Learned About My White
    Privilege.' No, It's the Year He Let Emotions Cloud His Judgement," *Daily
    Wire*, December 28, 2017, https://www.dailywire.com/news/max-boot
    -2017-was-year-i-learned-about-my-white-ben-shapiro.

23 Max Boot, "Here Are 18 Reasons Trump Could Be a Russian Asset,"
    Washington Post, January 13, 2019, https://www.washingtonpost.com/
    opinions/here-are-18-reasons-why-trump-could-be-a-russian
    -asset/2019/01/13/45b1b250-174f-11e9-88fe-f9f77a3bcb6c_story.html.

24 Max Boot, "The Joy of Chores," *Washington Post*, September 7, 2019,
    https://www.washingtonpost.com/opinions/2019/09/07/joy-chores.

25 Rich Lowry, "The Never Trump Delusion," *National Review*, March 30,
    2018, https://www.nationalreview.com/2018/03/never-trump-delusion
    -trumpism-not-going-to-disappear.

26 Jonah Goldberg and Ramesh Ponnuru, "Conservative Criticism of Trump
    Is Not Deluded," *National Review*, April 3, 2018, https://www
    .nationalreview.com/2018/03/never-trump-delusion-trumpism-not
    -going-to-disappear.

27 Jonah Goldberg, "Op-Ed: Why the Trump Presidency Will End Poorly,"
    LA Times, December 25, 2018, https://www.latimes.com/opinion/op-ed
    /la-oe-goldberg-trump-presidency-shutdown-20181225-story.html.

28 Jonah Goldberg, "The 'Deep State' Canard Spreads," *National Review*,
    November 29, 2019, https://www.nationalreview.com/2019/11/deep
    -state-canard-spreads-partisan-talking-point.

29 Jonah Goldberg, "Jeffery Epstein's Death and Our Age of Conspiracy
    Theories," *National Review*, August 14, 2019, https://www.nationalreview
    .com/2019/08/jeffrey-epstein-death-age-of-conspiracy-theories.

30 Jonah Goldberg, "The Never-ending Collusion Story," *National Review*,
    March 27, 2019, https://www.nationalreview.com/2019/03/trump-russia
    -collusion-story-political-polarization.

31 "Trump Calls Into Radio Show; Host Is a Member of #NeverTrump
    Movement," NPR, April 1, 2016, https://www.npr.org/2016/04/01
    /472639980/trump-calls-into-radio-show-finds-out-host-is-a-member
    -of-nevertrump-movement.

32 Erick Trickey, "Charlie Sykes' Air War," *Politico*, August 21, 2016, https://
    www.politico.com/magazine/story/2016/08/charlie-skyes-wisconsin
    -radio-conservatives-214175.

33 Charles J. Sykes, *How the Right Lost Its Mind* (New York: St. Martin's
    Press, 2017).

34 Nick Gillespie, "When It Comes to Trump, the Bulwark's Charlie Sykes
    Is 'All Out of Fucks to Give': Podcast," *Reason*, January 11, 2019, https://
    reason.com/podcast/charlie-sykes-podcast.

35 "Doing the Work McCain's People Can't or Won't Do," *New Republic*,

October 31, 2008, https://newrepublic.com/article/62900/doing-the
-work-mccains-people-cant-or-wont-do.

36 Ctown legend, "GOP Strategist Calls Trump Supporters 'Childless,
Single Men Who Masturbate to Anime,'" MSNBC, YouTube video, 01:15,
January 19, 2016, https://www.youtube.com/watch?v=5EFCh2JJG-c.

37 David Weigel, "'Concerned' Conservatives, Aiming to Build a Trump
Resistance, Call for GOP to Protect Mueller," *Washington Post*,
November 1, 2017, https://www.washingtonpost.com/news/powerpost
/wp/2017/11/01/concerned-conservatives-aiming-to-build-a-trump
-resistance-call-for-gop-to-protect-mueller.

38 Ben Terris, "She Works for Trump. He Can't Stand Him. This Is Life
with Kellyanne and George Conway," *Washington Post*, August 15, 2018,
https://www.washingtonpost.com/lifestyle/style/she-works-for
-trump-he-cant-stand-him-this-is-life-with-kellyanne-and-george
-conway/2018/08/15/3b89b82a-9b46-11e8-843b-36e177f3081c_story.html.

39 Hadas Gold, "Stephen Hayes Named Editor-in-Chief of the Weekly
Standard," *Politico*, December 12, 2016, https://www.politico.com/blogs
/on-media/2016/12/stephen-hayes-named-editor-in-chief-of-weekly
-standard-232531.

40 CBS News, "David Frum: The National Interview," YouTube video, 09:37,
January 22, 2018, https://www.youtube.com/watch?v=hTevzsOVvpo.

41 Ben Schreckinger, "Trump Attacks McCain, 'I Like People Who Weren't
Captured,'" *Politico*, July 18, 2015, https://www.politico.com/story/2015
/07/trump-attacks-mccain-i-like-people-who-werent-captured-120317.

42 "Meghan McCain's Emotional Eulogy at John McCain's Funeral:
'American Was Always Great,'" ABC 7, September 1, 2018, https://abc7
.com/politics/meghan-mccains-eulogy-at-dads-funeral-america-was
-always-great/4118240.

43 Bill Kristol (@BillKristol), "Obviously strongly prefer normal democratic
and constitutional politics. But if it comes to it, prefer the deep state to
the Trump state," Twitter, February 14, 2017, https://twitter.com
/BillKristol/status/831497364661747712.

CHAPTER 3: USEFUL IDIOTS FOR THE LEFT

1 Mona Charen, *Useful Idiots: How Liberals Got It Wrong in the Cold War
and Still Blame America First* (Washington, D.C.: Regnery, 2003).

2 Josef Adalian, "Joy Reid Wants to Argue with You," *Vulture*, September
2017, https://www.vulture.com/2017/09/joy-reid-wants-to-argue-with
-you.html.

3 David Korn, "Why Bush Is a Loser," *Washington Post*, July 17, 2007,
https://www.washingtonpost.com/wp-dyn/content/article/2007/07/17
/AR2007071701456.html.

4 "No Regrets from the Architects of Iraq War," MSNBC, March 21, 2013,
https://www.msnbc.com/msnbc/watch/no-regrets-from-the-architects
-of-iraq-war-23131203699.

5   American Forum, "Would Bill Kristol Prefer Obama to Trump?,"
     YouTube video, 01:35, April 19, 2017, https://www.youtube.com/watch
     ?v=zfjIA72VbtM.

6   Charlie Sykes and Stephen F. Hayes, "Stephen Hayes on Fighting for
     Fight's Sake," September 6, 2019, in Bulwark podcast, MP3 audio, 45:29,
     https://podcast.thebulwark.com/stephen-f-hayes-on-fighting-for
     -fightings-sake.

7   Jennifer Rubin, "20 Things for Hillary Clinton to Worry About,"
     Washington Post, June 1, 2015, https://www.washingtonpost.com/blogs
     /right-turn/wp/2015/06/01/20-things-for-hillary-clinton-to-worry
     -about.

8   Jennifer Rubin, "Trump Can Be Both Evil and Nuts," Washington Post,
     October 16, 2016, https://www.washingtonpost.com/blogs/right-turn
     /wp/2016/10/16/trump-can-be-both-evil-and-nuts.

9   Tim Hains, "WP's Jennifer Rubin: Trump Cabinet Made Up of
     'Ignoramuses, Billionaires, and a Few Generals,'" Real Clear Politics,
     December 11, 2016, https://www.realclearpolitics.com/video/2016/12/11
     /wps_jennifer_rubin_trump_cabinet_made_up_of_ignoramuses
     _billionaires_and_a_few_generals.html.

10 Donald Trump (@realDonaldTrump), "Highly untalented Wash Post
     blogger, Jennifer Rubin, a real dummy, never writes fairly about me,"
     Twitter, December 1, 2015, https://twitter.com/realDonaldTrump
     /status/671792600052027393.

11 Patrick Pexton, "Ombo Sauce: Advice for Jeff Bezos from the Post's
     Former In-house Critic," Washington City Paper, August 15, 2013, https://
     www.washingtoncitypaper.com/news/city-desk/blog/13067559/ombo
     -sauce-advice-for-jeff-bezos-from-the-posts-former-in-house-critic.

12 Julie Kelly, "Washington Post: Where Conservatism Dies in Bitterness,"
     American Greatness, December 8, 2017, https://amgreatness.com/2017
     /12/08/washington-post-where-conservatism-dies-in-bitterness.

13 Jennifer Rubin, "Economy Stuck in Neutral," Washington Post, April 26,
     2013, https://www.washingtonpost.com/blogs/right-turn/wp/2013/04/26
     /economy-stuck-in-neutral.

14 Jennifer Rubin, "After Huge Tax Breaks for the Rich, There's Not Enough
     for the Sick and Poor," Washington Post, December 4, 2017, https://www
     .washingtonpost.com/blogs/right-turn/wp/2017/12/04/after-huge-tax
     -breaks-for-the-rich-theres-not-enough-for-the-sick-and-poor.

15 Jennifer Rubin, "Is Obama Trying to Kill Coal and Senate Democrats?,"
     Washington Post, June 2, 2014, https://www.washingtonpost.com/blogs
     /right-turn/wp/2014/06/02/is-obama-trying-to-kill-coal-and-senate
     -democrats.

16 Jennifer Rubin, "Rip Van Winkle Republicans," Washington Post, June 4,
     2017, https://www.washingtonpost.com/blogs/right-turn/wp/2017
     /06/04/rip-van-winkle-republicans.

17 Sean Davis, "Washington Post's Fake Conservative Blogger Hated the

Paris Deal…Until Trump Agreed with Her," *Federalist*, June 1, 2017, https://thefederalist.com/2017/06/01/washington-posts-fake -conservative-blogger-hated-the-paris-deal-until-trump-opposed-it.

18 Jennifer Rubin, "The Iran Deal Makes It Clear It Pays to Enrich," *Washington Post*, November 24, 2013, https://www.washingtonpost.com /blogs/right-turn/wp/2013/11/24/the-iran-deal-makes-clear-it-pays-to -enrich.

19 Jennifer Rubin, "It's Not the Iran Deal That's at Risk. It's American Credibility," *Washington Post*, October 6, 2017, https://www .washingtonpost.com/blogs/right-turn/wp/2017/10/06/its-not-the-iran -deal-thats-at-risk-its-american-credibility.

20 Lawrence O'Donnell, "The Last Word with Lawrence O'Donnell, Transcript 10/5/17 'Dossier' Author Interviewed," MSNBC, October 5, 2017, http://www.msnbc.com/transcripts/the-last-word/2017-10-05.

21 Francis P. Cannon et al. to the *Washington Post* Editorial Board, American Principles Project, October 3, 2018, https:// americanprinciplesproject.org/wp-content/uploads/2018/10/WaPo -letter-Jennifer-Rubin-Is-No-Conservative.pdf.

22 David Roberts, "The *New York Times* Should Not Have Hired Climate Change Bullshitter Bret Stephens," Vox, May 1, 2017, https://www.vox .com/2017/5/1/15482698/new-york-times-bret-stephens.

23 Stefan Rahmstorf (@rahmstorf), "Why I cancelled my @nytimes subscription. @BretStephensNYT," Twitter, April 27, 2017, https://twitter .com/rahmstorf/status/857625862933540864.

24 Genevieve Guenther, "Tell the NY Times: Do Not Promote Climate Denial at Your Paper," Change.org, accessed October 2019, http://chng.it /n58fBLKCvj.

25 Bret Stephens, "The Great Global Warming Fizzle," *Wall Street Journal*, November 29, 2011, https://www.wsj.com/articles/SB1000142405297020 3935604577066183761315576.

26 Bret Stephens, "Climate of Complete Certainty," *New York Times*, April 28, 2017, https://www.nytimes.com/2017/04/28/opinion/climate-of -complete-certainty.html.

27 Bret Stephens, "Repeal the Second Amendment," *New York Times*, October 5, 2017, https://www.nytimes.com/2017/10/05/opinion/guns -second-amendment-nra.html.

28 Max Boot, "Consider the Cost of Your Dream Court, Conservatives," *Washington Post*, July 6, 2018, https://www.washingtonpost.com/news /global-opinions/wp/2018/07/06/so-you-want-a-conservative-supreme -court-consider-the-cost.

29 Max Boot (@MaxBoot), "If you want the Trump tax cuts and the judges, you've also signed up for the racism, the misogyny, the amorality, the lawlessness, the deranged tweets," Twitter, December 5, 2017, https:// twitter.com/MaxBoot/status/938052524761739264.

30 Max Boot, "I Came to This Country 41 Years Ago. Now I Feel Like I

Don't Belong Here," *Washington Post*, September 5, 2017, https://www
.washingtonpost.com/news/democracy-post/wp/2017/09/05/i-came-to
-this-country-41-years-ago-now-trump-is-making-me-feel-like-i-dont
-belong-here.

31   Max Boot, "I Was Wrong on Climate Change. Why Can't Other
     Conservatives Admit It, Too?," *Washington Post*, November 26, 2018,
     https://www.washingtonpost.com/opinions/global-opinions/i-was
     -wrong-on-climate-change-why-cant-other-conservatives-admit-it
     -too/2018/11/26/11d2b778-f1a1-11e8-bc79-68604ed88993_story.html.

32   Max Boot, "The Second Amendment Is Being Turned into a Suicide
     Pact," *Washington Post*, February 15, 2018, https://www.washingtonpost
     .com/opinions/the-second-amendment-is-being-turned-into-a-suicide
     -pact/2018/02/15/632f702c-128e-11e8-9570-29c9830535e5_story.html.

33   Max Boot, "Thanks, Beto. We Need to Debate an Assault-Weapon
     Buyback," *Washington Post*, September 17, 2019, https://www
     .washingtonpost.com/opinions/thanks-beto-we-need-to-debate-an
     -assault-weapon-buyback/2019/09/17/864d09a4-d964-11e9-a688
     -303693fb4b0b_story.html.

34   EWTN, "President Trump Defends the Unborn in Address to UN,"
     YouTube video, 04:21, September 24, 2019, https://www.youtube.com
     /watch?v=0b_mvJ55Ne4.

35   Gregory S. Schenider and Laura Vozzella, "Abortion Bill Draws GOP
     Outrage Against Va. Gov. Northam, Democratic Legislators," *Washington
     Post*, January 30, 2019, https://www.washingtonpost.com/local
     /virginia-politics/failed-abortion-bill-draws-gop-outrage-against-va
     -gov-northam-democratic-lawmakers/2019/01/30/4a18f022-24b2-11e9
     -ad53-824486280311_story.html.

36   Jennifer Rubin, "A Real Gaffe from Bernie Sanders," *Washington Post*,
     September 5, 2019, https://www.washingtonpost.com/opinions/2019
     /09/05/now-this-is-legitimate-graph.

37   Tom Nichols (@RadioFreeTom), "Even 'muh' judges isn't a policy,
     except to one-issue, anti-abortion voters who think of themselves as
     'conservatives,'" Twitter, July 10, 2019, https://twitter.com/RadioFreeTom
     /status/1149038293796970496.

38   David French (@DavidAFrench), "I appreciate Trump's pro-life actions,
     but he can't yet match GWB," Twitter, March 2, 2019, https://twitter
     .com/DavidAFrench/status/1101916314204102656.

39   David French (@DavidAFrench), "A thread on March for Life day about
     grassroots, person-by-person success of the pro-life movement," Twitter,
     January 24, 2020, https://twitter.com/DavidAFrench/status
     /1220783369929347082.

40   Bill Kristol (@BillKristol), "The GOP tax bill's bringing out my inner
     socialist. The sex scandals are bringing out my inner feminist," Twitter,
     November 21, 2017, https://twitter.com/BillKristol/status
     /933074207637991424.

41   John Harwood, "Bill Kristol Was Once the Voice of the Republican Party. Now He's One of Trump's Biggest Opponents," CNBC, January 25, 2018, https://www.cnbc.com/2018/01/24/speakeasy-with-john-harwood-bill -kristol-on-age-of-trump.html.

42   Shapiro, "Max Boot."

43   David French, "On Native-Born Ingrates," *National Review*, July 15, 2019, https://www.nationalreview.com/corner/gratitude-native-born-citizens -immigrants.

44   Jennifer Rubin, "If You Still Support Donald Trump," *Chicago Tribune*, August 17, 2017, https://www.chicagotribune.com/opinion/commentary /ct-trump-supporters-racist-deplorables-20170817-story.html.

45   David French, "The Alt-Right's Chickens Come Home to Roost," *National Review*, August 12, 2017, https://www.nationalreview.com /corner/alt-rights-chickens-come-home-roost.

46   John Podhoretz, "Charlottesville Proves Trump's Doubters Rights," *New York Post*, August 14, 2017, https://nypost.com/2017/08/14 /charlottesville-is-why-im-glad-i-dont-support-trump.

47   Stephen F. Hayes, "Hayes: Why Won't Trump Denounce White Supremacists?," *Washington Examiner*, August 12, 2017, https://www .washingtonexaminer.com/weekly-standard/hayes-why-wont-trump -denounce-white-supremacists.

48   Mona Charen, "False Racism Accusations Don't Excuse the Real Thing," *National Review*, July 19, 2019, https://www.nationalreview.com/2019/07 /false-racism-accusations-dont-excuse-real-thing.

49   Seth Mandel, "The Next Steps for 'Never Trump,'" *Atlantic*, January 11, 2018, https://www.theatlantic.com/politics/archive/2018/01 /nevertrump/550283.

50   Ian Hanchett, "Bill Kristol: Obama Set Race Relations Back," Breitbart, December 22, 2014, https://www.breitbart.com/politics/2014/12/22/bill -kristol-obama-set-race-relations-back.

51   Bill Kristol (@BillKristol), "I argued and voted against Barack Obama, and don't think highly of his presidency. But how much more impressive an American he is than Donald Trump, Jr.!," Twitter, March 10, 2018, https://twitter.com/BillKristol/status/972493137590587392; Bill Kristol (@BillKristol), "I'm no fan of the Obama administration, and intend to vote for a non-Trump Republican in 2020," Twitter, April 3, 2018, https:// twitter.com/BillKristol/status/981151789461508096.

52   Jennifer Rubin, "Gillespie's Cultural-Warrior Act Isn't Working," *Washington Post*, October 5, 2017, https://www.washingtonpost.com /blogs/right-turn/wp/2017/10/05/gillespies-cultural-warrior-act-isnt -working.

53   Evan McMullin (@EvanMcMullin), "@EdWGillespie was one of the good guys, but now he peddles fear and white nationalism. It's better for VA and America that he not prevail," Twitter, November 7, 2017, https:// twitter.com/EvanMcMullin/status/927887548344688642.

54 Benjamin Wallace-Wells, "Bill Kristol Wanders the Wilderness of Trump World," *New Yorker*, February 2, 2018, https://www.newyorker.com /culture/persons-of-interest/bill-kristol-wanders-the-wilderness-of -trump-world.

55 Bill Kristol (@BillKristol), "1. Doug Jones would be a better U.S. senator than Roy Moore. 2. Moore as a senator would be a constant embarrassment to the GOP," Twitter, October 18, 2017, https://twitter .com/billkristol/status/920763879390679040.

56 Alicia Parlapiano, "Wilson Andrews, Jasmine C. Lee, Rachel Shorey, How Each Senator Voted on Obamacare Repeal Proposals," *New York Times*, July 18, 2017, https://www.nytimes.com/interactive/2017/07/25/us /politics/senate-votes-repeal-obamacare.html.

57 Maegan Vazquez and Sunlen Serfaty, "Sasse Threatens to Pull Out of GOP Senate Fundraising Arm If It Backs Moore," CNN, December 6, 2017, https://www.cnn.com/2017/12/06/politics/sasse-nrsc-roy-moore /index.html.

58 John McCormack, "Could the Senate Expel Roy Moore If He Wins Election?," *Washington Examiner*, November 10, 2017, https://www .washingtonexaminer.com/weekly-standard/could-the-senate-expel-roy -moore-if-he-wins-election.

59 ABC World News Tonight with David Muir, "Ohio Gov. John Kasich Comments on Roy Moore Allegations," Facebook video, 0:29, November 12, 2017, https://www.facebook.com/WorldNewsTonight/videos /ohio-gov-john-kasich-comments-on-roy-moore-allegations /10155484991379818.

60 David French, "Evangelicals, Where Is Your Faith?," *National Review*, November 10, 2017, https://www.nationalreview.com/2017/11/roy -moore-evangelical-supporters-lack-faith.

61 "Doug Jones' Voting Record," Vote Smart, https://justfacts.votesmart .org/candidate/key-votes/176464/doug-jones, accessed November 2019.

62 Tom Nichols, "Want to Save the GOP, Republicans? Vote for Every Democrat on This Year's Ballot," *Washington Post*, September 4, 2018, https://www.washingtonpost.com/outlook/2018/09/04/want-save-gop -republicans-vote-every-democrat-this-years-ballot.

63 Tom Nichols, "Why I'm Leaving the Republican Party," *Atlantic*, October 7, 2018, https://www.theatlantic.com/ideas/archive/2018/10/tom -nichols-why-im-leaving-republican-party/572419.

64 Tom Nichols (@RadioFreeTom), "Local GOP candidate just knocked on my door. Couldn't process it when I said as a Never Trump Republican I am not voting for any Republicans this cycle," Twitter, August 28, 2018, https://twitter.com/RadioFreeTom/status/1034532813922594818.

65 "Arizona Special Election Spells Trouble for Republicans," MSNBC, April 25, 2018, http://www.msnbc.com/morning-joe/watch/arizona-special -election-spells-trouble-for-republicans-1218719299727.

66 Jonah Goldberg, "Will Russia Back the Democrats in 2018 Midterms?," Record Searchlight, August 8, 2018, https://www.redding.com/story /opinion/2018/08/08/jonah-goldberg-russia-back-democrats-2018 -midterms/929956002.

67 David Frum, Liz Mair, Jennifer Rubin, and Peter Wehner, "What's Left of the Right?," *Democracy Journal*, summer 2018, https://democracyjournal .org/magazine/49/whats-left-of-the-right.

68 Ana Navarro, "Why I'm Voting for Andrew Gillium (a Democrat!)," CNN, November 3, 2018, https://www.cnn.com/2018/11/02/opinions /why-im-voting-for-andrew-gillum-navarro/index.html.

69 George F. Will, "Vote Against the GOP This November," *Washington Post*, June 22, 2018, https://www.washingtonpost.com/opinions/vote -against-the-gop-this-november/2018/06/22/a6378306-7575-11e8-b4b7 -308400242c2e_story.html.

70 "Max Boot on How Trump Helped Drive Him from the Right," MSNBC, October 8, 2018, https://www.msnbc.com/morning-joe/watch/max -boot-on-how-trump-helped-drive-him-from-the-right-1339166787729.

71 Glenn Kessler, "What Is Socialism?," *Washington Post*, March 5, 2019, https://www.washingtonpost.com/politics/2019/03/05/what-is -socialism.

72 Tara Golshan, "Read: Bernie Sanders Defines His Vision for Democratic Socialism in the United States," Vox, June 12, 2019, https://www.vox .com/2019/6/12/18663217/bernie-sanders-democratic-socialism-speech -transcript.

73 Hannah Hartig, "Stark Partisan Divisions in Americans' Views of 'Socialism,' 'Capitalism,'" Pew Research Center, June 25, 2019, https:// www.pewresearch.org/fact-tank/2019/06/25/stark-partisan-divisions-in -americans-views-of-socialism-capitalism.

74 Tom Nichols, "Ex-Republican: Do We Still Agree on Beating Trump? After Your LGBTQ Forum, I'm Not Sure," *USA Today*, October 12, 2019, https://www.usatoday.com/story/opinion/2019/10/12/ousting-trump -2020-job-one-democrats-forgot-at-lgbtq-forum-column/3947332002.

75 Charles Sykes, "Dear Democrats, Here's How to Guarantee Trump's Reelection," *Politico*, June 25, 2019, https://www.politico.com/magazine /story/2019/06/25/democrats-trump-election-2020-227215.

CHAPTER 4: BUT GORSUCH!

[EPIGRAPH] "Senator Mitch McConnell on Merrick Garland Supreme Court Nomination," C-SPAN, March 16, 2016, https://www.c-span.org /video/?c4585255/senator-mitch-mcconnell-merrick-garland-supreme -court-nomination.

1 Alan Rappeport and Charlie Savage, "Donald Trump Releases List of Possible Supreme Court Picks," *New York Times*, May 18, 2016, https:// www.nytimes.com/2016/05/19/us/politics/donald-trump-supreme -court-nominees.html.

2   Philip Bump, "A Quarter of Republicans Voted for Trump to Get
    Supreme Court Picks—and It Paid Off," *Washington Post*, June 26, 2018,
    https://www.washingtonpost.com/news/politics/wp/2018/06/26/a
    -quarter-of-republicans-voted-for-trump-to-get-supreme-court-picks
    -and-it-paid-off.

3   Tom Nichols, "Are Trump Voters Ruining America for All of Us?," *USA
    Today*, April 27, 2017, https://www.usatoday.com/story/opinion/2017
    /04/27/trump-voters-ruining-america-tom-nichols-column/100926836.

4   David French (@DavidAFrench), "Evergreen Meme," Twitter, July 17,
    2017, https://twitter.com/davidafrench/status/887138529658249216.

5   Michael Lind, *The New Class War: Saving Democracy from the
    Managerial Elite* (New York: Portfolio/Penguin, 2020), 61.

6   Rich Lowry, "But Gorsuch...and Other Excellent Judicial Picks...and
    a Tax Cut...and Major Deregulatory Actions...and Immigration
    Enforcement...and the End of the Individual Mandate...and a Roll Back
    of the HHS Mandate...," *National Review*, December 3, 2017, https://
    www.nationalreview.com/corner/gorsuch-trump-administration
    -accomplishments.

7   Magnolia Pictures and Magnet Releasing, "The Final Year Clip—Last
    Time," YouTube video, 02:48, January 20, 2018, https://www.youtube
    .com/watch?v=nIhsJp1tyZ4.

8   Julie Kelly, "'The Final Year' Depicts the Chaotic Legacy of Obama's
    National Security Team," *Federalist*, January 29, 2018, https://
    thefederalist.com/2018/01/29/final-year-depicts-chaotic-legacy-obamas
    -national-security-team.

9   Tom Nichols, "After James Mattis Resigned, Trump's America Is
    Slinking Off the World Stage," *USA Today*, December 23, 2018, https://
    www.usatoday.com/story/opinion/2018/12/23/james-mattis-defense-
    resignation-donald-trump-afghanistan-syria-troops-column
    /2401206002.

10 David French, "Will the Nation Heed the Warning Jim Mattis Delivered
    Today?," *National Review*, December 20, 2018, https://www
    .nationalreview.com/corner/james-mattis-resignation-rebuke-to-trump.

11 Mona Charen, "Kim Jong-un Pulls the Wool over President Trump's
    Eyes," *National Review*, June 15, 2018, https://www.nationalreview.
    com/2018/06/north-korea-summit-failure-for-united-states/#slide-1.

12 Charles J. Sykes, "Republicans, Don't Just Tweet About It. Do
    Something," *New York Times*, July 21, 2018, https://www.nytimes
    .com/2018/07/21/opinion/sunday/republicans-trump-russia-putin.html.

13 Rick Wilson, "Trump Probably Gave Putin a Foot Massage," YouTube
    video, 04:56, July 17, 2018, https://www.youtube.com/watch?v
    =th58csVoopA.

14 MSNBC, "Kevin Baron on U.S. Troop Withdrawal from Syria: 'No One
    Wanted This' | Velshi & Ruhle | MSNBC," YouTube video, 10:02, https://
    www.youtube.com/watch?v=oEVNHEMdfaU.

15 Jonah Goldberg, "In Syria Withdrawal, Trump Wings It—as Usual,"
    National Review, October 16, 2019, https://www.nationalreview.
    com/2019/10/syria-withdrawal-trump-wings-it-on-foreign-policy.

16 *Washington Post*, "'Bloodstain on…American History': Romney Slams
    Trump over Syria Troop Withdrawal," *Washington Post* video, 02:07,
    October 17, 2019, https://www.msn.com/en-us/news/politics
    /bloodstain-on-american-history-romney-slams-trump-over-syria
    -troop-withdrawal/vi-AAIWFFF.

17 Mitt Romney, "Remarks at Virginia Military Institute," speech transcript,
    New York Times, October 8, 2012, https://www.nytimes.com/2012/10/09
    /us/politics/mitt-romney-remarks-at-virginia-military-institute.html.

18 Tom Nichols, "Iran's Smart Strategy," *Atlantic*, January 10, 2020, https://
    www.theatlantic.com/ideas/archive/2020/01/how-iran-deterred-us
    /604717.

19 David Frum, "We're Just Discovering the Price of Killing Soleimani,"
    Atlantic, January 9, 2020, https://www.theatlantic.com/ideas
    /archive/2020/01/were-just-discovering-price-killing-soleimani/604705.

20 David Frum, "We're Just Discovering the Price of Killing Soleimani,"
    Atlantic, January 10, 2020, https://www.theatlantic.com/ideas/archive
    /2020/01/trump-broke-it-he-owns-it/604780.

21 Tom Nichols, "From Stormy Daniels to John Bolton, Will America Ever
    Recover from Donald Trump?," *USA Today*, March 23, 2018, https://
    www.usatoday.com/story/opinion/2018/03/23/stormy-daniels-john
    -bolton-can-america-recover-donald-trump-column/450827002.

22 "Full Text: Trump's Speech on Afghanistan," *Politico*, August 21, 2017,
    https://www.politico.com/story/2017/08/21/trump-afghanistan-speech
    -text-241882.

23 Ruth Igielnik and Kim Parker, "Majorities of U.S. Veterans, Public Say the
    Wars in Iraq and Afghanistan Were Not Worth Fighting," Pew Research
    Center, July 10, 2019, https://www.pewresearch.org/fact-tank/2019/07
    /10/majorities-of-u-s-veterans-public-say-the-wars-in-iraq-and
    -afghanistan-were-not-worth-fighting.

24 Craig Whitlock, Leslie Shapiro, and Armand Emamdjomeh, "The
    Afghanistan Papers: A Secret History of the War," *Washington Post*,
    December 9, 2019, https://www.washingtonpost.com/graphics/2019
    /investigations/afghanistan-papers/documents-database.

25 Julie Kelly, "Mendacity, Hubris, and the Tragedy of Afghanistan,"
    American Greatness, January 16, 2020, https://amgreatness.
    com/2020/01/16/mendacity-hubris-and-the-tragedy-of-afghanistan.

26 Donald J. Trump (@realDonaldTrump), "The Trans-Pacific Partnership
    will lead to even greater unemployment. Do not pass it," Twitter, April 22,
    2015, https://twitter.com/realDonaldTrump/status/590983484518305793.

27 Robert E. Lighthizer to Charles E. Schumer et al., Office of the United
    States Trade Representative, May 18, 2017, https://ustr.gov/sites/default
    /files/files/Press/Releases/NAFTA%20Notification.pdf.

28 Bill Chappell, "U.S. Will Lift Tariffs on Steel and Aluminum from Canada and Mexico," NPR, May 17, 2019, https://www.npr.org/2019/05/17 /724357441/u-s-to-lift-tariffs-on-canadas-and-mexico-s-steel-and -aluminum.

29 Donald J. Trump (@realDonaldTrump), "I am a Tariff Man. When people or countries come in to raid the great wealth of our Nation, I want them to pay for the privilege of doing so," Twitter, December 4, 2018, https:// twitter.com/realDonaldTrump/status/1069970500535902208.

30 White House Office of Trade and Manufacturing Policy, "How China's Economic Aggression Threatens the Technologies and Intellectual Property of the United States and the World," June 2018, https://www. whitehouse.gov/wp-content/uploads/2018/06/FINAL-China -Technology-Report-6.18.18-PDF.pdf.

31 C-SPAN, Testimony to Senate Judiciary Committee on FBI Oversight, Washington, D.C., July 23, 2019, video, 2:58:58, xhttps://www.c-span.org /video/?462772-1/senate-judiciary-committee-hearing-fbi-oversight.

32 CNBC, "Secretary Mike Pompeo: We've Tried to Push Back Against Chinese IP Theft," CNBC, May 13, 2019, https://www.cnbc.com /video/2019/05/13/pompeo-tried-push-back-against-china-chinese-ip -intellectual-property-theft.html.

33 Henry I. Miller, "What's in Your Chinese-Supplied Medication?," *American Greatness*, March 11, 2020, https://amgreatness.com/2020 /03/11/whats-in-your-chinese-supplied-medication.

34 Bret Stephens, "What's Our China End Game?," *New York Times*, May 16, 2019, https://www.nytimes.com/2019/05/16/opinion/china-us-trade -war-tariffs.html.

35 Max Boot, "Imposing Tariffs Is Stupid Policy," *Washington Post*, March 5, 2018, https://www.washingtonpost.com/opinions/imposing-tariffs-is -stupid-policy/2018/03/05/b5512ea0-2093-11e8-86f6-54bfff693d2b_story .html.

36 Tom Nichols, "Flashback: Trump Promised a Trade War. Should We Let His Voters Get What They Asked For?," *USA Today*, June 6, 2018, https:// www.usatoday.com/story/opinion/2018/06/06/trade-war-ruin-donald -trump-voters-american-economy-column/674058002.

37 Dorcas Wong and Alexander Chipman Koty, "The US-China Trade War: A Timeline," *China Briefing*, January 16, 2020, https://www.china -briefing.com/news/the-us-china-trade-war-a-timeline.

38 "Fact Sheet," Economic and Trade Agreement the United States of America and the People's *Republic* of China, Office of the United States Trade Representative, January 15, 2020, https://ustr.gov/sites /default/files/files/agreements/phase%20one%20agreement/US_China _Agreement_Fact_Sheet.pdf.

39 Thomas Franck, "Mnuchin Says More Tariffs Will Be Rolled Back in Phase Two of Trade Deal," CNBC, January 15, 2020, https://www.cnbc

.com/2020/01/15/mnuchin-says-more-tariffs-will-be-rolled-back-in
-phase-two-of-trade-deal.html.

40 Agreement between the United States of America, the United Mexican
States, and Canada, 12/13/19 Text, Office of the United States Trade
Representative, December 14, 2019, https://ustr.gov/trade-agreements
/free-trade-agreements/united-states-mexico-canada-agreement
/agreement-between.

41 White House, "President Trump Delivers Remarks at a USMCA
Celebration with American Workers," YouTube video, 1:12:26, January 30,
2020, https://www.youtube.com/watch?v=TauWU1tCmko.

42 Josh Zumbrun and Anthony DeBarros, "Trade War with China Took Toll
on U.S., but Not Big One," *Wall Street Journal*, January 12, 2020, https://
www.wsj.com/articles/trade-war-with-china-took-toll-on-u-s-but-not
-big-one-11578832381.

43 Office of the High Commission, UN Human Rights, "Children Deprived
of Liberty—The United Nations Global Study," November 24, 2019,
https://www.ohchr.org/EN/HRBodies/CRC/StudyChildrenDeprived
Liberty/Pages/Index.aspx.

44 Howard Goller, ed., "Story on U.N. Study on Child Detentions
Withdrawn," Reuters, November 18, 2019, https://www.reuters.com
/article/us-un-rights-child-idUSKBN1XS1PC.

45 Rick Wilson, *Everything Trump Touches Dies: A* Republican *Strategist
Gets Real About the Worst President Ever* (New York: Free Press, 2018),
254, 252.

46 American Enterprise Institute, "It Came Apart: What's Next for a
Fractured Culture?," YouTube video, 1:16:19, February 2, 2017, https://
www.youtube.com/watch?v=bsoh9ieLPyw.

47 Bill Kristol (@BillKristol), "I'm aware a wall that keeps foreigners out is
different from a wall that keeps one's own citizens in," Twitter, December
22, 2018, https://twitter.com/BillKristol/status/1076585794960273408.

48 Bret Stephens, "Only Mass Deportation Can Save America," *New York
Times*, June 16, 2017, https://www.nytimes.com/2017/06/16/opinion
/only-mass-deportation-can-save-america.html.

49 "Mitt Romney Remarks," C-SPAN, January 27, 2012, https://www.c-span
.org/video/?303952-3/mitt-romney-remarks.

50 Mitt Romney, "Mitt Romney: The President Shapes the Public Character
of the Nation. Trump's Character Falls Short," *Washington Post*, January
1, 2019, https://www.washingtonpost.com/opinions/mitt-romney-the
-president-shapes-the-public-character-of-the-nation-trumps-character
-falls-short/2019/01/01/37a3c8c2-0d1a-11e9-8938-5898adc28fa2_story.
html.

51 Donald J. Trump, "Presidential Proclamation on Declaring a National
Emergency Concerning the Southern Border of the United States,"
February 15, 2019, https://www.whitehouse.gov/presidential-actions

/presidential-proclamation-declaring-national-emergency-concerning
-southern-border-united-states.

52 David French, "Defenses of Trump's Emergency Declaration Defy the
Plain Language and Clear Intent of the Law," *National Review*, January
10, 2019, https://www.nationalreview.com/2019/01/defenses-of-trumps
-emergency-declaration-defy-the-plain-language-and-clear-intent-of
-the-law.

53 "Mitt Romney Remarks."

54 Editors of the *National Review*, "Disapprove," *National Review*, March 13,
2019, https://www.nationalreview.com/2019/03/trump-border
-emergency-declaration-republicans-should-vote-disapprove.

55 Mitt Romney, "Romney Announces Vote to Disapprove of National
Emergency Declaration," press release, March 14, 2019, https://www
.romney.senate.gov/romney-announces-vote-disapprove-national
-emergency-declaration.

56 Tim Hains, "Sen. Mitt Romney on Immigration: 'The President Has
Tapped into Something Which the People Feel Very Deeply,'" April 7,
2019, RealClearPolitics, https://www.realclearpolitics.com
/video/2019/04/07/sen_mitt_romney_democrats_making_a_huge
_error_by_making_immigration_a_partisan_issue.html.

57 Rachel Bovard, "Congressional Republicans Punt on Sovereignty,"
American Greatness, June 24, 2018, https://amgreatness.
com/2018/06/24/congressional-republicans-punt-on-sovereignty.

58 Jennifer Rubin, "Jennifer Rubin: The Worst U.S. Human Rights Abuse in
Decades Isn't Over," *Salt Lake Tribune*, July 25, 2018, https://www.sltrib
.com/opinion/commentary/2018/07/24/jennifer-rubin-worst-us.

59 Jennifer Rubin, "Republicans Are Justifying the Unjustifiable,"
Washington Post, June 20, 2018, https://www.washingtonpost.com/blogs
/right-turn/wp/2018/06/20/republicans-are-justifying-the-unjustifiable.

60 Brad Wilmouth, "Rubin: Sarah Huckabee Sanders Should Be Harassed
Publicly as a 'Life Sentence,'" *MRC NewsBusters*, July 1, 2018, https://
www.newsbusters.org/blogs/nb/brad-wilmouth/2018/07/01/rubin-sarah
-huckabee-sanders-should-be-harassed-publicly-life.

61 Tom Nichols (@RadioFreeTom), "So much BS in the family separation
debate. A family enters the US illegally? Fine. Deport. Together," Twitter,
June 18, 2018, https://twitter.com/RadioFreeTom/status
/1008600311622197248.

62 Tom McGovern (@jefe_viejo), "You meant citizens, right," Twitter, July 3,
2018, https://twitter.com/jefe_viejo/status/1014225387193135104.

63 Rick Wilson (@TheRickWilson), "These people are essentially writing
erotic fanfic about Trump's executive power and are mute on this one,"
Twitter, June 17, 2018, https://twitter.com/TheRickWilson/status
/1008350798861012992.

64 Ana Navarro-Cárdenas (@ananavarro), "@IvankaTrump, lovely picture.
How nice that you get to hold your child in your arms and not face the

anguish of having him torn from you and left to God knows what fate. #WhereAreTheChildren," Twitter, May 27, 2018, https://twitter.com /ananavarro/status/1000901960898371584.

65 Evan McMullin (@EvanMcMullin), "The lies. The dictator adoration. The bigotry. The lawlessness. The indecency. The corruption," Twitter, July 19, 2018, https://twitter.com/EvanMcMullin/status/1009115693906890752.

66 David French, "Now Is the Time, Congress—End Family Separation," *National Review*, June 18, 2018, https://www.nationalreview.com /2018/06/family-separation-immigration-congress-end-it.

67 Julie Kelly, "Trump Works While NeverTrump Predicts Doom—Again," *American Greatness*, December 27, 2018, https://www.amgreatness .com/2018/12/27/trump-works-while-nevertrump-predicts-doom-again.

68 Bret Stephens, "For Once, I'm Grateful for Trump," *New York Times*, October 4, 2018, https://www.nytimes.com/2018/10/04/opinion/trump -kavanaugh-ford-allegations.html.

69 Jonah Goldberg, "You Idiot Reporters Are Making It Worse," *National Review*, October 2, 2018, https://www.nationalreview.com/2018/10 /kavanaugh-hearings-partisan-reporters-making-it-worse.

70 John Podhoretz, "Kavanaugh: The Surprise Ending," *Commentary*, October 5, 2018, https://www.commentarymagazine.com/politics-ideas /brett-kavanaugh-the-surprise-ending.

71 Seth Mandel (@SethAMandel), "I say this because it just morphed into a cultural reckoning of sorts, representative of something we haven't dealt with as a society and this is going to be the moment we do so," Twitter, September 17, 2018, https://twitter.com/SethAMandel/status /1041883767214952449.

72 Seth Mandel, "How the Kavanaugh Allegations Are Rallying Conservatives Behind Trump," *Atlantic*, October 1, 2018, https://www .theatlantic.com/ideas/archive/2018/10/kavanaugh-allegations-drive -support-trump/571756.

73 Nancy French, "If Kavanaugh Attacked Ford, What He's Done Since Doesn't Wipe the Slate Clean," *Washington Post*, September 20, 2018, https://www.washingtonpost.com/outlook/2018/09/20/if-kavanaugh -attacked-ford-what-hes-done-since-doesnt-wipe-slate-clean.

74 Robert Siegel and Nancy French, "Nancy French on Implications of Alabama Election for Christian Conservatives," December 13, 2017, in *All Things Considered*, MP3 audio, 8:00, https://www.npr.org/2017/12/13 /570603492/nancy-french-on-implications-of-alabama-election-for -christian-conservatives.

75 Charles J. Sykes, "The Anger of Brett Kavanaugh," *Washington Examiner*, October 2, 2018, https://www.washingtonexaminer.com/weekly-standard /the-anger-of-brett-kavanaugh.

76 Senator Ben Sasse, "The Important #MeToo Movement and Our Descent into Tribalism," YouTube video, 18:25, October 3, 2018, https://www .youtube.com/watch?time_continue=328&v=6bcWvixc_BU.

77 EWTN, "Why President Trump's Comments on Christine Blasey Ford Were 'Not Helpful,'-ENN," YouTube video, 03:16, October 3, 2018, https://www.youtube.com/watch?v=Q97NLjaMjQg.

78 Jennifer Rubin, "Why Brett Kavanaugh Should Not Be Confirmed," *Salt Lake Tribune*, September 28, 2018, https://www.sltrib.com/opinion/commentary/2018/09/28/jennifer-rubin-why-brett.

CHAPTER 5: WEAPONS OF MASS COLLUSION

[EPIGRAPH] Chris Buskirk and Lee Smith, "The Plot Against the President: How Devin Nunes Uncovered the Biggest Scandal in US History," October 31, 2019, in *The Chris Buskirk Show*, MP3 audio, 38:40, https://amgreatness.com/2019/10/31/the-chris-buskirk-show-episode-18-the-plot-against-the-president.

1 Post Opinion Staff, "A Transcript of Donald Trump's Meeting with the *Washington Post* Editorial Board," *Washington Post*, March 21, 2016, https://www.washingtonpost.com/blogs/post-partisan/wp/2016/03/21/a-transcript-of-donald-trumps-meeting-with-the-washington-post-editorial-board.

2 Lachlan Markay, "Trump Adviser Compared U.S.-Russia Policy to Slavery, Police Shootings," *Washington Free Beacon*, March 23, 2016, https://freebeacon.com/politics/trump-adviser-compared-u-s-russia-policy-to-slavery-police-shootings.

3 Glenn Simpson and Peter Fritsch, *Crime in Progress: Inside the Steele Dossier and the Fusion GPS Investigation of Donald Trump* (New York: Random House, 2019), 51.

4 Robert Zubrin, "Trump: The Kremlin's Favorite Candidate," *National Review*, April 4, 2016, https://www.nationalreview.com/2016/04/trump-kremlins-candidate.

5 Lee Smith, *The Plot Against the President: The True Story of How Congressman Devin Nunes Uncovered the Biggest Political Scandal in US History* (New York: Center Street, 2019), 42.

6 Noah Rothman, "Trump's Great Russia and Our Expense," *Commentary*, July 21, 2016, https://www.commentarymagazine.com/foreign-policy/europe/russia/donald-trump-dream-of-a-greater-russia.

7 William Kristol, "Putin's Party?," *Washington Examiner*, February 5, 2020, https://www.washingtonexaminer.com/weekly-standard/putins-party.

8 Tom Nichols (@RadioFreeTom), "On this Trump, Russia, and patriotism issue, let's do a thought experiment here, shall we? /1." Twitter, July 28, 2016, https://twitter.com/RadioFreeTom/status/758678201040302081.

9 Mona Charen, "Where Does a Patriot Turn in 2016,?" Creators, July 29, 2016, https://www.creators.com/read/mona-charen/07/16/where-does-a-patriot-turn-in-2016.

10 Jennifer Rubin, "Trump's Travesty," *Washington Post*, July 28, 2016,

https://www.washingtonpost.com/blogs/right-turn/wp/2016/07/28
/trumps-travesty.

11   "President Obama Roasts Donald Trump at White House
     Correspondents' Dinner!," YouTube video, 05:33, April 30, 2011, https://
     www.youtube.com/watch?v=k8TwRmX6zs4.

12   Mean Tweets-President Obama Edition #2," YouTube video, 01:56,
     October 24, 2016, https://www.youtube.com/watch?v=XvgnOqcCYCM.

13   Julie Kelly, "Obama's Shady Trump-Russia Spinmeister," *American
     Greatness*, October 31, 2017, https://amgreatness.com/2017/10/31
     /obamas-shady-trump-russia-spinmeister.

14   Joint Statement from the Department of Homeland Security and Office
     of the Director of National Intelligence on Election Security, October 7,
     2016, https://www.dhs.gov/news/2016/10/07/joint-statement
     -department-homeland-security-and-office-director-national.

15   Julie Kelly, "How a Former McCain Associate Obtained the Steele
     Dossier and Helped Advance the Russian-Collusion Narrative," *American
     Greatness*, March 18, 2019, https://amgreatness.com/2019/03/18/how
     -a-former-mccain-associate-obtained-the-steele-dossier-and-helped
     -advance-the-russian-collusion-narrative.

16   McCain, *The Restless Wave*, 237.

17   McCain, *The Restless Wave*, 238.

18   Simpson and Fritsch, *Crime in Progress*, 47.

19   McCain, *The Restless Wave*, 240.

20   Julie Kelly, "McCain's Key Role in Fueling Post-Election Trump-Russia
     Hysteria," *American Greatness*, March 20, 2019, https://amgreatness.
     com/2019/03/20/mccains-key-role-in-fueling-post-election-trump
     -russia-hysteria.

21   "Russian Hacking and Cybersecurity," C-SPAN, 2:44:00, January 5, 2017,
     https://www.c-span.org/video/?420936-1/senior-intelligence-officials
     -more-resolute-russian-role-election-year-hacking.

22   Julie Kelly, "Same People Behind Iraq War Lies Pushed Russian
     Collusion," *American Greatness*, April 8, 2019, https://amgreatness.
     com/2019/04/08/same-people-behind-iraq-war-lies-pushed-russian
     -collusion.

23   Howard Kurtz, "Bill Kristol, Keeping Iraq in the Cross Hairs,"
     Washington Post, March 18, 2003, https://www.washingtonpost.com
     /archive/lifestyle/2003/03/18/bill-kristol-keeping-iraq-in-the-cross
     -hairs/72191034-2d12-44a0-aaa1-39ecab6d9dce.

24   Bill Kristol (@BillKristol), "Lest we lose sight of the forest for the trees: It
     seems to me likely Mueller will find there was collusion between Trump
     associates and Putin operatives," Twitter, August 9, 2018, https://twitter
     .com/BillKristol/status/1027697368383348736.

25   John McCain, "Remarks Prior to the U.S. Invasion of Iraq," speech
     transcript, *Congressional Record*, vol. 149, p. S3955, March 19, 2003,

https://en.wikisource.org/wiki/Remarks_by_John_McCain_prior_to
_the_U.S._invasion_of_Iraq.

26 Nolan D. McCaskill, "McCain on Trump-Russia Probes: 'Lot of Shoes to
    Drop from This Centipede," *Politico*, March 12, 2017, https://www
    .politico.com/story/2017/03/mccain-russia-trump-235966.

27 Matthew Engel, "Proud Wife Turn 'Axis of Evil' Speech into a Resignation
    Letter," *Guardian*, February 26, 2002, https://www.theguardian.com
    /world/2002/feb/27/usa.matthewengel.

28 David Frum (@DavidFrum), "I never envisioned an Axis of Evil of which
    one of the members was the US National Security Advisor," Twitter,
    November 18, 2016, https://twitter.com/davidfrum/status
    /799587933531570176.

29 Max Boot, "Does America Need an Empire?," lecture transcript, 2003
    Fleet Admiral Chester Nimitz Memorial Lecture at UC Berkeley, March
    12, 2003, https://www.berkeley.edu/news/berkeleyan/2003/03/19_boot
    -transcript.shtml.

30 Max Boot, "The Collusion Case Against Trump Just Got a Lot Stronger,"
    Washington Post, January 9, 2019, https://www.washingtonpost.com
    /opinions/2019/01/09/collusion-case-against-trump-just-got-lot
    -stronger.

31 TheMiddleBlitz, "Earth to Liberals: Robert Mueller Lied to Us in the Iraq
    War," YouTube video, 04:09, August 6, 2017, https://www.youtube.com
    /watch?v=mNeqrTbkZmM.

32 Commission on the Intelligence Capabilities of the United States
    Regarding Weapons of Mass Destruction, Report to the President of the
    United States, March 31, 2005, https://fas.org/irp/offdocs/wmd_report
    .pdf.

33 Byron York, "In Trump-Russia Probe, Was It All About the Logan Act?,"
    Washington Examiner, December 3, 2017, https://www
    .washingtonexaminer.com/byron-york-in-trump-russia-probe
    -was-it-all-about-the-logan-act.

34 Burgess Everett, "McCain to Press White House on Why Pence Was
    'Lied To,'" *Politico*, February 15, 2017, https://www.politico.com
    /story/2017/02/michael-flynn-resign-pence-john-mccain-235048; ABC
    News Politics (@ABCPolitics), "NEW: @SenatorJohnMcCain: Flynn
    resignation 'raises further questions about the Trump administration's
    intentions toward Vladimir Putin's Russia,'" Twitter, February 14, 2017,
    https://twitter.com/ABCPolitics/status/831516980196831233.

35 Jake Tapper, "Sen. John McCain's Entire SOTU Interview," CNN, March
    12, 2017, https://www.cnn.com/videos/politics/2017/03/12/john-mccain
    -entire-state-of-the-union-interview-march-12-intv.cnn.

36 David French, "Donald Trump and Russia—What Do We Really Know?,"
    National Review, February 15, 2017, https://www.nationalreview
    .com/2017/02/donald-trump-russia-contacts-what-we-know.

37 Department of Justice, Office of Public Affairs, "Appointment of Special Counsel," press release, May 17, 2017, https://www.justice.gov/opa/pr /appointment-special-counsel.

38 Mark Landler and Eric Lichtblau, "Jeff Sessions Rescues Himself from Russia Inquiry," *New York Times*, March 2, 2017, https://www.nytimes .com/2017/03/02/us/politics/jeff-sessions-russia-trump-investigation -democrats.html.

39 Max Boot, "Trump Is Ignoring the Worst Attack on America Since 9/11," *Washington Post*, February 18, 2018, https://www.washingtonpost .com/opinions/trump-is-ignoring-the-worst-attack-on-america-since -911/2018/02/18/5ad888f2-14f3-11e8-8b08-027a6ccb38eb_story.html.

40 "Statement to GOP Leadership: Support Robert Mueller's Investigation," Niskanen Center, November 2, 2017, https://www.niskanencenter.org /statement-gop-leadership-support-robert-muellers-investigation.

41 Bill Kristol (@BillKristol), "I'm honored to be a founding director of Republicans for the Rule of Law," Twitter, April 10, 2018, https://twitter .com/BillKristol/status/983879111117606912.

42 Jennifer Rubin, "Comey's Testimony Changed Everything—and Not in Trump's Favor," *Washington Post*, June 9, 2017, https://www .washingtonpost.com/blogs/right-turn/wp/2017/06/09/comeys -testimony-changed-everything-and-not-in-trumps-favor.

43 "Stephens: 'The White House and the President Should Be Terrified,'" MSNBC, August 24, 2017, https://www.msnbc.com/deadline-white -house/watch/stephens-the-white-house-and-the-president-should-be -terrified-1031830083903.

44 Tom Nichols (@RadioFreeTom), "Pretty sure I've spent more time around this stuff than this guy," Twitter, May 3, 2019, https://twitter.com /RadioFreeTom/status/1124506754157621248.

45 The Lead CNN (@TheLeadCNN), "This is war. @BillKristol thinks the FBI raiding Trump attorney Michael Cohen's office 'shows that we are very close to the end game,'" Twitter, April 9, 2018, https://twitter.com /TheLeadCNN/status/983442733389041666.

46 Tim Hains, "Bill Kristol: Trump's Last Line of Defense Is 'It's Not Russia,' But How Do We Know It's Not Russia?," *Real Clear Politics*, August 22, 2018, https://www.realclearpolitics.com/video/2018/08/22/bill_kristol _with_cohen_and_manafort_guilty_reality_has_changed.html.

47 Charlie J. Sykes, "The Rot at the Top," *Washington Examiner*, August 23, 2018, https://www.washingtonexaminer.com/weekly-standard /republicans-will-answer-for-trump-manafort-and-cohen.

48 David French, "The Special Counsel's Cohen Sentencing Brief Is Ominous for Trump," *National Review*, December 7, 2018, https://www .nationalreview.com/corner/special-counsel-michael-cohen-sentencing -brief-trump-legal-problems.

49 Jo Becker, Matt Apuzzo, and Adam Goldman, "Trump's Son Met with Russian Lawyer After Being Promised Damaging Information on

Clinton," *New York Times*, July 9, 2017, https://www.nytimes.com/2017
/07/09/us/politics/trump-russia-kushner-manafort.html.

50 David French, "There Is Now Evidence That Senior Trump Attempted to
    Collude with Russia," *National Review*, July 11, 2017, https://www
    .nationalreview.com/2017/07/donald-trump-jr-e-mails-proof-trump
    -campaign-attempted-collusion-russia.

51 Ana Navarro-Cárdenas (@ananavarro), "Is Michael Flynn going to jail?
    Unlike Paul, can't make $11 Million bail," Twitter, December 1, 2017,
    https://twitter.com/ananavarro/status/936672847417741312.

52 Evan McMullin (@EvanMcMullin), "Big news: Mueller reportedly has
    evidence that Michael Cohen did travel to Prague in 2016," Twitter, April
    13, 2018, https://twitter.com/EvanMcMullin/status/984939001218990080.

53 Jonah Goldberg, "Conspiracy Theorists in Trump-Russia Investigation
    See Black and White in an Ocean of Gray," Townhall, May 23, 2018,
    https://townhall.com/columnists/jonahgoldberg/2018/05/23/conspiracy
    -theorists-in-trumprussia-investigation-see-black-and-white-in-an
    -ocean-of-gray-n2483264.

54 David French, "Republicans Must Reject 'Russia Hoax' Conspiracies and
    Examine the Evidence," *National Review*, December 10, 2018, https://
    www.nationalreview.com/2018/12/republicans-must-reject-russia-hoax
    -conspiracies-and-examine-the-evidence.

55 David French, "Yes. A Reasonable Prosecutor Would Have Ordered an
    Investigation of the Trump Campaign," *National Review*, May 22, 2018,
    https://www.nationalreview.com/2018/05/russia-investigation-robert
    -mueller-reach-natural-conclusion.

56 David French, "The FBI's Counterintelligence Investigation of Trump
    Was Prudent and Proper," *National Review*, January 15, 2019, https://
    www.nationalreview.com/2019/01/the-fbis-counterintelligence
    -investigation-of-trump-was-prudent-and-proper.

57 Tom Nichols, "GOP's Crazy Russia Probe Conspiracies Are Crushed
    in Fusion GPS Transcript," *USA Today*, January 11, 2018, https://www.
    usatoday.com/story/opinion/2018/01/11/fusion-gps-interview
    -debunks-republican-russia-probe-conspiracy-theories-tom-nichols
    -column/1023938001.

58 Julie Kelly, "The Only Subject Ben Sasse Won't Talk About: Spygate,"
    American Greatness, September 11, 2018, https://amgreatness.
    com/2018/09/11/the-only-subject-ben-sasse-wont-talk-about-spygate.

59 MSNBC, "Bill Kristol: Team Donald Trump 'Are the Most Sore Winners
    in the World,'" YouTube video, 03:02, March 26, 2019, https://www
    .youtube.com/watch?v=j1NfRHzcD1U.

60 Charles Sykes, "This Is What Obstruction Looks Like," Bulwark, April 18,
    2019, https://thebulwark.com/this-is-what-obstruction-looks-like.

61 Max Boot (@MaxBoot), "@DevinNunes seems to think that Trump
    opponents made up the Trump campaign's extensive links with Russia,"

Twitter, November 19, 2019, https://twitter.com/maxboot/status
/1196796068157149195.

CHAPTER 6: NEVERTRUMP'S ENEMIES LIST

[EPIGRAPH] Donald J. Trump (@realDonaldTrump), "The Never Trumper
Republicans, though on respirators with not many left," Twitter, October
23, 2019, https://twitter.com/realDonaldTrump/status
/1187063301731209220.

1   Smith, *Plot Against the President*, 252.
2   Smith, *Plot Against the President*, 253.
3   CNN, "Rep. Devin Nunes Explains White House Visit," YouTube video,
14:41, March 27, 2017, https://www.youtube.com/watch?v
=4DKGXZ7Sx_M.
4   Politicus Media, "Bill Kristol Explains Why Devin Nunes Has
Republicans in Big Trouble," YouTube video, 02:02, March 27, 2017,
https://www.youtube.com/watch?v=HdqSA8oNpaM.
5   Greta Van Susteren, "For the Record with Greta," MSNBC, March 30,
2017, http://www.msnbc.com/transcripts/for-the-record-with
-greta/2017-03-30.
6   Jennifer Rubin, "Nunes Shows Why He's Incapable of Running an
Investigation," *Washington Post*, March 23, 2017, https://www
.washingtonpost.com/blogs/right-turn/wp/2017/03/23/nunes-shows
-why-hes-incapable-of-running-an-investigation.
7   Jennifer Rubin, "End the Nunes Charade, and Follow the Russian Money,"
Washington Post, March 29, 2017, https://www.washingtonpost.com
/blogs/right-turn/wp/2017/03/29/end-the-nunes-charade-and-follow
-the-russian-money.
8   Rebecca Savransky, "McCain: Nunes' Actions 'Very Disturbing,'" *The Hill*,
March 23, 2017, https://thehill.com/homenews/senate/325374-mccain
-nunes-actions-very-disturbing.
9   Savransky, "McCain: Nunes' Actions."
10 "McCain: Select Committee on Russia Now a 'Requirement,'" MSNBC
video, 10:36, March 22, 2017, https://www.msnbc.com/for-the
-record-with-greta/watch/mccain-select-committee-on-russia-now-a
-requirement-904215619769.
11 David French, "Devin Nunes Should Step Down As Chairman of the
House Intelligence Committee," *National Review*, March 28, 2017,
https://www.nationalreview.com/2017/03/devin-nunes-trump
-surveillance-campaign-investigation-house-intel-committee-russia.
12 Stephanie Ruhle, "The Political Divide Surrounding the Nunes Memo,"
MSNBC, February 1, 2018, https://www.msnbc.com/stephanie-ruhle
/watch/the-political-divide-surrounding-the-nunes-memo
-1151246403966.
13 Dan Nowicki and Ronald J. Hansen, "McCain, Flake Oppose Nunes

Memo Release," *Republic*, February 2, 2018, https://www.azcentral.com /story/news/politics/arizona/2018/02/02/john-mccain-and-jeff-flake -oppose-memos-release-but-other-gop-members-support-move /301178002.

14 Bill Kristol (@BillKristol), "When the history of Trump's presidency (and impeachment?) is written, the Nunes memo will be a minor footnote," Twitter, February 2, 2018, https://twitter.com/BillKristol/status /959445948530388992.

15 Max Boot, "The Nunes Memo Wasn't Meant to Win Over Everyone— Just 34 Senators," *Washington Post*, February 3, 2018, https://www .washingtonpost.com/opinions/the-nunes-memo-wasnt-meant-to-win -over-everyone--just-34-senators/2018/02/03/607531d6-085d-11e8-b48c -b07fea957bd5_story.html.

16 David French, "The Big Flaw in the Memo," *National Review*, February 2, 2018, https://www.nationalreview.com/2018/02/nunes-memo-big-flaw -confirms-new-york-times-story.

17 David French, "The Schiff Memo Undermines Republican Claims of FISA Abuse," *National Review*, February 26, 2018, https://www .nationalreview.com/2018/02/the-schiff-memo-undermines-republican -claims-of-fisa-abuse.

18 "Andrew C. McCarthy, Respectfully Disagreeing with David French on FISA Abuse," *National Review*, February 28, 2018, https://www .nationalreview.com/2018/02/schiff-memo-russia-investigation-fisa -abuse-david-french-analysis.

19 Julie Kelly, "Where Is House Ethics Probe Into Adam Schiff?" *American Greatness*, February 28, 2019, https://amgreatness.com/2019/02/28 /where-is-house-ethics-probe-into-adam-schiff.

20 Bret Stephens, "Devin Nunes's Nothingburger," *New York Times*, February 2, 2018, https://www.nytimes.com/2018/02/02/opinion/devin -nunes-memo.html.

21 Bret Stephens, "The Conservative Case for Impeachment—and Removal," *New York Times*, December 18, 2019, https://www.nytimes .com/2019/12/18/opinion/trump-impeachment-fbi.html.

22 Office of the Inspector General, "Review of Four FISA Applications and Other Aspects of the FBI's Crossfire Hurricane Investigation," originally issued December 9, 2019, revised December 20, 2019, https://oig.justice .gov/reports/2019/020012.pdf.

23 Office of the Inspector General, "Review."

24 Office of the Inspector General, "Review."

25 "Sen. Hawley to Horowitz: Why Would FBI Lie to FISA Court?," Fox News video, 08:12, December 18, 2019, https://video.foxnews.com /v/6116851669001#sp=show-clips.

26 Order Regarding Handling and Disposition of Information, In Re

Carter W. Page, Foreign Intelligence Surveillance Court, January 7, 2020, https://www.fisc.uscourts.gov/sites/default/files/FISC%20 Declassifed%20Order%2016-1182%2017-52%2017-375%2017-679%20%20 200123.pdf.

27 David French (@DavidAFrench), "Pay no attention to malicious grifters. I don't know any serious person who hasn't been calling for a thorough investigation," Twitter, December 10, 2019, https://twitter.com /DavidAFrench/status/1204426450914418688.

28 Jennifer Rubin (@JRubinBlogger), "all unfit for office, have violated their oaths. voters take down names, please," Twitter, May 22, 2018, https:// twitter.com/JRubinBlogger/status/998952659901140992.

29 Bill Kristol (@BillKristol), "Watching Rep. Jordan harass Deputy AG Rosenstein. I knew Jim Jordan before he was a reckless demagogue," Twitter, June 28, 2018, https://twitter.com/BillKristol/status /1012359047373258752.

30 Haley Byrd, "Trump's Favorite Wrestler," *Washington Examiner*, August 16, 2018, https://www.washingtonexaminer.com/weekly-standard /freedom-caucus-co-founder-jim-jordan-wants-to-be-speaker-of-the -house.

31 Sarah K. Burris, "Republican Gobsmacked By 'Intelligent and Responsible Congressman' Who Switched to a 'Devotee of the Trump Cult,'" Raw Story, July 13, 2018, https://www.rawstory.com/2018/07 /republican-gobsmacked-intelligent-responsible-congressman-switched -devotee-trump-cult.

32 Jennifer Rubin, "Schiff Goes on Offense," *Washington Post*, February 5, 2018, https://www.washingtonpost.com/blogs/right-turn/wp/2018/02 /05/schiff-goes-on-offense.

33 Jennifer Rubin, "Dear Cowering Republicans: What Are You Waiting For?," *Washington Post*, October 4, 2019, https://www.washingtonpost .com/opinions/2019/10/04/awol-republicans-their-staff-its-time.

34 Max Boot, "Will the GOP's Born-Again Trumpers Ever Pay the Price for Selling Out?," *Washington Post*, December 10, 2019, https://www .washingtonpost.com/opinions/2019/12/10/will-gops-born-again -trumpers-ever-pay-price-selling-out.

35 Quin Hilyer, "These GOP House Members Just Made Themselves the Antifa of Capitol Hill," *Washington Examiner*, October 23, 2019, https:// www.washingtonexaminer.com/opinion/these-gop-house-members -just-made-themselves-the-antifa-of-capitol-hill.

36 Nick Givas, "Rick Wilson Refers to Trump Supporters as His 'Rube, 10-Tooth Base' for Believing Border Wall Promise," Daily Caller, January 4, 2019, https://dailycaller.com/2019/01/04/rick-wilson-trump-base-cnn.

37 Tom Nichols (@RadioFreeTom), "When today's conservative writers signed up in the 1980s and 1990s, they could imagine their core audience

being well-off," Twitter, August 13, 2019, https://twitter.com /RadioFreeTom/status/1161412837996150784.

38 Chris Buskirk, "Scholars & Writers for Trump," *American Greatness*, September 28, 2016, https://amgreatness.com/2016/09/28/writes -scholars-for-trump.

39 Michael Anton, phone conversation with the author, October 2019.

40 Publius Decius Mus [Michael Anton], "The Flight 93 Election," *Claremont Review of Books*, September 5, 2016, https:// claremontreviewofbooks.com/digital/the-flight-93-election.

41 Anton, phone conversation, October 2019.

42 Bill Kristol (@BillKristol), "1/ 'The Flight 93 Election' is elegantly-written garden-variety sophistry. I presume the author is Mike Anton," Twitter, September 8, 2016, https://twitter.com/BillKristol/status /773905549557719040.

43 Michael Warren, "The Anonymous Pro-Trump 'Decius' Now Works Inside the White House," *Washington Examiner*, February 2, 2017, https://www.washingtonexaminer.com/weekly-standard/the -anonymous-pro-trump-decius-now-works-inside-the-white-house.

44 Bill Kristol (@BillKristol), "From Carl Schmitt to Mike Anton: First time tragedy, second time farce," Twitter, February 3, 2017, https://twitter .com/BillKristol/status/827560738109718528.

45 Gabriel Schoenfeld, "Michael Anton Is Back to Remind Us That There's Such a Thing as a 'Trump Intellectual,'" Bulwark, February 12, 2019, https://thebulwark.com/michael-anton-is-back-to-remind-us-that -theres-such-a-thing-as-a-trump-intellectual.

46 Tom Nichols (@RadioFreeTom), "This is the natural outcome of the utterly dishonest 'All Flight 93, all the time' culture warrior approach, in which trifling things like the Constitution must be pushed aside because guns and abortion and drag queens and stuff. /7," Twitter, September 6, 2019, https://twitter.com/RadioFreeTom/status/1170141316753346560.

47 Julie Kelly, "When Cabin Boys Attack," *American Greatness*, March 13, 2019, https://amgreatness.com/2019/03/13/when-cabin-boys-attack.

48 Gabriel Schoenfeld, "Expose Trump's Enablers: How Many People Who Should Know Better Are Making It Easier for Him to Lie to the American People," *Daily News*, October 31, 2016, https://www .nydailynews.com/opinion/gabriel-schoenfeld-expose-trump-enablers -article-1.2852461.

49 Tom Nichols (@RadioFreeTom), "I think it's really important to separate the good academic work someone has done from their personality, and I admire a lot of Hanson's writings on ancient Greece. But he is also a tragic case, as this shows, of an intellectual selling his soul for pennies on the dollar," Twitter, February 20, 2019, https://twitter.com /RadioFreeTom/status/1098426106917634049.

50 Tom Nichols (@RadioFreeTom), "Of all the intellectuals and academics who've done great work but now tumble down the craptious sluices of

Trumpism," Twitter, March 7, 2019, https://twitter.com/RadioFreeTom
/status/1103680989035986948; Tom Nichols (@RadioFreeTom), "The sad
decline of Victor Davis Hanson accelerates, like an asteroid that can't
wait to make its first and only crater," Twitter, April 20, 2019, https://
twitter.com/RadioFreeTom/status/1119792416758870016.

51 Max Boot, "Republicans Have No Convincing Argument Against
    Impeachment," *Washington Post*, November 12, 2019, https://www
    .washingtonpost.com/opinions/2019/11/12/republicans-have-no
    -convincing-argument-against-impeachment.

52 David French, "From David French: Building the Idiocracy, One Word
    Salad at a Time," *French Press* (blog), *Dispatch*, November 14, 2019,
    https://frenchpress.thedispatch.com/p/from-david-french-building-the
    -idiocracy.

53 Victor Davis Hanson, "The Wages of Trump Fixation," *American
    Greatness*, November 17, 2019, https://amgreatness.com/2019/11/17/the
    -wages-of-trump-fixation.

54 Mona Charen, "Claremont's New Class of Fellows Would Make Its
    Founders Weep," *National Review*, July 12, 2019, https://www
    .nationalreview.com/2019/07/claremont-would-make-its-founders-weep.

55 Charles Sykes, Gabriel Schoenfeld, and Mona Charen, "Mona Charen
    and Gabriel Schoenfeld on Claremont and the New Nationalism," July 12,
    2019, in Bulwark podcast, MP3 audio, 42:14, https://podcast.thebulwark
    .com/mona-charen-and-gabriel-schoenfeld-on-claremont-and-the-new
    -nationalism.

56 Anton, phone conversation, October 2019.

57 Tim Hains, "David French: Awful Lot of People Are 'Desperate' to
    Believe Trump/Russia Collusion Is All 'Nonsense,'" *Real Clear Politics*,
    May 20, 2018, https://www.realclearpolitics.com/video/2018/05/20
    /david_french_awful_lot_of_people_are_desperate_to_believe
    _trumprussia_collusion_is_all_nonsense.html.

58 Brad Wilmouth, "MSNBC-Style 'Conservative' Charlie Sykes Bashes
    GOP 'Cult,' Fox News," *MRC NewsBusters*, June 24, 2017, https://www
    .newsbusters.org/blogs/nb/brad-wilmouth/2017/06/24/msnbc-style
    -conservative-charlie-sykes-bashes-gop-cult-fox-news.

59 Jennifer Rubin, "Five Better Uses of Michael Bloomberg's Money,"
    Washington Post, November 10, 2019, https://www.washingtonpost.com
    /opinions/2019/11/10/all-things-bloombergs-money-could-be-better
    -spent.

60 Paul Farhi, "CNN Settles Libel Lawsuit with Covington Catholic
    Student," *Washington Post*, January 7, 2020, https://www
    .washingtonpost.com/lifestyle/style/cnn-settles-libel-lawsuit-with
    -covington-catholic-student/2020/01/07/fob21842-319e-11ea-91fd
    -82d4e04a3fac_story.html.

61 Colby Hall, "Max Boot Calls for Advertisers to Boycott Fox News 'Until
    They Pull Back from the Hate,'" *Mediaite*, October 29, 2018, https://www

.mediaite.com/tv/max-boot-calls-for-advertisers-to-boycott-fox-news -until-they-pull-back-from-the-hate.

62   CNN (@CNN), "A Florida woman who ran a Trump supporters page that unwittingly promoted a Russian-coordinated event on Facebook says she doesn't believe that she was influenced by Kremlin-linked trolls," Twitter, February 20, 2018, https://twitter.com/CNN/status/966134015337140229.

63   Tom Nichols (@RadioFreeTom), "It's tough to be old. I've watched my father and my relatives pass on," Twitter, May 10, 2018, https://twitter .com/RadioFreeTom/status/994721564410155008.

64   Michael M. Grynbaum, "A Rightward Tilt and Big Ratings at Fox News," *Media Memo* (blog), November 12, 2017, https://www.nytimes.com/2017 /11/12/business/media/fox-news-roy-moore.html.

65   National Conservatism, "Tucker Carlson: Big Business Hates Your Family—National Conservatism Conference," YouTube video, 53:37, July 17, 2019, https://www.youtube.com/watch?v=AXG0WtK1NnY.

66   Bill Kristol (@BillKristol), "They started by rationalizing Trump. They ended by rationalizing slavery," Twitter, August 15, 2017, https://twitter .com/BillKristol/status/897648303348862977.

67   Ian Schwartz, "Tucker Carlson Rips Bill Kristol: 'Like a Slot Machine Junkie' Using Twitter to Say I Rationalized Slavery," *Real Clear Politics*, August 17, 2017, https://www.realclearpolitics.com/video/2017/08/17 /tucker_carlson_rips_bill_kristol_like_a_slot_machine_junkie_using _twitter_to_say_i_rationalized_slavery.html.

68   Jeremy Binckles, "Bill Kristol Slams Tucker Carlson, Fox News, for 'Ethno-Nationalism,'" *Salon*, https://www.salon.com/2018/01/25/bill -kristol-slams-tucker-carlson-fox-news-for-ethno-nationalism.

69   "'You Specialize in Moral Outrage': Sparks Fly as Tucker Battles Romney Adviser on Russia Threat," *Fox News Insider* (blog), June 12, 2017, https:// insider.foxnews.com/2017/07/12/tucker-carlson-max-boot-russia -collusion-donald-trump-jr-foreign-policy-romney.

70   "Tucker: America's Goal Is Happiness, but Leaders Show No Obligation to Voters," Fox News video, 15:13, January 3, 2019, https://video.foxnews .com/v/5985464569001?playlist_id=5198073478001#sp=show-clips.

71   David French, "The Right Should Reject Tucker Carlson's Victimhood Populism," *National Review*, January 4, 2019, https://www.nationalreview .com/2019/01/the-right-should-reject-tucker-carlsons-victimhood -populism.

72   Elaina Plott, "What Does Tucker Carlson Believe?," *Atlantic*, December 15, 2019, https://www.theatlantic.com/politics/archive/2019/12/tucker -carlson-fox-news/603595.

73   Plott, "What Does Tucker Carlson Believe?"

74   "Conservative Writer: 'A Disgrace' Religious Leaders Defending Trump," MSNBC video, 0:50, January 26, 2018, https://www.msnbc.com

/deadline-white-house/watch/conservative-writer-a-disgrace-religious
-leaders-defending-trump-1147058243557.

75 Jennifer Rubin, "Evangelical Conservatives Are Proving Their Harshest
Critics Right," *Washington Post*, October 11, 2017, https://www
.washingtonpost.com/blogs/right-turn/wp/2017/10/11/evangelical
-conservatives-are-proving-their-harshest-critics-right.

76 Tom Nichols (@RadioFreeTom), "This comes up a lot, along with the
usual liberal carping about the 'Southern strategy' and it's worth a
moment of comment," Twitter, February 25, 2019, https://twitter.com
/RadioFreeTom/status/1100157241460703233.

77 Pam Key, "Ana Navarro: Pearl-Clutching Fox-Viewing Trump Voters
Have 'Lowered' America's Standards," Breitbart, March 11, 2019, https://
www.breitbart.com/clips/2019/03/11/ana-navarro-pearl-clutching-fox
-viewing-trump-voters-have-lowered-americas-standards.

78 Wilson, *Everything Trump Touches Dies*, 66.

79 David French, "An Open Letter to Trump's Evangelical Defenders," *The
Corner* (blog), *National Review*, May 3, 2018, https://www
.nationalreview.com/corner/donald-trump-evangelical-supporters
-stormy-daniels.

80 David French, "Evangelicals Are Supporting Trump Out of Fear Not
Faith," *Time*, June 27, 2019, https://time.com/5615617/why-evangelicals
-support-trump.

81 David French (@DavidAFrench), "Too many of our nation's Evangelical
leaders haven't just tolerated wrongdoing by Trump, they've rationalized
and minimized it," Twitter, April 25, 2019, https://twitter.com
/DavidAFrench/status/1121485310016262144.

82 "Sign Our Petition Supporting Rev. Franklin Graham," American Family
Radio, May 6, 2019, https://www.afa.net/activism/action-alerts/2019
/sign-our-petition-supporting-rev-franklin-graham.

83 Chris Buskirk, "Yes, Christians Can Support Trump Without Risk to
Their Witness," *American Greatness*, May 8, 2019, https://www
.amgreatness.com/2019/05/08/yes-christians-can-support-trump
-without-risk-to-their-witness.

84 Mark Galli, "Trump Should Be Removed from Office," *Christianity
Today*, December 19, 2019, https://www.christianitytoday.com/ct/2019
/december-web-only/trump-should-be-removed-from-office.html.

85 Nancy French, "*Christianity Today*'s Op-Ed Isn't Attacking Trump. It's
Defending Christianity," *Washington Post*, December 21, 2019, https://
www.washingtonpost.com/outlook/2019/12/21/christianity-todays-op
-ed-isnt-attacking-trump-its-defending-christianity.

86 "Nancy French CNN," YouTube video, 04:45, December 22, 2019, https://
www.youtube.com/watch?v=OKvYzdCIVPY.

87 David and Nancy French, *Home and Away: A Story of Family in a Time of
War* (New York: Center Street, 2011), 29.

88   David French, "*Christianity Today* Exposed the Reality of Evangelical Division," *French Press* (blog), *Dispatch*, December 22, 2019, https://frenchpress.thedispatch.com/p/christianity-today-exposed-the-reality.

89   David French, "There Is Always a Reason to Be Mad," *French Press* (blog), *Dispatch*, January 28, 2020, https://frenchpress.thedispatch.com/?utm_source=substack&utm_medium=menu.

CHAPTER 7: NEVERTRUMP SPLITS UP

[EPIGRAPH]   Bret Stephens, "The NeverTrump Vindication," *New York Times*, November 1, 2019, https://www.nytimes.com/2019/11/01/opinion/trump-republicans.html.

1   Charles C.W. Cooke, "Jennifer Rubin Is Everything She Hates About Trump Worshippers," *National Review*, December 18, 2017, https://www.nationalreview.com/2017/12/jennifer-rubin-trump-obsession-mindless-opponent.

2   Charles C.W. Cooke, "No, Trump's Conservative Critics Have Not Been 'Destroyed' or Silenced," *National Review*, December 14, 2016, https://www.nationalreview.com/2016/12/never-trump-conservatives-donald-trump-election-ayn-rand-jonathan-chait.

3   David Frum, "Conservatism Can't Survive Donald Trump Intact," *Atlantic*, December 19, 2017, https://www.theatlantic.com/politics/archive/2017/12/conservatism-is-what-conservatives-think-say-and-do/548738.

4   Charles C.W. Cooke, "David Frum Proves My Point," *The Corner* (blog), *National Review*, December 19, 2017, https://www.nationalreview.com/corner/david-frum-proves-my-point.

5   David Brooks, "The Failures of Anti-Trumpism," *New York Times*, April 9, 2018, https://www.nytimes.com/2018/04/09/opinion/trump-republicans.html.

6   Rich Lowry, "The Never Trump Delusion," *Politico*, March 28, 2018, https://www.politico.com/magazine/story/2018/03/28/never-trump-rich-lowry-217756.

7   Jonah Goldberg and Ramesh Ponnuru, "Conservative Criticism of Trump Is Not Deluded," *National Review*, April 3, 2018, https://www.nationalreview.com/2018/04/conservative-criticism-donald-trump-can-be-valid.

8   Bret Stephens, "Fights Worth Having," *New York Times*, March 1, 2018, https://www.nytimes.com/2018/03/01/opinion/mona-charen-never-trumper.html.

9   Joshua Rhett Miller, "Bret Stephen Challenges Troll: 'Call Me a Bedbug to My Face,'" *New York Post*, August 27, 2019, https://nypost.com/2019/08/27/nyt-columnist-challenges-troll-call-me-a-bedbug-to-my-face.

10   MSNBC, "Bret Stephens Explains 'Bedbug' Controversy, Why He Quit Twitter," MSNBC video, 02:16, August 27, 2019, https://www.msnbc

.com/msnbc/watch/bret-stephens-explains-bedbug-controversy-why
-he-quit-twitter-67545157765.

11 Bret Stephens, "Why I'm Still a NeverTrumper," *New York Times*,
December 29, 2017, https://www.nytimes.com/2017/12/29/opinion/why
-im-still-a-nevertrumper.html.

12 Seth Mandel, "The Next Steps for 'NeverTrump,'" *Atlantic*, January 11,
2018, https://www.theatlantic.com/politics/archive/2018/01
/nevertrump/550283.

13 John McCain, "Read John McCain's Farewell Statement," *New York
Times*, August 27, 2018, https://www.nytimes.com/2018/08/27/us
/politics/john-mccain-farewell-statement.html.

14 John McCain "McCain TV Ad: 'Complete the Danged Fence,'" YouTube
video, 0:30, May 7, 2010, https://www.youtube.com/watch?v
=rolwusMxiHc.

15 Jonah Goldberg, "Goldberg: How McCain's Patriotism Can Still Best
Trump's Nationalism," *Baltimore Sun*, August 31, 2018, https://www
.baltimoresun.com/opinion/op-ed/bs-ed-op-0902-goldberg-mccain
-20180830-story.html.

16 Bill Kristol (@BillKristol), "I'm proud to have voted three times for John
McCain (in the Virginia GOP primary in 2000 and 2008, and in the 2008
general election) and never for Donald Trump," Twitter, August 25, 2018,
https://twitter.com/BillKristol/status/1033348522274443265.

17 Bill Kristol (@BillKristol), "McCain points to some of what is best in
America, Trump to much of what is worst. It's up to us to decide which
man to emulate, whose path to follow," Twitter, August 31, 2018, https://
twitter.com/BillKristol/status/1035384145386594304.

18 Jennifer Rubin, "Three Men Unfit to Eulogize John McCain," *Washington
Post*, August 31, 2018, https://www.washingtonpost.com/news/opinions
/wp/2018/08/31/three-men-unfit-to-eulogize-mccain.

19 Rick Wilson (@TheRickWilson), "The Trump-right is mocking and
trolling McCain's death," Twitter, August 26, 2018, https://twitter.com
/TheRickWilson/status/1033572314745434114.

20 Max Boot, "Republicans Rejected McCain and Embraced Trump, What
Does That Say About Them?," *Washington Post*, August 29, 2018, https://
www.washingtonpost.com/news/global-opinions/wp/2018/08/29
/republicans-rejected-mccain-and-embraced-trump-what-does-that
-say-about-them.

21 Associated Press, "Trump Remarks on the Death of Arizona Sen. John
McCain," AP News, August 27, 2018, https://apnews.com
/dd2e3b97c51a4c14bc3a91a371df5e54.

22 *New York Times* News, "Full Video: John McCain's Memorial Service,"
YouTube video, 3:57:39, September 1, 2018, https://www.youtube.com
/watch?v=O2kzx8gxt_w.

23 Andrew Dugan, "John McCain Well-Known, Well-Liked for Much of His

Career," *Gallup*, August 26, 2018, https://news.gallup.com/opinion/gallup/237764/john-mccain-known-liked-career.aspx.

24 Julie Kelly (@julie_kelly2), "Don't forget. The Left doesn't just want to destroy you. They want to humiliate, disgrace and banish your children forever," Twitter, January 19, 2019, https://twitter.com/julie_kelly2/status/1086823154440421378.

25 Michael Green (@andmichaelgreen), "Plus side: A face like that never changes. This image will define his life. No one need ever forgive him," Twitter, January 19, 2019, https://twitter.com/andmichaelgreen/status/1086698655225020416.

26 Nicholas Frankovich, "The Covington Kids Might as Well Have Just Spit on the Cross," *Corner* (blog), *National Review*, January 20, 2019, accessed at https://archive.md/tlwIV#selection-1225.142-1225.308.

27 Rich Lowry (@RichLowry), "Having now seen other angle, I take point of @timcast," Twitter, January 19, 2019, https://twitter.com/RichLowry/status/1086821100351307776.

28 Ace of Spades HQ, "Trump: LOL I'm Authorizing $7+ Billion for the Wall GFY," January 24, 2019, http://ace.mu.nu/archives/379379.php.

29 Ana Navarro-Cárdenas (@ananavarro), "Must Watch: Native-American elder taunted by racist MAGA-hat wearing teens, speaks and cries for America, the country he defended and sacrificed and wore the uniform for," Twitter, January 19, 2019, https://twitter.com/ananavarro/status/1086699541611581441.

30 Timothy Meads, "So-Called Adults Apoplectically Overreact to Covington Catholic Kids," Townhall, January 20, 2019, https://townhall.com/tipsheet/timothymeads/2019/01/20/so-called-adults-apoplectically-over-react-to-the-covington-high-school-kids-n2539329.

31 Rich Lowry, "The Lincoln Memorial Hoax," *The Corner* (blog), *National Review*, January 20, 2019, https://www.nationalreview.com/corner/the-lincoln-memorial-hoax.

32 Ken Meyer, "Meghan McCain, After Viral Covington Video: I Don't Know If There's Any Coming Back from 'How Divided We Are,'" *Mediaite*, January 22, 2019, https://www.mediaite.com/tv/abby-huntsman-condemns-media-for-jumping-on-buzzfeed-report-the-greatest-gift-to-trump.

33 Julie Kelly, "Call-Out Conservatives Join the Left's Lynch Mob," *American Greatness*, January 21, 2019, https://amgreatness.com/2019/01/21/call-out-conservatives-join-the-lefts-lynch-mob.

34 Charles R. Kesler, "An Interview with Norman Podhoretz," *Claremont Review of Books*, April 16, 2019, https://claremontreviewofbooks.com/digital/an-interview-with-norman-podhoretz.

35 Max Boot, "Get a Grip, White People. We're Not the Victims," *Washington Post*, August 6, 2019, https://www.washingtonpost.com/opinions/2019/08/06/get-grip-white-people-were-not-victims.

36 John Hirschauer, "Max Boot Fans the Flames of Racial Hatred," *National Review*, August 12, 2019, https://www.nationalreview.com/2019/08/max -boot-fans-the-flames-of-racial-hatred.

37 Rich Lowry (@RichLowry), "Now @maxboot is portraying this analysis by @baseballcrank as some sort of white nationalist screed—how completely dishonest and thoroughly pathetic," Twitter, August 13, 2019, https://twitter.com/RichLowry/status/1161454357189206017.

38 "Author Warns of Dangers of 'White Victimhood Complex,'" CNN video, 01:47, August 14, 2019, https://www.msn.com/en-us/weather/topstories /author-warns-of-dangers-of-white-victimhood-complex/vi-AAFMAxQ.

39 Max Boot, "*National Review*'s Ugly Attack on Me Reflects the Trumpification of Conservatism," *Washington Post*, August 13, 2019, https://www.washingtonpost.com/opinions/2019/08/13/national -reviews-ugly-attack-me-reflects-trumpification-conservatism.

40 Seth Mandel (@SethAMandel), "Boot's full-on Chernobyl meltdown is here, and it is quite a thing to watch," Twitter, August 13, 2019, https:// twitter.com/SethAMandel/status/1161461595597352960.

41 Tom Nichols (@RadioFreeTom), "These intellectuals tried to adopt the camouflage of bib-overalls and Hee Haw straw hats; this was a very, very bad gamble," Twitter, August 13, 2019, https://twitter.com /RadioFreeTom/status/1161412834942685185.

42 Kyle Smith, "Meet the World Expert on All Things: Tom Nichols," *National Review*, September 3, 2019, https://www.nationalreview .com/2019/09/meet-the-world-expert-on-all-things-tom-nichols.

43 Charles Sykes, "Dear Democrats, Here's How to Guarantee Trump's Reelection," *Politico*, June 25, 2019, https://www.politico.com/magazine /story/2019/06/25/democrats-trump-election-2020-227215.

44 Tom Nichols, "Never Trumper: I'll Vote for Almost Any Democrat, but Lurching Left Won't Beat Trump," *USA Today*, July 1, 2019, https://www .usatoday.com/story/opinion/2019/07/01/donald-trump-referendum-all -democrats-need-to-win-2020-column/1611561001.

45 Bret Stephens, "A Wretched Start for Democrats," *New York Times*, June 28, 2019, https://www.nytimes.com/2019/06/28/opinion/democrats -debate-2020.html.

46 David Brooks, "Dems, Please Don't Drive Me Away," *New York Times*, June 27, 2019, https://www.nytimes.com/2019/06/27/opinion /democratic-debate-2020.html.

47 Mona Charen, "How a Democrat Can Win Over a Never-Trumper," *Politico*, July 9, 2019, https://www.politico.com/magazine/story/2019 /07/09/never-trumpers-2020-democrats-227255.

48 Nichols, "Never Trumper: I'll Vote."

49 Chris Hayes (@chrislhayes), "We should just ditch this whole primary thing and just have a small panel of Never Trump Republicans solomonically decide which Democrat would make them most

comfortable," Twitter, June 28, 2019, https://twitter.com/chrislhayes
/status/1144619034937348103.

50 Calvin Stowell (@calvinstowell), "It's hilarious that never trumpers
    think they are entitled to an audience when it comes to their political
    opinions," Twitter, June 28, 2019, https://twitter.com/calvinstowell/status
    /1144619388248711169.

51 Jeet Heer, "Democrats Don't Need David Brooks," *Nation*, July 3, 2019,
    https://www.thenation.com/article/archive/david-brooks-never-trump.

CHAPTER 8: THE DEATH OF THE *WEEKLY STANDARD*

[EPIGRAPH] Chris Buskirk, "Death of *The Weekly Standard* Signals Rebirth of
the Right," *American Greatness*, December 17, 2018, https://www
.amgreatness.com/2018/12/17/death-of-the-weekly-standard-signals
-rebirth-of-the-right.

1   Jason Schwartz, "*The Weekly Standard*, Conservative Outlet that
    Criticized Trump, to Shut Down," *Politico*, December 14, 2018, https://
    www.politico.com/story/2018/12/14/the-weekly-standard-to-shut
    -down-1064753.

2   Stephen Hayes (@stephenfhayes), "I am profoundly disappointed in the
    decision to close *The Weekly Standard*," Twitter, December 14, 2018,
    https://twitter.com/stephenfhayes/status/1073623117459845120.

3   Bret Baier (@BretBaier), "Congrats to @stephenfhayes—many people
    could talk about a young family overseas for a year—but very few people
    would actually do it," Twitter, July 9, 2018, https://twitter.com/BretBaier
    /status/1016459291291680771.

4   Jennifer Rubin, "Distinguished Persons of the Week: Goodbye to the
    Weekly Standard," *Washington Post*, December 16, 2018, https://www
    .washingtonpost.com/opinions/2018/12/16/distinguished-persons-week
    -goodbye-weekly-standard.

5   David Brooks, "How We Are Ruining America," *New York Times*, July 11,
    2017, https://www.nytimes.com/2017/07/11/opinion/how-we-are
    -ruining-america.html.

6   David Brooks, "Who Killed the Weekly Standard?," *New York Times*,
    December 15, 2018, https://www.nytimes.com/2018/12/15/opinion
    /weekly-standard-closing-conservatism.html.

7   John Podhoretz, "The Murder of the Weekly Standard," *Commentary
    Magazine*, December 14, 2018, https://www.commentarymagazine.com
    /politics-ideas/murder-weekly-standard.

8   Donald J. Trump (@realDonaldTrump), "The pathetic and dishonest
    Weekly Standard, run by failed prognosticator Bill Kristol (who, like
    many others, never had a clue), is flat broke and out of business," Twitter,
    December 15, 2018, https://twitter.com/realDonaldTrump/status
    /1073974873939169282.

9   William Kristol, "Country First," *Washington Examiner*, January 27, 2017,
    https://www.washingtonexaminer.com/weekly-standard/country-first.

10 Stephen F. Hayes, "Comey, Trump and the GOP," *Washington Examiner*, May 21, 2017, https://www.washingtonexaminer.com/weekly-standard /comey-trump-and-the-gop.

11 "Editorial: The Surrender," *Washington Examiner*, October 27, 2017, https://www.washingtonexaminer.com/weekly-standard/editorial-the -surrender.

12 Sho Chandra, "U.S. Consumer Confidence Just Hit Its Highest Level in Almost 17 Years," Bloomberg, October 31, 2017, https://www.bloomberg .com/news/articles/2017-10-31/u-s-consumer-confidence-index-rises-to -highest-level-since-2000.

13 Fox News, "House Passes 20-Week Abortion Ban, with Trump White House Support," October 3, 2017, https://www.foxnews.com/politics /house-passes-20-week-abortion-ban-with-trump-white-house-support.

14 Jonathan Easley, "Religious Right Notches Gains Under Trump," *Hill*, October 10, 2017, https://thehill.com/homenews/administration/354629 -religious-right-notches-gains-under-trump.

15 "Editorial: Scott Pruitt and His Enemies," *Washington Examiner*, May 14, 2018, https://www.washingtonexaminer.com/weekly-standard/editorial -scott-pruitt-should-resign-from-the-epa.

16 Chris White, "Soros-Backed Group Is Behind Lawsuit Targeting Trump's EPA Pick," Daily Caller, February 8, 2017, https://dailycaller. com/2017/02/08/soros-backed-group-is-behind-lawsuit-targeting -trumps-epa-pick.

17 Charles J. Sykes, "The Mystery of Scott Pruitt's Mattress," *Washington Examiner*, June 7, 2018, https://www.washingtonexaminer.com/weekly -standard/why-did-scott-pruitt-want-a-mattress-from-trump-hotel.

18 Stephen F. Hayes, "Rand Paul, Russian Stooge," *Washington Examiner*, August 21, 2018, https://www.washingtonexaminer.com/weekly-standard /rand-paul-russian-stooge.

19 John McCormack, "The Neo-Trumper," *Washington Examiner*, June 22, 2018, https://www.washingtonexaminer.com/weekly-standard/the-neo -trumper.

20 Andrew Egger, "Sasse Rises Above," *Washington Examiner*, September 4, 2018, https://www.washingtonexaminer.com/weekly-standard/sasse -rises-above.

21 Haley Byrd, "Is Jeff Flake's Summer Vacation Sabotaging Trump's Nominees?," *Washington Examiner*, August 1, 2018, https://www .washingtonexaminer.com/weekly-standard/is-jeff-flakes-summer -vacation-sabotaging-trumps-judicial-nominees.

22 Julie Kelly, "The Unmasking of the *Weekly Standard*," *American Greatness*, July 31, 2018, https://amgreatness.com/2018/07/31/the -unmasking-of-the-weekly-standard.

23 Haley Byrd, "Confirmed: Jim Jordan Still Carrying Water for Nunes Memo," *Washington Examiner*, July 24, 2018, https://www

.washingtonexaminer.com/weekly-standard/jim-jordan-defends
-nunes-memo-after-carter-page-fisa-applications-are-released.

24 David Byler, "Can Rick Scott Survive Ron DeSantis?," *Washington Examiner*, September 26, 2018, https://www.washingtonexaminer.com /weekly-standard/florida-midterm-election-can-rick-scott-survive -ron-desantis; Hayley Byrd, "Matt Gaetz Knows How to Get President Trump's Attention," *Washington Examiner*, February 9, 2018, https:// www.washingtonexaminer.com/weekly-standard/matt-gaetz-knows -how-to-get-president-trumps-attention.

25 Grant Wishard, "All Along the Rio Grande," *Washington Examiner*, May 31, 2018, https://www.washingtonexaminer.com/weekly-standard/u-s -mexico-border-why-a-wall-wont-fix-the-problems-in-remote-texas -region.

26 Colin Grabow, "Didn't Republicans Use to Believe in Free Trade?," *Washington Examiner*, January 9, 2018, https://www .washingtonexaminer.com/weekly-standard/didnt-republicans-use -to-believe-in-free-trade.

27 Thomas Joscelyn, "Trump and Syria," *Washington Examiner*, April 6, 2018, https://www.washingtonexaminer.com/weekly-standard/trump -and-syria.

28 Thomas Joscelyn, "Losing a War," *Washington Examiner*, August 27, 2018, https://www.washingtonexaminer.com/weekly-standard/losing-a-war.

29 Lee Smith, phone conversation with the author, December 2019.

30 Smith, phone conversation, December 2019.

31 Luisa Kroll and Kerry A. Dolan, "The Forbes 400: The Definitive Ranking of the Wealthiest Americans," *Forbes*, October 2, 2019, https://www .forbes.com/forbes-400.

32 Omidyar Network Fund, Inc., Form 990-PF: Return of Private Foundation, 2017, https://www.omidyar.com/sites/default/files /financials/ONFI%202017%20990-PF.pdf.

33 "Soros Clones: 5 Liberal Mega-Donors Nearly As Dangerous as George Soros," Media Research Center, https://www.mrc.org/special-reports /soros-clones-5-liberal-mega-donors-nearly-dangerous-george-soros, accessed February 2, 2020.

34 Omidyar Network, "Omidyar Network Commits $30 Million to High-Impact Entrepreneurship at Clinton Global Initiative Annual Meeting," press release, September 22, 2009, https://www.omidyar.com/news /omidyar-network-commits-30-million-high-impact-entrepreneurship -clinton-global-initiative.

35 NeverTrump PAC, "Top Donors 2016 Cycle," Center for Responsive Politics, https://www.opensecrets.org/outsidespending/contrib. php?cmte=C00610907&cycle=2016, accessed February 2, 2020.

36 Democracy Fund, "2018 Letter from Our President: A $100 Million Commitment to Healthy Democracy," press release, 2018, https://www

.democracyfund.org/vision/entry/2018-letter-from-our-president.

37 "Welcome," Democracy Fund Voice, https://democracyfundvoice.org, accessed February 18, 2020.

38 Charlie Sykes (@SykesCharlie), "False. I was on advisory committee. But term has expired. Never on board," Twitter, February 18, 2020, https://twitter.com/SykesCharlie/status/1229801648886775810.

39 "About Us," Stand Up Republic, https://standuprepublic.com/about-us.

40 Democracy Fund, "Stand Up Republic," press release, May 9, 2017, https://democracyfundvoice.org/stand-up-republic.

41 David Weigel, "Anti-Trump Conservatives Place $500,000 Ad Buy Against Roy Moore," *Washington Post*, December 8, 2017, https://www.washingtonpost.com/news/powerpost/wp/2017/12/08/anti-trump-conservatives-place-500000-ad-buy-against-roy-moore.

42 "Senate Republicans Refused to Do Their Jobs. Let's Do Ours," Stand Up Republic (blog), January 31, 2020, https://standuprepublic.com/senate-republicans-refused-to-do-their-jobs-lets-do-ours.

43 "What Is the Threat?," Protect Democracy, https://protectdemocracy.org/the-threat, accessed February 2, 2020.

44 "Democracy Threat Index," Protect Democracy, https://protectdemocracy.org/threat-index, accessed February 18, 2020.

45 "Protect Democracy Project," Democracy Fund, https://www.democracyfund.org/portfolio/entry/protect-democracy-project, accessed February 18, 2020.

46 "2000+ DOJ Alumni Condemn Abuse of Power and Call for New Leadership at Justice," Protect Democracy, February 16, 2020, https://protectdemocracy.org/update/1100-doj-alumni-condemn-abuse-of-power-and-call-for-new-leadership-at-justice.

47 "Securing Democracy Is a Global Necessity," Alliance for Securing Democracy, https://securingdemocracy.gmfus.org, accessed February 18, 2020.

48 Mollie Hemingway, "How the Media Enable Rep. Adam Schiff's Russian Conspiracy Theories," *Federalist*, February 21, 2018, https://thefederalist.com/2018/02/21/how-the-media-enable-rep-adam-schiffs-russian-bot-conspiracy-theories.

49 "German Marshall Fund: Alliance for Securing Democracy," Democracy Fund, https://www.democracyfund.org/portfolio/entry/alliance-for-securing-democracy, accessed February 18, 2020.

50 "The Niskanen Center," Democracy Fund, https://www.democracyfund.org/portfolio/entry/the-niskanen-center, accessed February 18, 2020.

51 "Niskanen Center funding," Niskanen Center, December 1, 2019, https://www.niskanencenter.org/wp-content/uploads/2019/12/Niskanen-Center-funding-12-1-2019.pdf.

52 "Conspectus," Niskanen Center, https://niskanen.s3.amazonaws.com/Niskanen%20Center%20Conspectus.pdf.

53   Niskanen Center, "Starting Over: The Center-Right After Trump," December 18, 2018, https://www.niskanencenter.org/starting-over-the -center-right-after-trump.

54   "About Us," Defending Democracy Together, https://www. defendingdemocracytogether.org/about-us, accessed February 18, 2020.

55   "Protect the Mueller Investigation," YouTube video, 0:30, April 10, 2018, https://www.youtube.com/watch?v=e0AUus59QhE.

56   Democracy Fund, "Defending Democracy Together," press release, May 3, 2018, https://democracyfundvoice.org/defending-democracy-together.

57   Julie Kelly, "NeverTrump's Billionaire Benefactors," *American Greatness*, November 14, 2018, https://amgreatness.com/2018/11/14/nevertrumps -billionaire-leftist-benefactors.

58   Bill Kristol (@BillKristol), "Grateful to all—left, right, and center—who are willing to step up to defend liberal democracy and the rule of law," Twitter, November 14, 2018, https://twitter.com/BillKristol/status /1062795174282256384.

59   Smith, phone conversation, December 2019.

60   "Charles Sykes," Bulwark, https://thebulwark.com/author/charlessykes, accessed February 18, 2020.

61   Jennifer Rubin, "A Bulwark Against Trump and Trumpism," *Washington Post*, January 8, 2019, https://www.washingtonpost.com /opinions/2019/01/08/bulwark-against-trump-trumpianism.

62   Rachael Larimore, "How AOC Owns the Cons," Bulwark, January 6, 2019, https://thebulwark.com/how-aoc-owns-the-cons.

63   Charles Sykes, "The 'Crisis' Isn't at the Border," Bulwark, January 8, 2019, https://thebulwark.com/the-crisis-isnt-at-the-border.

64   "Southwest Border Migration FY 2020," US Customs and Border Protection, January 9, 2020, https://www.cbp.gov/newsroom/stats /sw-border-migration.

65   Linda Chavez, "The Trump Who Cried Wolf," Bulwark, April 5, 2019, https://thebulwark.com/the-trump-who-cried-wolf.

66   Liz Mair, "William Weld Could Make 2020 Interesting. Here's How," Bulwark, February 14, 2019, https://thebulwark.com/william-weld-could -make-2020-interesting-heres-how.

67   Jonathan V. Last, "Three Horsemen Are Coming for Trump," Bulwark, September 10, 2019, https://thebulwark.com/three-horsemen-are -coming-for-trump.

68   Tim Miller, "The Fourth of July Is an Idea and Donald Trump Doesn't Understand It," Bulwark, July 3, 2019, https://thebulwark.com/the -fourth-of-july-is-an-idea-and-donald-trump-doesnt-understand-it.

69   Philip Rotner, "The R Word," Bulwark, September 5, 2019, https:// thebulwark.com/the-r-word.

70   Jerry Taylor, "What Changed My Mind About Climate Change?," Bulwark, May 21, 2019, https://thebulwark.com/what-changed-my -mind-about-climate-change.

71 Buskirk, "Death of *The Weekly Standard*."

72 "About," *Dispatch*, https://thedispatch.com/about, accessed February 18, 2020.

73 Seth Mandel (@SethAMandel), "It's like 2016 all over again. Watching the right devolve into the hunt for moles and turncoats and saboteurs," Twitter, October 2, 2019, https://twitter.com/SethAMandel/status /1179545069688365057.

74 Quin Hillyer, "How Republicans Could Benefit from Evicting Trump," *Washington Examiner*, December 3, 2019, https://www .washingtonexaminer.com/opinion/how-republicans-could -benefit-from-evicting-trump.

75 Sebastian Gorka, *The War for America's Soul: Donald Trump, the Left's Assault on America, and How We Take Back Our Country* (Washington, D.C.: Regnery, 2019), 183.

CHAPTER 9: TRUMP 2020

[EPIGRAPH] Jonathan Martin and Alexander Burns, "Republican Shadow Campaign for 2020 Takes Shape as Trump Doubts Grow," *New York Times*, August 5, 2017, https://www.nytimes.com/2017/08/05/us /politics/2020-campaign-president-trump-cotton-sasse-pence.html.

1 Joe Concha, "Bill Kristol Building 'War Machine' to Challenge Trump in 2020 Primary," *Hill*, September 14, 2018, https://thehill.com/homenews /media/406790-bill-kristol-building-war-machine-seeking-candidate-to -challenge-trump-in-2020.

2 Julie Kelly, "Revenge of NeverTrump: Mr. Murphy Makes a War Room," *American Greatness*, March 29, 2018, https://amgreatness.com/2018 /03/29/revenge-of-nevertrump-mr-murphy-makes-a-war-room.

3 Chris Cillizza, "Why One Big-Time Republican Consultant Thinks Trump Won't Be President by 2019," *The Point* (blog), CNN, August 22, 2017, https://www.cnn.com/2017/08/22/politics/donald-trump-gop -mike-murphy/index.html.

4 Nate Cohn, "One Year From Election, Trump Trails Biden but Leads Warren in Battlegrounds," *New York Times*, November 4, 2019, https:// www.nytimes.com/2019/11/04/upshot/trump-biden-warren-polls.html.

5 Tom Nichols (@RadioFreeTom), "The bright spot here is that this is not 'Civil War 2.0' or a fascist movement. That would require commitment and bravery from the Trumpist inner circle," Twitter, November 3, 2019, https://twitter.com/RadioFreeTom/status/1191200578254315521.

6 Bill Kristol (@BillKristol), "Here's a question that's increasingly been pre-occupying me: If Mueller doesn't find grounds to impeach, what then," Twitter, August 10, 2017, https://twitter.com/BillKristol/status /895669823799140352.

7 Bill Kristol (@BillKristol), "To Republicans who have the honor (and it is or should be an honor!) of serving in the United States Congress: Now is

the time to step up," Twitter, September 24, 2019, https://twitter.com/BillKristol/status/1176454748947570688.

8 Kristol (@BillKristol), "To Republicans."

9 Seth Mandel (@SethAMandel), "1. Trump says we do a lot for Ukraine, Zelensky says yes," Twitter, September 25, 2019, https://twitter.com/SethAMandel/status/1176862742931824640.

10 Jennifer Rubin, "Trump's Call with the Ukrainian President Should Seal His Fate," *Washington Post*, September 25, 2019, https://www.washingtonpost.com/opinions/2019/09/25/trumps-call-should-seal-his-fate.

11 Jonah Goldberg, "Ukraine-Biden Whistleblower Affair Shows What Team Trump Thinks of Us," *St. Louis Post-Dispatch*, September 25, 2019, https://www.stltoday.com/opinion/columnists/national/jonah-goldberg-ukraine-biden-whistleblower-affair-shows-what-team-trump/article_1be29efc-50b6-5dd7-be40-ed86196cf924.html.

12 "Will Meghan McCain Vote for Joe Biden in 2020?," YouTube video, 0:48, September 24, 2019, https://www.youtube.com/watch?v=1fG9yFkWdy8.

13 Tim Miller, "Joe Biden Deserves Better Than This," Bulwark, April 9, 2019, https://thebulwark.com/joe-biden-deserves-better-than-this.

14 Jennifer Rubin (@JRubinBlogger), "Biden speech finely crafted, extremely well delivered," Twitter, August 7, 2019, https://twitter.com/JRubinBlogger/status/1159181089539313664; Paul Bois, "'Morning Joe': Accept Biden or Suffer a Rust Belt 'Blowout,'" *Daily Wire*, November 21, 2019, https://www.dailywire.com/news/morning-joe-accept-biden-or-suffer-a-rust-belt-blowout.

15 Katie Glueck, "These Are the Democrats Winning the 'Never Trump' Republican Primary," *McClatchy DC*, February 11, 2019, https://www.mcclatchydc.com/news/politics-government/election/campaigns/article225994695.html.

16 "Ana Navarro Defends Joe Biden Iowa Outburst," YouTube video, 02:32, December 6, 2019, https://youtu.be/pl9_0_A7OBI.

17 Mona Charen, "Charen: Trump Thinks He's Above the Law," *Casper Star Tribune*, October 11, 2019, https://trib.com/opinion/columns/charen-trump-thinks-he-s-above-the-law/article_688b6c9e-b539-504e-a8fb-e6b0e49c3548.html.

18 Jonah Goldberg, "Jonah Goldberg: Trump Can Avoid Impeachment—by Apologizing," *Indy Star*, November 10, 2019, https://www.indystar.com/story/opinion/2019/11/10/jonah-goldberg-trump-can-avoid-impeachment-apologizing/4166715002.

19 Jonah Goldberg and David French, "Episode 144: The David French Experience," October 22, 2019, in *Remnant*, podcast, MP3 audio, 1:17:00, https://podcasts.apple.com/us/podcast/episode-144-the-david-french-experience/id1291144720?i=1000454514400.

20 David French, "Trump's Actions in Ukraine Weren't Just Wrong, They

Were Dangerous," *Time*, November 20, 2019, https://time.com/5732777
/trumps-actions-ukraine-dangerous.

21 "Face the Nation: Robert O'Brien, Stephen Hayes, Margaret Talev,
Antjuan Seawright, Jeffrey Goldberg," Bing video, 23:08, November 10,
2019, https://binged.it/31t9glB.

22 Impeaching Donald John Trump, President of the United States, for high
crimes and misdemeanors, H.R. Res., 116th Cong. (2019).

23 Karl W. Smith, "Trump's Economy Is Working for Minorities,"
Bloomberg, November 6, 2019, https://www.bloomberg.com/opinion
/articles/2019-11-06/trump-s-economy-is-historically-good-for
-minorities.

24 Lucia Mutikani, "U.S. Housing Starts, Building Permits Scale 12-Year
High," Reuters, September 18, 2019, https://www.reuters.com/article
/us-usa-economy-housingstarts-idUSKBN1W31LF.

25 Amy Furr, "Retailers Make Historic $34.4 Billion During Super Saturday
Sales," Breitbart, December 24, 2019, https://www.breitbart.com
/economy/2019/12/24/retailers-make-historic-34-4-billion-during-super
-saturday-sales.

26 Burgess Everett, "Trump Tightens Grips on Judges as McConnell Wins
50th Circuit Pick," *Politico*, December 12, 2019, https://www.politico
.com/news/2019/12/12/trump-judges-mcconnell-circuit-082836.

EPILOGUE

1   Bill Kristol (@BillKristol), "Not presumably forever; not perhaps for a day
after Nov. 3, 2020; not on every issue or in every way until then," Twitter,
February 1, 2010, https://twitter.com/BillKristol/status
/1223639550209200129.

2   Julie Kelly, "A Week of Political Karma for the Democrats," *American
Greatness*, February 5, 2020, https://amgreatness.com/2020/02/05
/a-week-of-political-karma-for-the-democrats.

3   Phillip M. Bailey, "Iowa Poll Cancelled After a Pete Buttigieg Supporter
Says the Candidate's Name Was Omitted During a Poll Call," *Des Moines
Register*, February 1, 2020, https://www.desmoinesregister.com/story
/news/politics/iowa-poll/2020/02/01/iowa-poll-pulled-after-presidential
-candidate-pete-buttigieg-name-omitted-during-call/4638527002.

4   Brianne Pfannenstiel, "Iowa Caucus 2020: Inside the Iowa Democratic
Party's 'Boiler Room' Where 'Hell' Preceded the Results Catastrophe,"
Des Moines Register, February 9, 2020, https://www.msn.com/en-us
/news/elections-2020/iowa-caucus-2020-inside-the-iowa-democratic
-party-s-boiler-room-where-hell-preceded-the-results-catastrophe/ar
-BBZNrKh.

5   Tom Perez (@TomPerez), "Enough is enough," Twitter, February 6, 2020,
https://twitter.com/TomPerez/status/1225468833458245632.

6   Jeffrey M. Jones, "Trump Job Approval at Personal Best 49%," *Gallup*,

February 4, 2020, https://news.gallup.com/poll/284156/trump-job
-approval-personal-best.aspx.

7   Justin McCarthy, "New High of 90% of Americans Satisfied with Personal
     Life," *Gallup*, February 6, 2020, https://news.gallup.com/poll/284285
     /new-high-americans-satisfied-personal-life.aspx.

8   R.J. Reinhart, "Record-High Optimism on Personal Finances in U.S.,"
     Gallup, February 5, 2020, https://news.gallup.com/poll/284264/record
     -high-optimism-personal-finances.aspx.

9   Greg Robb, "Here's How Economists Are Interpreting a January Report
     That Shows the U.S. Added 225,000 Jobs," *MarketWatch*, February 7,
     2020, https://www.marketwatch.com/story/heres-how-economists
     -are-interpreting-a-january-report-that-shows-the-us-added-225000
     -jobs-2020-02-07.

10   Ian Schwartz, "Pelosi: Trump Looked Like He Was 'A Little Sedated' at
     State of the Union, He Looked That Way Last Year," *Real Clear Politics*,
     February 6, 2020, https://www.realclearpolitics.com/video/2020/02/06
     /pelosi_trump_looked_like_he_was_a_little_sedated_at_state_of_the
     _union_he_looked_that_way_last_year.html.

11   Joe Biden (@JoeBiden), "Former Mayor Pete doesn't think very highly
     of the Obama-Biden record. Let's compare," Twitter, February 8, 2020,
     https://twitter.com/JoeBiden/status/1226189752598171648.

12   Robert Costa and Philip Rucker, "'Tempted to Despair,' Trump's
     Resilience Causes Democrats to Sound the Alarm," *Washington Post*,
     February 8, 2020, https://www.washingtonpost.com/politics
     /tempted-to-despair-trumps-resilience-causes-democrats-to-sound
     -the-alarm/2020/02/08/8301b71a-4906-11ea-b4d9-29cc419287eb_story
     .html.

13   Fox News, "Trump Addresses the Nation on Senate Impeachment
     Aquittal," YouTube video, 1:03:37, February 6, 2020, https://www.youtube
     .com/watch?v=IREknOdkPbA.

14   Fox News, "Trump Addresses the Nation."

15   Joe Concha, "Bill Kristol Building 'War Machine' to Challenge Trump in
     2020 Primary," *Hill*, September 14, 2018, https://thehill.com/homenews
     /media/406790-bill-kristol-building-war-machine-seeking-candidate-to
     -challenge-trump-in-2020.

16   Michael Graham, "EXCLUSIVE: NeverTrump-Funded Phone Calls Push
     GOP-Leaning Independents to Vote in NH Dems Primary," *NH Journal*,
     February 9, 2020, https://www.insidesources.com/nevertrump-funded
     -phone-calls-push-gop-leaning-independents-to-vote-in-nh-dems
     -primary.

17   Parker Molloy, "Why Should Anyone Care What 'Never Trump'
     Republicans Think About the Democratic Primary?," Media Matters for
     America, February 23, 2020, https://www.mediamatters.org/jennifer
     -rubin/why-should-anyone-care-what-never-trump-republicans-think
     -about-democratic-primary.

INDEX

abortion: pro-life advocacy of Trump,
53–54, 142–43. *See also* Covington
Catholic High School; infanticide
Access Hollywood tape, 18–20, 82
Afghanistan, Trump's foreign policy
and, 71–72
After the Flight 93 Election (Anton),
114
Ailes, Roger, 117
Alabama, 2017 senate race in, 59–60,
82, 146–47
al-Assad, Bashir, 68
al-Baghdadi, Abu Bakr, 71
Alliance for Securing Democracy, 147
American Family Association, 122
American Greatness, 21, 113, 122, 149,
153; quotations from, 78, 80, 109,
133
Anschutz, Phil, 140–41, 150
Anton, Michael (Publius Decius
Mus): "Flight 93 Election"
and, 21–22, 113–14, 153; on
future of NeverTrumpers, 116;
NeverTrumpers' criticism of,
112–14
Atlantic Monthly, 35, 39, 44, 61, 71,
119–20, 126
Avenatti, Michael, 82

Barr, Bill, 100, 147
Beck, Glenn, 10, 126
Bezos, Jeff, 49
Biden, Hunter, 158, 159, 160
Biden, Joe: election of 2020 and, 162,

164, 165, 167; impeachment of
Trump and, 151, 159–61; Obama
administration and, 76
Biggs, Andy, 111
Bird, Haley, 143
Black, Conrad, 153
Blitzer, Wolf, 105
Bloomberg, Michael, 117, 145, 167
Bongino, Dan, 153
Boot, Max: on Carlson, 119; on Fox
News, 118; on Gaetz, 111; on
Hanson, 115; Iraq War and, 94; on
Jordan, 111; Kavanaugh nomination
and, 84; liberal media and, 48, 52–
53; McCain's death and, 129–30; as
NeverTrumper, 28, 41; on Nunes,
108, 111; race-baiting of, 134–35;
Russian collusion hoax and, 94,
96, 101; support of Democratic
Party candidates, 62; Trump's trade
policy and, 74; "white privilege"
and, 28, 41, 56
Bork, Robert, 82
Born Alive Abortion Survivors Act,
60
Bovard, Rachel, 78
Bozell, Brent III, 12–13, 126
Breitbart News, 12, 153
Brennan, John, 92
Broaddrick, Juanita, 19
Brooks, David: Democratic candidates
and, 136; as NeverTrumper, 127;
Weekly Standard and, 140–41
Buckley, William F. Jr., 10, 12

Buffett, Warren, 145
Bulwark, ix–x, 100, 150–52, 160;
    Anton and, 114; Kristol and, 100,
    150; Sykes and, 42, 101, 116, 150
Burisma, 158–59, 160
Bush, Billy, 18
Bush, George H.W., 1, 8, 20, 36
Bush, George W., 14, 36, 38, 72, 129
Bush, Jeb, 13, 156
Buskirk, Chris, 122, 152
"But Gorsuch" meme, 66–67
Buttigieg, Pete, 151, 163–64, 165, 167

Canada, Trump's trade policy and,
    73, 75
Carlson, Tucker: Iraq War and, 13;
    NeverTrumpers and liberal media,
    118–20; on Trump, 37
Carville, James, 164
Case for Trump, The (Hanson), 36, 114
Charen, Mona: Bulwark and, 150;
    on Claremont Institute, 116;
    Defending Democracy Together
    and, 148; Democratic candidates
    and, 137; impeachment of Trump
    and, 160; Kavanaugh nomination
    and, 83–84; as NeverTrumper,
    40–41; Protect Democracy and,
    147; Russian collusion hoax and,
    96; on Trump, 11, 58; Trump's
    foreign policy and, 70; Useful
    Idiots: How Liberals Got It Wrong
    in the Cold War and Still Blame
    America First, 47
Charlottesville, VA, melee, 55, 56–57,
    131, 156
Chavez, Linda: Bulwark and, 151;
    Defending Democracy Together
    and, 148; Niskanen Center and,
    148; Protect Democracy and, 147
Chertoff, Michael, 147
child detention. See family separation
    policy
China, Trump's trade policy and,
    72–75
Christianity Today, 123

Clapper, James, 91–92
Claremont Institute, 112, 113, 116
Claremont Review of Books, 21–22,
    113
climate change: Boot and, 53;
    NeverTrumpers and liberal media,
    50–51
Clinton, Bill: character issues, 19–20;
    election of 1992, 8; McCain and,
    129; Trump and, 10
Clinton, Hillary: character issues,
    19–20; conservative concerns
    about presidency of, 21–22, 65–66;
    election of 2016, 12, 15, 16, 17, 18,
    21–22, 34, 86–87; email server of,
    89; Kristol and 1993 health plan of,
    1–2, 7, 8; McCain and, 129; Rubin's
    support for, 49; Russian collusion
    hoax and, 99; trade policy and, 73;
    Trump and, 10
Clovis, Sam, 99
Cohen, Michael, 97–98, 157
Collins, Gail, 52
Collins, Susan, 16, 60
Columbia Journalism Review, 40
Comey, James: French on, 108;
    Russian collusion hoax and, 45,
    88–91, 95, 97, 99, 105, 108, 115, 142;
    Trump's firing of, 107, 142, 157,
    165–66
Commentary, 11, 39, 44, 87, 88, 141
Comstock, Barbara, 18
conservative media: Trump's
    reconfiguration of, 152–54. See
    also specific individuals and
    publications
Continetti, Matthew, 86, 87
Conway, George, 43
Conway, Kellyanne, 17, 153
Cooke, Charles, 125–27
Corn, David, 48
coronavirus, ix–x, 74
Costa, Robert, 165
Covington Catholic High School,
    students at March for Life rally, 3,
    117–18, 130–33

Crime in Progress (Fritsch), 91
"Crossfire Hurricane," 89, 110
CrowdStrike, 99
Crowley, Candy, 20
Crowley, Michael, 9
Cruz, Ted, 12, 88
cyber espionage, China and, 73–74

Daily Caller, 153
Daniels, Stormy, 39, 82, 120, 121, 157
Davis, Sean, 51
Death of Expertise, The (Nichols), 39
"deep state": Flynn and, 45; Goldberg's
    mocking of idea of, 31, 42; Kristol's
    preference for, 45, 134; Trump and,
    114
Defending Democracy Together,
    148–50
Delegates Unbound, 16
Democracy Fund, 145–47, 149, 150
Democracy Fund Voice, 146, 149
Democratic Party candidates,
    NeverTrumpers' support of,
    58–62, 163
DeSantis, Ron, 61, 104, 111, 144
Dionne, E.J., 61
Dispatch, 30, 31, 39, 54, 115, 152–54
Domenech, Ben, 126
Doss, April, 143
Douthat, Ross, 35
Dowd, Matthew, 147
Drudge Report, 152

Earnest, Josh, 89
election of 1984, 34
election of 1992, 1, 8
election of 2000, 14
election of 2008, 43, 129
election of 2012, 20, 22, 34
election of 2016: alternate
    candidates of NeverTrumpers,
    15–18; evolution of NeverTrump
    movement and, 2, 7–23; Hillary
    Clinton and, 12, 15, 16, 17, 18, 21–
    22, 34, 65–66, 86–87; Republican
    primary candidates, 88; results

as repudiation of Republican
    establishment, 12, 33–37
election of 2018, NeverTrumpers'
    support of Democratic Party
    candidates, 58–62
election of 2020: NeverTrumpers'
    suggested candidates, 155–56;
    primaries and, 163–64, 166–67
Erickson, Erick, 126
Ethics and Public Policy Center, 40
evangelicals, NeverTrumpers' attacks
    on, 36, 60, 120–23
Everett, Burgess, 162
Everything Trump Touches Dies
    (Wilson), 43

Falwell, Jerry Jr., 120
family separation policy, 53, 75–76,
    79–80
Farhi, Paul, 37
Federalist, 4, 39, 51, 126, 153
Feingold, Russ, 42
Final Year, The (HBO film), 67–68
Finn, Mindy, 41, 146, 147, 148
Fiorina, Carly, 18
Fischer, Deb, 18, 19
Flake, Jeff, 44, 143
"Flight 93 Election, The" (Anton),
    21–22, 113
Flynn, Mike, 45, 87, 89, 94–95, 98, 129
Ford, Christine Blasey, 81, 82
Foreign Intelligence Surveillance Act
    (FISA), 95, 107, 108
Foreign Intelligence Surveillance
    Court, 90, 95, 105, 110
foreign policy of Trump,
    NeverTrumpers' plan to frustrate,
    67–72, 80
Fox News, NeverTrumpers' criticism
    of, 112, 116–20
Frankovich, Nick, 131, 132
French, David: on *Access Hollywood*
    tape, 18–19; as alternate candidate
    in 2016, 15; "But Gorsuch"
    meme, 66; *Dispatch* and, 152;
    evangelicals and, 36, 60, 121–23;

on Fox News, 116, 119–20; on
    Hanson, 115; immigrants and, 56;
    impeachment of Trump and, 160;
    as NeverTrumper, 20, 30, 38–39;
    on Nunes, 107, 108, 110; racial
    politics and, 57; Russian collusion
    hoax and, 95, 98, 99; Trump's
    border policy and, 77, 80; Trump's
    foreign policy and, 69, 71; Trump's
    pro-life advocacy and, 54; 2017
    Alabama senate race and, 60
French, Nancy: on evangelicals,
    122–23; Kavanaugh nomination
    and, 82–83
Fritsch, Peter, 91
Frum, David: Cooke and, 126, 127;
    on Fox News, 118; Iraq War and,
    93; liberal media and, 48; as
    NeverTrumper, 44; Niskanen
    Center and, 148; Russian collusion
    hoax, 93; support of Democratic
    Party candidates, 61; Trump's
    foreign policy and, 71
Fund, John, 16
Fusion GPS, 86–87, 89, 90, 99, 104,
    111. *See also* Simpson, Glenn

Gaetz, Matt, 111, 144
Galli, Mark, 123
Garland, Merrick, 65
Gillespie, Ed, 54, 59
Gillum, Andrew, 61
Goldberg, Jonah: Anton and, 22;
    Dispatch and, 39, 152; election
    of 2016 and, 19, 34; on Hanson,
    115; impeachment of Trump and,
    158, 160; Kavanaugh nomination
    and, 81–82; on McCain, 129;
    as NeverTrumper, 31, 42; on
    Republican voters, 127; Russian
    collusion hoax and, 99; support of
    Democratic Party candidates, 61;
    Trump's foreign policy and, 71
Goldman, Joe, 145–46
Gorka, Seb, 153
Gorsuch, Neil, 66

GQ, 15
Graham, Franklin, 120, 122
Graham, Lindsay, 20, 44, 128, 143, 149
Grand New Party (Salam and
    Douthat), 35
gun rights (Second Amendment), 52,
    53

Hamilton, 68, 147
Hannity, Sean, 116, 117, 153
Hanson, Victor Davis, 153; *The
    Case for Trump*, 36, 114;
    NeverTrumpers' criticism of, 112,
    114–15, 148
Harwood, John, 55
Hayden, Michael, 17
Hayes, Chris, 137
Hayes, Stephen: *Dispatch* and, 39,
    152; election of 2016 results and,
    33; impeachment of Trump and,
    160; liberal media and, 48; racial
    politics and, 58; on Rand Paul, 143;
    at *Weekly Standard*, 44; on *Weekly
    Standard*'s closing, 139–40
Hemingway, Mollie, 153
Hewitt, Hugh, 58
Higher Loyalty, A (Comey), 107
Hillyer, Quin, 112
Hogan, Larry, 155
Holder, Eric, 58
Horowitz, Michael, 109–10
House Freedom Caucus, 111
How the Right Lost Its Mind (Sykes),
    42

immigrants: Charen and, 58; French
    and, 56; Kristol and, 56; Obama's
    policies, 75–76, 79–80; Trump's
    border policy and, 75–80
impeachment, of Trump, 157–62
infanticide: Born Alive Abortion
    Survivors Act, 60; liberal media
    and, 54; Northam and, 59
intellectuals, NeverTrumpers'
    criticism of Pro-Trump, 112–16
Intercept, The, 146

Internal Revenue Service, Tea Party and, 89

Iowa caucuses, in 2020, 163–64, 165, 166

Iran: Rubin and Obama's nuclear deal, 51; Trump's foreign policy and, 71

Iraq War, 13–14, 72; Kristol and, 8, 48, 93; questions of weapons of mass destruction, 92–94

Johnson, Ron, 42

Joint Comprehensive Plan of Action (JCPOA), 51

Jolly, David, 146

Jones, Doug, 59–60

Jones, Paula, 19

Jong-Fast, Molly, 150

Jordan, Jim, 104, 111, 143–44

Kasich, John, 16, 18, 60, 88, 155

Kavanaugh, Brett: Jones and, 60; Left's character assassination of, 3, 81–84; N. French and, 122; Rubin and, 51; *Weekly Standard* and, 143

Kennedy, John, 110

Kerry, John, 51

Kessler, Glenn, 63

Kimball, Roger, 112, 115

Kim Jong Un, 70

Kimmel, Jimmy, 88

King, John, 11

Kislyak, Sergey, 95

Klobuchar, Amy, 167

Kramer, David, 90, 91, 147

Kristol, Bill: Alliance for Securing Democracy and, 147; alternate candidates in 2016 and, 15–18; Anton and, 22, 113; Bulwark and, 100, 150; candidates for 2020 and, 155–56; on Carlson, 118–19; Covington Catholic High School student and, 132; Defending Democracy Together and, 148; on DeSantis, 111; election of 2016 and, 22–23, 86; election of 2020 and, 166; Hillary Clinton's 1993 health plan and, 1–2, 7, 8; immigrants and, 56; impeachment of Trump and, 157, 158, 160; Iraq War and, 8, 48, 93; Kavanaugh nomination and, 84; liberal media and, 48, 55; on McCain, 129; as neoconservative, 1–2; as NeverTrumper, 4, 26; Niskanen Center and, 148; Northam and Virginia gubernatorial race, 59; on Nunes, 105–6, 108; on Obama, 48, 58–59; Omidyar and, 137–38, 144–45, 149; praise of Obama, 58–59; Russian collusion hoax and, 87, 93, 96; support of Democratic Party candidates, 61, 163; Trump's border policy and, 76; 2017 Alabama senate race and, 59; *Weekly Standard* and, 140, 141–42, 149–50

Kristol, Irving, 8, 134

Lachlan, Markay, 85–86, 88

Langwell, Sarah, 150

Lemon, Don, 43

Levin, Mark, 153

liberal media: Boot and, 52–53; embrace of socialism, 62–64; inaccurate tropes of racism, 55–58; NeverTrumpers' pivot from conservatism to liberalism, 9, 47–64; pro-Democrat activism of, 58–62; Rubin and, 49–51; Stephens and, 51–52; Trump's pro-life policies and, 53–54. *See also* conservative media; *specific individuals and publications*

Lighthizer, Robert, 73

Limbaugh, Rush, 153

Lind, Michael, 67

Liu He, 74–75

Loesch, Dana, 126

Logan Act, 94–95

Lowry, Rich, 42, 127; "But Gorsuch" meme, 67; Covington Catholic High School student and, 131–32;

National Review's "Against Trump"
    issue and, 10–12
Lynch, Loretta, 88

Maher, Bill, 117
Manafort, Paul, 87, 89, 97
Mandel, Seth: on Boot, 135;
    impeachment of Trump and, 158;
    Kavanaugh nomination and, 82;
    as NeverTrumper, 44, 128; racial
    politics and, 58; *Washington
    Examiner* and, 150, 152
Martin, Jonathan, 19
Mattis, Jim, 69
McCabe, Andrew, 99
McCain, Cindy, 159
McCain, John: character of, 11,
    128; election of 2008, 43, 121;
    NeverTrumpers and death of,
    128–30; on Nunes, 106–7, 108;
    Obamacare and, 60; Russian
    collusion hoax and, 44, 90–95
McCain, Meghan: Biden and, 159;
    Covington Catholic High School
    student and, 132–33; father's death
    and, 44, 160; impeachment of
    Trump and, 159; Russian collusion
    hoax and, 90–95
McCarthy, Andrew, 108, 109
McConnell, Mitch: confirmation
    of judges during Trump
    impeachment, 161–62; Defending
    Democracy Together and, 148–49;
    Garland nomination and, 65;
    McCain's death and, 129
McLaughlin, Dan, 19
McMullin, Evan: as alternate
    candidate in 2016, 17–18; on
    evangelicals, 121; Graham
    and, 20; as NeverTrumper, 41;
    NeverTrumpers and liberal media,
    134; Niskanen Center and, 148; on
    Nunes, 106; Protect Democracy
    and, 147; Russian collusion hoax
    and, 96, 98; Stand Up Republic
    and, 146; Trump's border

policy and, 79; 2017 Virginia
    gubernatorial race and, 59
Meadows, Mark, 104, 111
media. *See* conservative media; liberal
    media
Mexico, Trump's trade policy and,
    73, 75
Militant Normals (Schlichter), 5
military commitments, Trump's
    foreign policy and, 71–72
Miller, Tim, 160
Molloy, Parker, 167
Moore, Roy, 59–60, 82, 146–47
Moore, Russell, 11
MoveOn.org, 107
Mueller, Robert: Defending
    Democracy Together and, 148;
    Goldberg on, 42; Russian collusion
    and, 3, 16–17, 94–100, 152, 157, 158
Murdoch, Rupert, 117
Murkowski, Lisa, 60
Murphy, Mike, 156

National Emergencies Act, 77
National Review: Boot and, 135;
    Charen and, 70, 116; Goldberg
    and, 152; Lowry and, 67; Pruit and,
    143; Republican Party's lack of
    conservatism and, 12; Rubin and,
    87–88; Russian collusion hoax
    and, 86, 98, 99; "Against Trump"
    issue, 2, 9–13, 16, 19, 113, 126, 132;
    Trump's border policy and, 77–78,
    80
Navarro, Ana: Covington Catholic
    High School student and, 132; on
    evangelicals, 121; impeachment of
    Trump and, 160; as NeverTrumper,
    44; Russian collusion hoax and,
    98; support of Democratic Party
    candidates, 61; Trump's border
    policy and, 79
NeverTrump movement: fault lines
    between voters and conservative
    establishment, 14–18; incorrect
    warnings about Trump, 2–3, 155;

Iraq War and, 8, 13–14; "Meeting of the Concerned" in 2017, 43; motivations and goals of, 6, 157; prominent supporters of, 5, 38–45; as right flank of Left's resistance to Trump, 3–4, 136–37; status before 2020 election, 167–68

New York Post, 44, 57, 58

New York Times, 8, 12, 19, 41, 98, 156; Brooks and, 127, 141; Douthat and, 35; Stephens and, 40, 51–52, 74

Nichols, Tom: abortion and, 54; on Anton, 114; Boot and, 135; "But Gorsuch" meme, 66; contempt for Trump voters, 157; Democratic candidates and, 136, 137; on evangelicals, 120–21; on Fox News, 118; on Hanson, 115; impeachment of Trump and, 160; Kavanaugh nomination and, 84; as NeverTrumper, 39; Niskanen Center and, 148; Russian collusion hoax and, 87, 97; Smith on, 135–36; socialism and, 63; support of Democratic Party candidates, 61; Trump's border policy and, 79; Trump's foreign policy and, 69, 71; Trump's trade policy and, 74; on Trump supporters, 112

Niskanen Center, 147–48

Northam, Ralph, 54, 59

North American Free Trade Agreement (NAFTA), 73, 75

North Korea, Trump's foreign policy and, 70

Nunes, Devin: as target of NeverTrumpers, 99, 104–11, 143–44; Trump and, 166

Obama, Barack: child detention and, 75–76, 78; election of 2012, 20, 22, 34–36; impeachment of Trump and, 161; Kristol's criticism and praise of, 48, 58–59; McCain and, 129; Nunes and allegations about, 107, 109; policies inherited by Trump, 33, 67–68, 70; Rubin's criticism of, 50, 51; Rubin's support for Iran nuclear deal, 51; trade policy of, 73; Trump and, 88–89, 90

Obama, Michelle, 58–59

Ocasio-Cortez, Alexandria, 62, 63, 112, 150

O'Donnell, Lawrence, 51

Ohr, Bruce, 99

Omar, Ilhan, 4, 62, 112

Omidyar, Pierre, political organizations funded by, 144–50, 158

Omidyar Network, 145

One America News Network (OANN), 153

Open Society Foundation, 148

O'Rourke, Beto, 53

Page, Carter, 95, 105, 107–10, 143

Page, Lisa, 99

Papadopoulos, George, 89, 99

Paul, Rand, 143

Pavlich, Katie, 126

Pelosi, Nancy, 75, 112, 117, 151; election of 2018 and, 62, 63; impeachment of Trump and, 161; Trump's 2020 State of the Union speech and, 164, 165

Pence, Mike, 18

Perez, Tom, 164

Pexton, Patrick, 49–50

Phillips, Nathan, 132–33

Pittsburgh synagogue shooting, 117–18

Plot Against the President, The (Smith), 86, 105

Podesta, John, 18, 147

Podhoretz, John: on closing of *Weekly Standard*, 141; on evangelicals, 120; Kavanaugh nomination and, 82; as NeverTrumper, 44, 134; on Trump, 11, 57

Podhoretz, Norman, 11, 134

Pompeo, Mike, 74

Ponnuru, Ramesh, 127
Posobiec, Jack, 116
Powell, Colin, 20, 94
Power, Samantha, 67–68
Prager, Dennis, 153
Protect Democracy, 147
Pruitt, Scott, 143
Publius Decius Mus. *See* Anton,
    Michael (Publius Decius Mus)
Putin, Vladimir: Obama and, 68;
    Trump and Russian collusions
    hoax, 70, 87–88, 90–91, 93, 95–96,
    100, 108

Quayle, Dan, 1, 7

racial politics, NeverTrumpers and
    liberal media, 55–58, 134–35
Reagan, Ronald, 12, 16, 34, 76, 79, 144
Reid, Joy, 48
Reno, R.R., 113
Republicans for the Rule of Law, 96,
    158
Restless Wave, The (McCain), 90–91
Rhodes, Ben, 68
Ridge, Tom, 17
Roberts, David, 52
Rogin, Josh, 17
Romney, Mitt: as alternate candidate
    in 2016, 16; election of 2012 and,
    20, 34; impeachment of Trump
    and, 158; as NeverTrumper, 39, 45,
    119; Trump's border policy and,
    77–78
Rosenstein, Rod, 95–96, 111
Rothman, Noah, 87
Rubin, Jennifer: abortion and,
    54; Cooke on, 125–26, 127; on
    evangelicals, 120; on Fox News,
    117; on House Freedom Caucus,
    111; impeachment of Trump and,
    158, 160; Kavanaugh nomination
    and, 84; left turn in "Right Turn"
    Washington Post blog, 49–51;
    liberal media and, 48; McCain's
    death and, 129; as NeverTrumper,

27, 39–40; Niskanen Center and,
    148; on Nunes, 106; racial politics
    and, 56; Russian collusion hoax
    and, 87, 97; on Schiff, 111; support
    for Democratic Party candidates,
    49, 61; Sykes and, 150; 2017 Virginia
    gubernatorial race and, 59; *Weekly
    Standard* and, 140
Rubio, Marco, 88
Rucker, Philip, 165
Russian collusion hoax, 85–101; Boot
    and, 41; Iraq and WMDs and,
    92–94; McCain and, 44, 90–95;
    Mueller and his report, 94–100,
    152, 157, 158; NeverTrumpers and,
    3, 85–88, 104–11; Obama and,
    88–89, 90; Weber and, 16–17
Ryan, Paul, 18, 23, 34, 61, 96

Salam, Reihan, 35
Sanders, Bernie: abortion and, 54;
    election of 2016 and, 167; election
    of 2020 and, 163–64, 166; socialism
    and, 63; supporter's shooting of
    Scalise, 56–57, 112
Sanders, Sarah, 40, 79
Sandmann, Nicholas, 117, 132–33
Sanford, Mark, 151
Sasse, Ben: as 2020 candidate, 155;
    impeachment of Trump and,
    158; Kavanaugh nomination and,
    83, 143; Moore and, 44–45, 60;
    Russian collusion hoax and, 99
Scalia, Antonin, 65, 66
Scalise, Steve, 56–57, 112
Scarborough, Joe, 7
Schiff, Adam, 96, 167; impeachment
    of Trump and, 158–59; Nunes and,
    107, 108, 109, 111–12
Schlichter, Kurt, 5
Schoenfeld, Gabe: on Anton, 114;
    on Hanson, 114; on Kimball, 115;
    Niskanen Center and, 148
Scowcroft, Brent, 20
Second Amendment, 52, 53
Sessions, Jeff, 59, 78, 95–96

Shapiro, Ben, 132
Ship of Fools (Carlson), 37
Simpson, Glenn, 86, 89, 91, 97, 98, 110
Singer, Paul, 86
Smith, Kyle, 135–36
Smith, Lee, 86, 105, 144, 149–50
socialism, NeverTrumpers' embrace of, 62–64
Soleimani, Qasem, 71
Sopko, John, 72
Soros, George, 145, 148
Sowell, Thomas, 10
Squad, the, 58, 62–63
Stand Up Republic, 146–47
Steele, Christopher, and dossier of, 86–87, 89–91, 97–99, 108–10
Stefanik, Elise, 95
Stephens, Bret: and comparison of NeverTrumpers to freedom fighters, 127–28; Democratic candidates and, 136; Kavanaugh nomination and, 81; liberal media and, 51–52; as NeverTrumper, 40; Nunes and, 109; Russian collusion hoax and, 97; Trump's border policy and, 76–77; Trump's foreign policy and, 70; Trump's trade policy and, 74
Steyer, Tom, 145
Strzok, Peter, 99
Supreme Court: Kavanaugh nomination, 81–84; 2016 voters' concerns about future nominees to, 65–66
Sykes, Charlie: Bulwark and, 150; Democratic candidates and, 136; Fox News and, 117; Kavanaugh nomination and, 83; liberal media and, 48; as NeverTrumper, 42; Nunes and, 107–8; Posobiec and, 116; Pruit and, 143; Russian collusion hoax and, 97, 101; socialism and, 63; Stand Up Republic and, 146; Trump's foreign policy and, 70

Syria, Trump's foreign policy and, 68, 70–71

Tapper, Jake, 95
tax cut, by Trump, 27, 45, 48, 50–51, 53, 55, 63, 67, 142
Tea Party, Internal Revenue Service and, 89
Thomas, Cal, 10
Thomas, Clarence, 66, 82
Tlaib, Rashida, 4, 58, 62
Todd, Chuck, 78
trade policy, of Trump, 72–75, 80
Trans-Pacific Partnership, 73
Trump, Donald: accomplishments as president, 155, 161–62, 164–65; after impeachment trial, 165–66; Iraq War and, 13–14; on *National Review*, 12; NeverTrumpers and border policy of, 75–80; NeverTrumpers and foreign policy of, 67–72, 80; NeverTrumpers and tax policy of, 27, 45, 48, 50–51, 53, 55, 63, 67, 142; NeverTrumpers and trade policy of, 72–75, 80; reconfiguration of conservative media and, 152–54; on Rubin, 49; on *Weekly Standard*, 141
Trump, Donald Jr., 98
Trump, Ivanka, 79
Turley, Jonathan, 77

Ukraine, impeachment of Trump and, 158–61
USA Today, 39, 66
Useful Idiots: How Liberals Got It Wrong in the Cold War and Still Blame America First (Charen), 47
US-Mexico-Canada Agreement (USMCA), 75

Van Susteren, Greta, 106
Veselnitskaya, Natalia, 98
Virginia, 2017 gubernatorial race and, 54, 59
voters, fault lines between

conservative establishment and,
14–18
Vox, 15, 52

Wallace, Chris, 15
Wall Street Journal: hostile
commentary on Trump
administration, 152; Stephens and,
40, 51; Trump's trade policy and, 75
Walsh, Joe, 151, 166
War for America's Soul, The (Gorka),
153
Washington Examiner, 44, 112, 150,
152–53
Washington Free Beacon, 85–87, 88
Washington Post: *Access Hollywood*
tape and, 18; Boot and, 28, 41, 53,
56; Collins and, 16; Farhi and, 37;
Kessler and, 63; McMullin and,
17; N. French and, 82–83; Nichols
and, 61; Page and, 95; Rogin and,
17; Romney and, 29, 77; Rubin
and, 27, 39–40, 49–51, 53, 87, 106,
125–26, 140; sued by Sandmann,
117; Trump's border policy and,
77–78; Trump's foreign policy and,
72; Weigel and, 43
Weber, Vin, 16–17
Weekly Standard: anti-Trump
sentiments in, 2, 141–45; Anton

and, 113; election of 2016 and, 12,
33, 37–38; Kristol steps down as
editor, 44; launch of, 1, 8, 26; racial
politics and, 58; Russian collusion
hoax and, 87–88; shutdown of, 4,
137, 149–50; staff comments on
closing of, 139–41; 2017 Alabama
senate race and, 60
Wehner, Peter, 61
Weigel, David, 43
Weld, William, 151
"white privilege," Boot and, 28, 41, 56
Whitman, Christine Todd, 148
Whitman, Meg, 156
Will, George, 15, 61
Wilson, Rick: on evangelicals, 121;
McCain's death and, 129; as
NeverTrumper, 17, 43; Trump's
border policy and, 76; Trump's
foreign policy and, 70; on Trump
supporters, 112
Wood, Andrew, 90
Wray, Christopher, 74
Wright, Jeremiah, 43, 104, 121

Zelensky, Volodymyr, 159
Zubrin, Robert, 86